PEARLS OF
DAILY BIBLE READING AND COMMENTARY

VOLUME 1

"The Bible is the Word of God. When a word appears in the Bible once, it is important. When twice, it is very important. When three times, it is very, very important. When many times, it is extremely important. In this book, through compilation and reflection on the Bible verses compiled according to key word(s)/phrase, let's hear the extremely important messages God has spoken to us in the Bible."

Joseph Zhou

Again, the kingdom of heaven is like a merchant looking for fine pearls. When he found one of great value, he went away and sold everything he had and bought it. Matthew 13:45-46

PEARLS OF WISDOM

DAILY BIBLE READING AND COMMENTARY

VOLUME 1

JOSEPH ZHOU

Pearls of Wisdom VOLUME 1 by Joseph Zhou
Copyright © 2025 by Joseph Zhou
All Rights Reserved
ISBN: 978-1-59755-842-6

Published by: ADVANTAGE BOOKS
                Orlando, FL, www.advbookstore.com

All rights reserved. No portion of this book may be reproduced, stored in a retrieval system, or transmitted in any form or by any means—electronic, photocopy, recording, scanning, or other—except for brief quotations in critical reviews or articles, without the prior written permission of the publisher.

All Scripture quotations, unless otherwise indicated, are taken from The Holy Bible, New International Version, NIV. Copyright 1973, 1978, 1984, 2011 by Biblica, Inc. Used by permission of Zondervan. All rights reserved worldwide. www.Zondervan.com. The "NIV" and "New International Version" are trademarks registered in the United States Patent and Trademark Office by Biblica, Inc.

Library of Congress Catalog Number: 2025950745	
Name:	Zhou, Joseph., Author
Title:	*Pearls of Wisdom VOLUME 1*
	Joseph Zhou
	Advantage Books, 2025
Identifiers:	ISBN Paperback: 9781597558726
	ISBN eBook: 9781597558624
Subjects:	Books: Religion: Christian Life – Devotional
	Books › Religion: Christian Life: Spiritual Growth
	Books › Religion: Christian Life – Personal Growth

First Printing: January 2026
26 27 28 29 30 31   10 9 8 7 6 5 4 3 2 1

Endorsements

The *Pearls of Wisdom* was born out of that deeply personal encounter of the author with God's love and truth.

This devotional is more than a collection of reflections; it is an invitation to walk daily with the Lord, to uncover the riches of His Word, and to allow His Spirit to shape your heart. Each entry in *Pearls of Wisdom* pairs carefully selected Scriptures with meditations drawn from the author's journey of faith—a journey marked by awe at God's faithfulness, humility in His presence, and gratitude for His unending grace. My prayer is that these pages will draw believers of all ages closer to the Lord.

As you read, you will find assurance in God's promises, strength in His power, and freedom in His truth. The reflections, rooted in passages such as Philippians 4:7 and Ephesians 3:20, remind us that God's peace guards our hearts, His providence meets our needs, and His power exceeds our wildest expectations. Through these daily meditations, you will be encouraged not only to read the Word but to live it—to let it transform your thoughts, guide your actions, and deepen your love for Christ.

My hope is that *Pearls of Wisdom* will be a faithful companion on your spiritual journey, offering fresh insight and renewed hope each day. May it inspire you to pursue a deeper relationship with God, to trust in His unchanging promises, and to reflect His love in all you do. As you turn these pages, may you discover the joy of knowing Him more and the strength to walk faithfully in His light.

With heartfelt prayers for your growth in Christ,

Rev. Kim Voon Yee, Pastor
Vancouver Basel Hakka Lutheran Church

Rev. Kim Voon Yee has served as pastor of Vancouver Basel Hakka Lutheran Church since 2009 and has been actively involved in online training with Chinese Christian Mission since 2017. Born in Malaysia in 1962, he came to faith in 1978 out of a traditional religious background. Before moving to Canada, he spent 12 years in Malaysia serving both as an Old Testament lecturer and as a pastor. He is married and blessed with four children.

Undoubtedly, the Word of God is a pearl of wisdom—offering insight into knowing God, discerning His will, understanding life, and learning how to live it well. It is the sole source that keeps us connected to our divine Origin and anchors our hope in an eternal destiny. Along life's journey, Scripture serves as our spiritual GPS, guided by the Holy Spirit, transforming us into Christ's likeness. From reshaping our worldview and reforming our character to realigning our priorities and renewing our purpose, the Scriptures play a vital and transformative role in cultivating faith, hope, and love.

As lifelong students of God's Word, meditation and reflection are irreplaceable spiritual disciplines that allow us to dig deep and commune intimately with our Sovereign God. We are deeply grateful to Rev. Joseph Zhou for dedicating countless hours to immersing himself in Scripture, drawing forth the *Pearl of Wisdom* through his faithful meditation and reflection.

Daily journaling is a powerful spiritual discipline. By meditating each day on God's love letter to us—His Word—we open our hearts to encounter Him more deeply. This consistent practice nurtures vibrant spiritual growth and strengthens our relationship with the Lord, serving as a nourishing diet for the soul. It is my prayer that this book will inspire and encourage readers—especially ministry leaders—not only to receive fresh spiritual insights and nourishment, but also to adopt this rhythm as a pathway toward a fruitful and transformative spiritual journey. In doing so, they may become more effective ministers of God's Word.

Rev. Dr. Roland Shum, Pastor
Evangel Baptist Church

Rev. Dr. Roland Shum serves as the senior pastor of Evangel Baptist Church in Edmonton, Alberta, Canada. His ministry spans multiple roles, including church planter, pastor, Bible teacher, counselor, gospel radio broadcaster, and mentor to seminary graduates. Responding to the call of the missional God, he has devoted his life to embodying missional living and cultivating missional communities. In recent years, Dr. Shum has actively participated in a church planting movement in Cuba and has led pastoral retreats in Alberta.

Pearls of Wisdom VOLUME 1

TABLE OF CONTENTS

JANUARY

JANUARY 1: CALLED TO SUFFER	13
JANUARY 2: SELF, CROSS, AND CHRIST	14
JANUARY 3: CRUCIFIXION, RESURRECTION, AND NEW CREATION	15
JANUARY 4: GARBAGE AND TREASURES	17
JANUARY 5: THE WHOLE MEASURE OF THE FULLNESS OF CHRIST	18
JANUARY 6: BEAR FRUIT (I)	19
JANUARY 7" BEAR FRUIT (II)	20
JANUARY 8: SORROW AND JOY	22
JANUARY 9: WHAT IS ETERNAL LIFE	23
JANUARY 10: CHRIST, THE WORD OF LIFE	24
JANUARY 11: SUFFERING AND HOLINESS	25
JANUARY 12: SUFFER ACCORDING TO GOD'S WILL	26
JANUARY 13: SUFFERING AND COMFORT	28
JANUARY 14: OBEDIENCE AND SACRIFICE	29
JANUARY 15: OBEDIENCE THAT IS WORTHWHILE	30
JANUARY 16: OBEDIENCE IN THE MIDST OF SUFFERING	32
JANUARY 17: TRUST IN THE LORD	33
JANUARY 18: JESUS CHRIST IS THE GOAL OF OUR SPIRITUAL RACE	34
JANUARY 19: THE MEANING OF JOY	35
JANUARY 20: THE FULLNESS OF CHRIST	36
JANUARY 21: OBEDIENCE AND RIGHTEOUSNESS	38
JANUARY 22: THE REVELATION OF THE MYSTERY OF CHRIST	39
JANUARY 23: A LIFE HIDDEN WITH CHRIST IN GOD	40
JANUARY 24: FAITH, OBEDIENCE, AND GUIDANCE OF GOD	42

JANUARY 25: THE FRUIT OF RIGHTEOUSNESS AND THE TREE OF LIFE	43
JANUARY 26: GOD'S GRACE	44
JANUARY 27: THE FULLNESS OF HIS GRACE	46
JANUARY 28: CALL TO THE LORD	47
JANUARY 29: JESUS, THE PERFECTER	48
JANUARY 30: THE FULL MEASURE OF THE BLESSING OF CHRIST	49
JANUARY 31: FAITH, HOPE, AND LOVE THAT ARE IN CHRIST	50

FEBRUARY

FEBRUARY 1: TRUE ASSURANCE (I)	51
FEBRUARY 2: TRUE ASSURANCE (II)	52
FEBRUARY 3: TRUE ASSURANCE (III)	53
FEBRUARY 4: SUFFERING AND PERFECTION	54
FEBRUARY 5: THE SUPREMACY OF CHRIST	55
FEBRUARY 6: CHRIST AND ALL CREATION	56
FEBRUARY 7: FIX OUR EYES ON JESUS	57
FEBRUARY 8: CHRIST, THE HOPE OF GLORY	59
FEBRUARY 9: THE GLORIOUS RICHES OF THIS MYSTERY	60
FEBRUARY 10: CHRIST AND THE MYSTERY OF GOD	61
FEBRUARY 11: THE BOUNDLESS RICHES OF CHRIST	62
FEBRUARY 12: DEVOTEDNESS IN PRAYER	63
FEBRUARY 13: AN AROMA PLEASING TO THE LORD	64
FEBRUARY 14: DEATH AND BAPTISM	65
FEBRUARY 15: LIFE AND CHRIST	67
FEBRUARY 16: THE TREASURES OF WISDOM AND KNOWLEDGE	68
FEBRUARY 17: SUFFERING AND GLORY	69
FEBRUARY 18: THE KNOWLEDGE OF GOD	71
FEBRUARY 19: CHRIST AND THE GLORY OF GOD	72

FEBRUARY 20: CHRIST AND THE IMAGE OF GOD	73
FEBRUARY 21: BLESSINGS OF GOD AND GOD OF BLESSINGS	75
FEBRUARY 22: DEATH AND LIFE	76
FEBRUARY 23: THE GLORY OF GOD	77
FEBRUARY 24: THE MAJESTY OF THE LORD	79
FEBRUARY 25: CHRIST HAS THE MAJESTY OF GOD	80
FEBRUARY 26: SPLENDOR AND MAJESTY	81
FEBRUARY 27: THE GLORIOUS SPLENDOR OF THE KINGDOM	83
FEBRUARY 28: THE ETERNAL KINGDOM	84

MARCH

MARCH 1: HE WHO PROMISED IS FAITHFUL	86
MARCH 2: THE COVENANTS OF THE PROMISE	87
MARCH 3: PRECEPTS AND PROMISES	89
MARCH 4: THE OFFER OF LIFE AND DEATH	90
MARCH 5: A COVENANT SEALED WITH AN OATH	92
MARCH 6: COVENANT OF LOVE	93
MARCH 7: CHRIST AND THE PROMISES OF GOD	94
MARCH 8: EVERLASTING COVENANT	95
MARCH 9: SIGN OF COVENANT	97
MARCH 10: TERMS OF THE COVENANT	99
MARCH 11: LOOKING FOR HIS PROMISES	100
MARCH 12: THE LORD REMEMBERS HIS COVENANT	101
MARCH 13: GOD'S UNFAILING LOVE	102
MARCH 14: TRUTH AND LOVE	103
MARCH 15: PAUL AND CHRIST (I)	105
MARCH 16: PAUL AND CHRIST (II)	106
MARCH 17: PROPHECIES AND PROMISES	107

MARCH 18: LOSS OR GAIN	108
MARCH 19: THE TRINITY (I)	109
MARCH 20: THE TRINITY (II)	111
MARCH 21: THE TRINITY (III)	112
MARCH 22: THE SPIRIT OF GOD (I)	113
MARCH 23: THE SPIRIT OF GOD (II)	114
MARCH 24: THE SON AND THE SPIRIT (I)	115
MARCH 25: THE SON AND THE SPIRIT (II)	117
MARCH 26: CHILDREN OF GOD	118
MARCH 27: CRUCIFIXION	119
MARCH 28: GOD AND THE SPIRIT (I)	120
MARCH 29: GOD AND THE SPIRIT (II)	122
MARCH 30: THE LAW OF THE SPIRIT OF LIFE	123
MARCH 31: RESURRECTION	125

APRIL

APRIL 1: GOD REVEALS	127
APRIL 2: THE REVELATION OF JESUS CHRIST	128
APRIL 3: THE MYSTERY OF GOD	129
APRIL 4: TWO CREATIONS (I)	131
APRIL 5: TWO CREATIONS (II)	132
APRIL 6: TWO COVENANTS (I)	133
APRIL 7: TWO COVENANTS (II)	134
APRIL 8: TWO CREATIONS AND TWO COVENANTS	135
APRIL 9: NEW CREATION	137
APRIL 10: THE CREATOR OF HEAVEN AND EARTH	138
APRIL 11: THE LORD OF THE HEAVENS AND THE EARTH	139
APRIL 12: THE KING OF THE HEAVENS AND THE EARTH	141

APRIL 13: THE JUDGE OF THE HEAVENS AND THE EARTH	142
APRIL 14: THE HEAVENS VS. THE EARTH	143
APRIL 15: THE DOOM OF HEAVENS AND THE EARTH	144
APRIL 16: THE NEW HEAVENS AND THE NEW EARTH	146
APRIL 17L: ALL THINGS (I)	147
APRIL 18: ALL THINGS (II)	148
APRIL 19: THE WORD AND THE WORLD	149
APRIL 20: A COPY AND SHADOW	151
APRIL 21: THE NEW ORDER (I)	152
APRIL 22: THE NEW ORDER (II)	154
APRIL 23: FAITH IS KNOWING WHO JESUS IS (I)	155
APRIL 24: FAITH IS KNOWING WHO JESUS IS (II)	156
APRIL 25: FAITH IS KNOWING WHO JESUS IS (III)	157
APRIL 26: CLEANSING	159
APRIL 27: PURIFICATION (I)	160
APRIL 28: PURIFICATION (II)	162
APRIL 29: SANCTIFICATION	163
APRIL 30: ETERNAL LIFE IS THE LIFE OF HOLINESS	164

MAY

MAY 1: THE SPLENDOR OF HIS HOLINESS	166
MAY 2: HOLINESS	167
MAY 3: THE BREAD OF LIFE	168
MAY 4: WHEAT AND BREAD	170
MAY 5: THE SPIRIT AND LIFE	171
MAY 6: THE MOST HOLY PLACE (I)	172
MAY 7: THE MOST HOLY PLACE (II)	174
MAY 8: THE THRONE OF GRACE	175

MAY 9: GOD IS LOVE	176
MAY 10: GOD'S LOVE (I)	177
MAY 11: GOD'S LOVE (II)	178
MAY 12: LOVE AND FAITHFULNESS (I)	180
MAY 13: LOVE AND FAITHFULNESS (II)	181
MAY 14: RIGHTEOUSNESS AND FAITHFULNESS	182
MAY 15: RIGHTEOUSNESS AND FAITH	183
MAY 16: RIGHTEOUSNESS AND JUSTICE (I)	184
MAY 17: RIGHTEOUSNESS AND JUSTICE (II)	185
MAY 18: FAITH AND PROMISE	186
MAY 19: THE PROMISE AND THE COVENANT	188
MAY 20: THE PROMISE AND THE LAW	189
MAY 21: LAW AND COVENANT	191
MAY 22: LAW AND CHRIST	192
MAY 23: LAW AND SIN (I)	193
MAY 24: LAW AND SIN (II)	194
MAY 25: LAW AND SIN (III)	195
MAY 26: WISDOM AND UNDERSTANDING (I)	196
MAY 27: WISDOM AND UNDERSTANDING (II)	198
MAY 28: FOR THE LORD'S NAME'S SAKE	199
MAY 29: SEEK THE LORD	200
MAY 30: SERVE THE LORD (I)	202
MAY 31: SERVE THE LORD (II)	202

JUNE

JUNE 1: THE ARK OF THE COVENANT AND THE MIRACLES	204
JUNE 2: THE ARK OF THE COVENANT AND THE LEVITES	205
JUNE 3: THE ARK OF THE COVENANT AND HIS DWELLING PLACE	206

JUNE 4: THE ARK OF THE COVENANT AND THE TABERNACLE	207
JUNE 5: THE ARK OF COVENANT AND THE LORD'S PRESENCE	208
JUNE 6: THE GOSPEL (I)	209
JUNE 7: THE GOSPEL (II)	210
JUNE 8: THE GOSPEL (III)	212
JUNE 9: THE GOSPEL (IV)	213
JUNE 10: FEAR OF THE LORD (I)	215
JUNE 11: FEAR OF THE LORD (II)	216
JUNE 12: GLORY AND POWER (I)	217
JUNE 13: GLORY AND POWER (II)	218
JUNE 14: PROPHECY (I)	219
JUNE 15: PROPHECY (II)	220
JUNE 16: SALVATION (I)	221
JUNE 17: SALVATION (II)	223
JUNE 18: SALVATION (III)	224
JUNE 19: SALVATION (IV)	225
JUNE 20: JOHN THE BAPTIST	227
JUNE 21: JESUS AND BAPTISM	228
JUNE 22: BAPTISM (I)	229
JUNE 23: BAPTISM (II)	230
JUNE 24: THE BLOOD OF CHRIST (I)	231
JUNE 25: THE BLOOD OF CHRIST (II)	232
JUNE 26: THE BLOOD OF CHRIST (III)	233
JUNE 27: BLOOD AND COVENANT (I)	235
JUNE 28: BLOOD AND COVENANT (II)	236
JUNE 29: THE DAY OF THE LORD (I)	237
JUNE 30: THE DAY OF THE LORD (II)	239

Pearls of Wisdom VOLUME 1

January 1

Called to Suffer

But if you suffer for doing good and you endure it, this is commendable before God. To this you were called, because Christ suffered for you, leaving you an example, that you should follow in his steps. (1 Peter 2:20-21)

It has been granted to us on behalf of Christ not only to believe in Him, but also to suffer for Him (Phil. 1:29). When we are called by Christ to follow Him, we are called simultaneously to suffer for His name as Paul was (Acts 9:15-16). However, when Peter and Andrew as well as John and James were called by Jesus to follow Him (Matt. 4:18-22; Mark 1:16-20), they might not be aware at that point that they were called simultaneously to suffer for His name. When Philip and Nathanael were called (John 1:43-51), they might not be aware of this either. Neither might Matthew (Matt. 9:9-13).

When Jesus told Peter that he would follow Him later (John 13:36), Peter seemed not to understand what Jesus meant (John 13:37). When Jesus prophesied how Peter would die, Peter did not understand Jesus again. Then Jesus called Peter again to follow Himself (John 21:18-22). Finally, when Peter wrote his epistles, he came to realize that we Christians were called to suffer for Christ's name (1 Pet. 2:20-21).

Paul was so blessed that as soon as he was chosen and called, he would be shown that he must suffer for Christ's name (Acts 9:15-16). Whether we accept or not, the reality is, as soon as we are called by Christ to follow Him, we are called to suffer for His name by taking up His cross (Luke 9:23-24). When Christ called us to follow him, he had left us an example by suffering for us; and we shall follow in his step by suffering for righteousness (1 Pet. 2:20-21).

When we receive God's calling to be His messengers of the gospel, we will receive His calling to suffer for His name simultaneously, because suffering is the method God forges His chosen instruments (Acts 9:15-16).

Suffering for His name is a divine calling, "for it has been granted to you on behalf of Christ not only to believe on him, but also to suffer for him." (Phil. 1:29)

Reflection: Suffering is a pervasive theme in the Scriptures which defines the Christian life. It is at the heart of the Christian experience. No Christian is exempted from it. Neither did the Patriarchs in the Old Testament nor did the Son of God in the New Testament, neither did the prophets in the Old Testament, nor did the apostles in the New

Testament enter into glory without following the path of suffering, because the path to glory is the path of suffering. The Scriptures clearly tells us, "We must go through many hardships to enter the kingdom of God" (Acts 14:22). Thus, as Christians we should never be surprised when trials come our way. The Lord came to give His life as a ransom for many (Matt. 20:28; Mark 10:45). He came to the cross to suffer where the Son of Man must be lifted up (John 3:14). And He showed Paul "how much he must suffer" for Christ's sake (Acts 9:16). Paul saw in sharing his Lord's sufferings the true path of displaying Christ's resurrection power, "I want to know Christ—yes, to know the power of his resurrection and participation in his sufferings, becoming like him in his death, and so, somehow, attaining to the resurrection from the dead." (Phil. 3:10-11). And that power works in us, the disciples of Christ, not in spite of suffering, but through our suffering! We are called to walk in His steps, which is a path of suffering. We are called to suffer because of righteousness, to suffer persecution and opposition and hardship for the gospel (Matt. 5:10-12; John 15:18-20). And we will be persecuted as long as we want to live a godly life in Jesus Christ (2 Tim. 3:12). The call of cross is the call of suffering. We are called to suffer for His name by taking up His cross. And He has called every Christian to suffer. Without suffering for His name, we cannot come to cross. Jesus has never called anyone to believe in Him, but to follow Him. To follow Him means to follow in His step by suffering for righteousness.

January 2

Self, Cross, and Christ

Then Jesus said to his disciples, "Whoever wants to be my disciple must deny themselves and take up their cross and follow me. For whoever wants to save their life will lose it, but whoever loses their life for me will find it." (Matthew 16:24-25)

Then he called the crowd to him along with his disciples and said: "Whoever wants to be my disciple must deny themselves and take up their cross and follow me. For whoever wants to save their life will lose it, but whoever loses their life for me and for the gospel will save it. What good is it for someone to gain the whole world, yet forfeit their soul? Or what can anyone give in exchange for their soul? (Mark 8:34-37)

Then he said to them all: "Whoever wants to be my disciple must deny themselves and take up their cross daily and follow me. For whoever wants to save their life will lose it, but whoever loses their life for me will save it. What good is it for someone to gain the whole world, and yet lose or forfeit their very self? (Luke 9:23-25)

Reflection: To a person in the first century, the cross represented nothing but the most painful and humiliating death. When Jesus took up his cross, He carried his own execution device. He was willfully giving his life up for redemption of the world. He was consenting to suffering, humiliation, torture and ultimately his death. And, finally He died on the cross. Nevertheless, God exalted him to the highest place and gave Him the name that is above every name (Phil. 2:9). Likewise, Paul lost his safety, security, and comfort but he gained Christ (2 Cor. 11:24-28; Phil. 3:8). To us, disciples of Christ, "Take up your cross and follow Me" means being willing to die in order to follow Jesus. It means we are willing to follow Jesus at the price of losing some close friends, alienation from our families, losing our reputation, jobs, or even lives. However, the reward is worth the price. Our Lord Jesus Christ has promised with the gift of life in Christ for those who have responded to His call of death to self (Matt. 16:24-25; Mark 8:34-37; Luke 9:23-25). In other words, the giving of our lives results in the saving of our lives. This is a spiritual paradox. As a matter of fact, there is another spiritual paradox conveyed in today's verses, which is the paradox of ownership. Without disowning ourselves, we cannot own cross. Disowning results in owning. This is also an issue of being owned and owning. Without being owned by Christ, we cannot own eternal life. We can own eternal life, but we cannot own Christ. Instead, we can only be owned by Christ.

January 3

Crucifixion, Resurrection, and New Creation

I have been crucified with Christ and I no longer live, but Christ lives in me. The life I live in the body, I live by faith in the Son of God, who loved me and gave himself for me. (Galatians 2:20)

We always carry around in our body the death of Jesus, so that the life of Jesus may also be revealed in our body. For we who are alive are always being given over to death for Jesus' sake, so that his life may also be revealed in our mortal body. So then, death is at work in us, but life is at work in you (2 Cor. 4:10-12).

You, however, are not in the realm of the flesh but are in the realm of the Spirit, if indeed the Spirit of God lives in you. And if anyone does not have the Spirit of Christ, they do not belong to Christ. But if Christ is in you, then even though your body is subject to death because of sin, the Spirit gives life because of righteousness. And if the Spirit of him who raised Jesus from the dead is living in you, he who raised Christ from the dead will also give life to your mortal bodies because of his Spirit who lives in you. Therefore, brothers and sisters, we have an obligation—but it is not to the flesh, to live according to it. For if you live according to the flesh, you will die; but if by the Spirit you put to death the misdeeds of the body, you will live." (Rom 8:9-13).

Therefore, if anyone is in Christ, the new creation has come: The old has gone, the new is here! (2 Cor. 5:17)

Reflection: Life and death are apparently a pair of antitheses that starkly contrast with each other. Their relationship is a significant paradox in the Scriptures, and a key teaching throughout the New Testament. The death of the old nature leads to the new life (Gal. 2:20). This death-life paradox is a secret to the kingdom of heaven which has been disclosed by the Apostle Paul, "We always carry around in our body the death of Jesus, so that the life of Jesus may also be revealed in our body. For we who are alive are always being given over to death for Jesus' sake, so that his life may also be revealed in our mortal body. So then, death is at work in us, but life is at work in you." (2 Cor. 4:10-12). Likewise, crucifixion and resurrection are also a pair of antitheses that convey spiritual paradox. Christ's crucifixion was followed by His resurrection. Without His crucifixion through which He atoned for sin, there would not have been resurrection through which He defeated the power of death. Jesus' crucifixion precedes resurrection. Likewise, a believer's crucifixion of his old nature precedes his resurrection as a new creation. There is no new life in a believer without the death of his old nature. The Apostle Paul teaches us, "You, however, are not in the realm of the flesh but are in the realm of the Spirit, if indeed the Spirit of God lives in you. And if anyone does not have the Spirit of Christ, they do not belong to Christ. But if Christ is in you, then even though your body is subject to death because of sin, the Spirit gives life because of righteousness. And if the Spirit of him who raised Jesus from the dead is living in you, he who raised Christ from the dead will also give life to your mortal bodies because of his Spirit who lives in you. Therefore, brothers and sisters, we have an obligation—but it is not to the flesh, to live according to it. For if you live according to the flesh, you will die; but if by the Spirit you put to death the misdeeds of the body, you will live." (Rom 8:9-13). It is necessary to point out that, in the physical world, life comes first, then does death. In the spiritual world, death comes first, then does life. In short, without crucifixion of our old self, without Christ's resurrection in our life, we won't be a new creation (2 Cor. 5:17).

Pearls of Wisdom VOLUME 1

January 4

Garbage and Treasures

I consider everything a loss because of the surpassing worth of knowing Christ Jesus my Lord, for whose sake I have lost all things. I consider them garbage, that I may gain Christ and be found in him. (Philippians 3:8-9)

But whatever were gains to me I now consider loss for the sake of Christ. What is more, I consider everything a loss because of the surpassing worth of knowing Christ Jesus my Lord, for whose sake I have lost all things. I consider them garbage, that I may gain Christ and be found in him, not having a righteousness of my own that comes from the law, but that which is through faith in Christ—the righteousness that comes from God on the basis of faith. I want to know Christ—yes, to know the power of his resurrection and participation in his sufferings, becoming like him in his death, and so, somehow, attaining to the resurrection from the dead (Phil 3:7-11).

The kingdom of heaven is like treasure hidden in a field. When a man found it, he hid it again, and then in his joy went and sold all he had and bought that field. Again, the kingdom of heaven is like a merchant looking for fine pearls. When he found one of great value, he went away and sold everything he had and bought it (Matt. 13:44-46).

My goal is that they may be encouraged in heart and united in love, so that they may have the full riches of complete understanding, in order that they may know the mystery of God, namely, Christ, in whom are hidden all the treasures of wisdom and knowledge. (Col. 2:2-3)

Reflection: The secrets of the kingdom are full of spiritual paradoxes. We Christians realize the vanity of the worldly life (Eccl.1:2). However, we are not resolving to pursue the state of emptiness, instead, we are resolving to pursue the fullness of life in Christ, the abundant life. We disown the "self" in order to gain Christ. This is a paradox of loss and gain. Garbage and treasures look like another pair of antitheses that convey spiritual paradox. The Apostle Paul regards his moral and religious achievements as garbage when compared to Christ. He deems three things superior to everything he has: (1) knowing Christ, (2) gaining Christ, and (3) being found in Christ. Knowing Christ is not only the rational but the relational knowledge of his Lord. Enjoying an intimate and robust relationship with Christ means more to Paul than any treasures, including his Jewish privileges. To gain Christ is his ultimate goal of life. To gain Christ is to be united to Christ by faith alone, and to experience the resurrection power of Christ in his daily walk (Phil. 3:10). Christ is not only the treasure Paul cherishes but the one who provides the right to have the treasure. To be found in Christ is to be in union with Christ by coming to the end of self, the end of Adam and the old age. To know Christ, gain Christ, and be found in Christ is all he wants. In fact, Christ means everything to him.

January 5

The Whole Measure of the Fullness of Christ

and the Fruit of the Spirit

Until we all reach unity in the faith and in the knowledge of the Son of God and become mature, attaining to the whole measure of the fullness of Christ. (Ephesians 4:13)

So Christ himself gave the apostles, the prophets, the evangelists, the pastors and teachers, to equip his people for works of service, so that the body of Christ may be built up until we all reach unity in the faith and in the knowledge of the Son of God and become mature, attaining to the whole measure of the fullness of Christ (Eph. 4:11-13).

But the fruit of the Spirit is love, joy, peace, forbearance, kindness, goodness, faithfulness, gentleness and self-control. Against such things there is no law. Those who belong to Christ Jesus have crucified the flesh with its passions and desires. Since we live by the Spirit, let us keep in step with the Spirit (Gal. 5:22-25)

Reflection: Unless our sinful nature is dying, our godly characters are not growing. "He must become greater; I must become less." (John 3:30) The only way to pursue holiness is to extinguish our sins (Rom. 6:22). But this is a process. When you are filled with Spirit, you will experience the fullness of Christ. To be filled with Spirit is to attain to the whole measure of the fullness of Christ. We disown the "self" in order to gain Christ. Not only to gain Christ, but to attain to the whole measure of fullness of Christ. The index of the whole measure of the fullness of Christ is the fruit of the Spirit. When we bear the fruit of Spirit, we will demonstrate the whole measure of the fullness of Christ. What is the fullness of Christ? What might be the "whole measure" of this fullness? In the Scriptures, "the fullness of God" (Eph. 3:19) and "the fullness of Christ" (Eph. 4:13) seem to be two interchangeable expressions. As a matter of fact, "the fullness of Christ" is a spiritual life fully saturated with Christ, fully relating to Christ, and fully united with Christ. However, how to attain to the whole measure of fullness of Christ? First of all, we must have desire to be filled with the fullness of Christ. Secondly, we must seek to expand our capacity to be filled with the fullness of Christ. We must enlarge the place of our tent, stretch our tent curtains wide (Isa. 54:2). Last but not least, we must abide in Christ, the true vine, before bearing fruit of the Spirit. We must have intimate relationship and vital union with Christ. We must grow in the knowledge of the Son of God, and grow in spiritual maturity. To experience Christ's fullness, we must spend time developing our intimate relationship and nurturing our vital union with Him. We must allow Christ dwell in our hearts through faith, and allow the Holy Spirit to cultivate the soil of our hearts and thus the fruit of the Spirit yields in our spiritual lives. The fruit of the Spirit is the sign of the whole measure of the fullness of Christ in our spiritual lives. It is the sign that we are filled with the fullness of Christ when the Holy Spirit indwells in us, and we are filled with the Spirit.

January 6

Bear Fruit (I)

Then God said, "Let the land produce vegetation: seed-bearing plants and trees on the land that bear fruit with seed in it, according to their various kinds." And it was so. (Genesis 1:11)

Then God said, "Let the land produce vegetation: seed-bearing plants and trees on the land that bear fruit with seed in it, according to their various kinds." And it was so. The land produces vegetation: plants bearing seed according to their kinds and trees bearing fruit with seed in it according to their kinds. And God saw it was good. (Gen. 1:11-12). Fruit trees of all kinds will grow on both banks of the river. Their leaves will not wither, nor will their fruit fail. Every month they will bear fruit, because the water from the sanctuary flows to them. Their fruit will serve for food and their leaves for healing (Ezek. 47:12). The trees are bearing their fruit; the fig tree and the vine yield their riches (Joel 2:22).

Once more a remnant of the kingdom of Judah will take root below and bear fruit above (2 Kings 19:30; Isa. 11:1). They will be like tree planted by the water that sends out its roots by the stream. It does not fear when heat comes; its leaves are always green. It has no worries in a year of drought and never fails to bear fruit (Jer. 17:8). They will bear fruit in old age, they will stay fresh and green (Ps. 92:14). A shoot will come up from the stump of Jesse; from his roots a Branch will bear fruit (Isa. 11:1). It will produce branches and bear fruit and become a splendid cedar. Birds of every kind will nest in it; they will find Shelter in the shade of its branches (Ezek. 17:23). It had been planted in good soil by abundant water so that it would produce branches, bear fruit and become a splendid vine (Ezek. 17:8).

Reflection: In the Scriptures, fruit plays an important metaphor to spiritual life. It connotes the productivity and abundance of our spiritual life. Because the fruit and the spiritual life have many similarities, fruit perfectly serves as a simile of the spiritual life. For instance, the secrets of bearing fruit remind us of the secrets of growing spiritual life. One of the secrets of bearing fruit is that the tree must be planted in good soil by abundant water (Ezek. 17:8), that is the rivers of living water (John 7:38). And the rivers of living water signify the Holy Spirit. The Holy Spirit, like the life-giving sap will flow up the trunk of a tree to all its branches so they can yield fruit! And we, like a tree planted by streams of water, will yield our fruits in season, and our leaf will not wither (Ps. 1:1). Every month, the fruit trees of all kinds will bear fruits, because the water from the sanctuary flows to them. The spiritual significance is that, our lives won't bear the fruit of the Spirit if the rivers of living water (John 7:38) don't flow to us. On the other hand, if we receive the living water from Jesus, it will become in us a spring of water welling up to eternal life. If we, like a tree, take root below, and deeply root our spiritual life in Jesus Christ, we will bear fruit above, and stay fresh and green. We must root our spiritual life in good soil which is an open heart that crave for the word of God, by abundant water which is the rivers of living water – the Son and the Spirit. The water comes from the sanctuary where the throne of God is located. We must approach the throne of grace with confidence, so that we may receive mercy and find grace to help us in our time of need (Heb. 4:16).

January 7

Bear Fruit (II)

Remain in me, as I also remain in you. No branch can bear fruit by itself; it must remain in the vine. Neither can you bear fruit unless you remain in me. I am the vine; you are the branches. If you remain in me and I in you, you will bear much fruit; apart from me you can do nothing. (John 15:4-5)

Every good tree bears good fruit, but a bad tree bears bad fruit. A good tree cannot bear bad fruit, and a bad tree cannot bear good fruit (Matt. 7:17-18). No good tree bears bad fruit, nor does a bad tree bear good fruit (Luke 6:43).

Seeing a fig tree by the road, he (Jesus) went up to it but found nothing on it except leaves. Then he said to it. "May you never bear fruit again!" Immediately the tree withered (Matt. 21:19). Every tree that does not bear good fruit is cut down and thrown into fire (Matt. 7:17-19). If it bears fruit next year, fine! If not, then cut it down (Luke 13:9). He (the Father) cuts off every branch in me (Jesus) that bears no fruit, while every branch that does bear fruit he prunes so that it will be even more fruitful (John 15:2). Remain in me, as I also remain in you. No branch can bear fruit by itself; it must remain in the vine. Neither can you bear fruit unless you remain in me. I am the vine; you are the branches. If you remain in me and I in you, you will bear much fruit; apart from me you can do nothing (John 15:4-5). This is my Father's glory, that you bear much fruit, showing yourselves to be my disciples (John 15:8). You did not choose me, but I chose you and appointed you so that you might go and bear fruit – fruit that will last – and so that whatever you ask in my name the Father will give you (John 15:16).

My brothers and sisters, you also died to the law through the body of Christ, that you might belong to another, to him who was raised from the dead, in order that we might bear fruit for God (Rom. 7:4). The gospel is bearing fruit and growing throughout the whole world (Col. 1:6), bearing fruit in every good work, growing in the knowledge of God (Col. 1:10).

Reflection: Another secret of bearing fruit, actually, is identical to the previous one in essence, which is abiding in Christ. Jesus Christ reminds us to remain in Him again and again. Because He is the vine, and we are branches. Only by remaining in the vine, the branches receive the nutrition that sustains their lives. No branch can bear fruit by itself; it must remain in the vine. Neither can we bear fruit unless we abide in Christ. Upon leaving the vine, branches will become dry wood. Without abiding in Christ, our spiritual life will wither away. "Abiding in Christ" depicts dynamics that secures our vital relationship with the Lord. We have to deepen our relationship with the Lord in order to grow our spiritual life. When we abide in Christ, the law of the Spirit that gives life will impart us righteousness. As a result, we will bear fruit, and much fruit. The Word of Life not only created life, but also changes life. Jesus, the Word of Life came to the world in order to give us life, abundant life. Eternal life is in essence the abundant life, the life of righteousness and of holiness. The full measure of blessing is manifested in the fruit of the Spirit, which is love, joy, peace, forbearance, kindness, goodness, faithfulness, gentleness, and self-control (Gal. 5:22-23). The full measure of blessing is actually the whole measure of the fullness of Christ (Eph. 4;13). In order to help us bear fruit, the Lord always put us in trials, and let us experience suffering and difficulties. He cuts off every branch in us that bears no fruit, while every branch that does bear fruit He prunes so that it will be even more fruitful (John 15:2). After our spiritual life is pruned as the branches, we will bear fruit, and much fruit for God. We will bear fruit in every good work, and grow in the knowledge of God.

January 8

Sorrow and Joy

And those the Lord has rescued will return. They will enter Zion with singing; everlasting joy will crown their heads. Gladness and joy will overtake them, and sorrow and sighing will flee away. (Isaiah 35:10; 51:11)

When the Jews got relief from their enemies, and when their sorrow was turned into joy and their mourning into a day of celebration, Mordecai wrote them to observe the days as days of feasting and joy and giving presents of food to one another and gifts to the poor (Esth. 9:22). And those the Lord has rescued will return. They will enter Zion with singing; everlasting joy will crown their heads. Gladness and joy will overtake them, and sorrow and sighing will flee away (Isa. 35:10; 51:11). They will come and shout for joy on the heights of Zion; they will rejoice in the bounty of the Lord— the grain, the new wine and the olive oil, the young of the flocks and herds. They will be like a well-watered garden, and they will sorrow no more (Jer. 31:12). Then young women will dance and be glad, young men and old as well. (This is what the Lord says,) I will turn their mourning into gladness; I will give them comfort and joy instead of sorrow (Jer. 31:13).

Very truly I tell you, you will weep and mourn while the world rejoices. You will grieve, but your grief will turn to joy (John 16:20). So with you: Now is your time of grief, but I will see you again and you will rejoice, and no one will take away your joy (John 16:22).

Reflection: Zion is another name of Jerusalem. For the people of Israel, Zion means the source of their joy, the highest joy (Ps. 137:6). Songs of joy are songs of Zion (Ps. 137:3). The Psalmist sings, "Great is the LORD, and most worthy of praise, in the city of our God, his holy mountain. Beautiful in its loftiness, the joy of the whole earth, like the heights of Zaphon is Mount Zion, the city of the Great King" (Ps. 48:1-2). That is why prophets prophesized that when the Israelites returned to Zion, they would enter Zion with singing; everlasting joy would crown their heads, and sorrow and sighing would flee away; they would come and shout for joy on the heights of Zion, and they would sorrow no more. The Psalmist sings, "Those who sow with tears will reap with songs of joy." (Ps. 126:5). In the history of Israel, the Israelites have suffered from slavery and captivity, war and disaster. They have experienced bitter sorrow, despair, humiliation, and abuse. As a small and weak nation, they have been enslaved and oppressed by the powers of the time. However, although sowing in tears, they have reaped in joy. In the time of deliverance from the Lord, God of Israel, their sorrow was turned into joy and their mourning into a day of celebration. Likewise, when we diligently labor for the gospel with blood, toil, tears and sweat, we will reap in joy in the time of redemption from Christ.

January 9

What is Eternal Life

And this is the testimony: God has given us eternal life, and this life is in his Son. He who has the Son has life; he who does not have the Son of God does not have life. (I John 5:11-12)

What is eternal life? Eternal life is like a tree planted by streams of water. (Ps. 1:3). And the streams of water are River of Life (Rev. 22.). He who has the Son has life (1 John 5:12). He who believes in the name of the Son of God has eternal life (1 John 5:13). Eternal life is to have the life of the Son. If someone has the life of the Son, "streams of living water will flow from within him." (John 7:38).

To have eternal life is to have the life of the Son. Eternal life is not only the status of life which is everlasting, but the quality of life which is of holiness. "To those who by persistence in doing good seek glory, honor and immortality, he will give eternal life." (Rom. 2:7). And the quality of life is expressed in one's characters. In other words, eternal life is the characters of Christ that are manifested in the fruit of the Spirit: love, joy, peace, forbearance, kindness, goodness, faithfulness, gentleness and self-control (Gal. 5:22-23). However, eternal life is indeed everlasting, since the characters of Christ or the fruit of the Spirit is everlasting (Heb. 7:3; Gal. 6:8). The quality of such life determines the eternality of such life.

Reflection: Jesus came to give us life, and abundant life. Eternal life is abundant life, a life abundant with holiness. Eternal life will be bestowed to one who pursues holiness. Eternal life is the life of holiness. Eternal life is a life which is lived to God, and is dead to sin but alive to God in Christ Jesus (Rom. 6:10-11). Eternal life is Christ-centered life, a life of new self which has been created to be like God in true righteousness and holiness (Eph. 4:24). Eternal life is a life of beatitudes, which reflects the characters of the Son of God. Eternal life is a fruitful life, which bears the fruit of the Spirit. In other words, eternal life is the life of the Son of God, its expressions are the beatitudes, and the fruit of the Spirit. "Eternal life is the life which Jesus Christ exhibited on the human level. And it is this same life, not simply a copy of it, which is made evident in our mortal flesh when we are born again...The life that was in Jesus becomes ours because of His Cross, once we make the decision to be identified with Him." (Oswald Chambers). God gave us eternal life and this life is in His Son (1 John 5:11). "Eternal life is not a gift from God; eternal life is the gift of God." (Oswald Chambers). To receive this amazing gift, we simply need to believe in the name of the Son of God (1John 5:13). As a matter of fact, the way to have the Son is to believe in the name of the Son (1 John 5:12-13). He who has the Son has life (1 John 5:12).

JANUARY 10

CHRIST, THE WORD OF LIFE

That which was from the beginning, which we have heard, which we have seen with our eyes, which we have looked at and our hands have touched—this we proclaim concerning the Word of life. The life appeared; we have seen it and testify to it, and we proclaim to you the eternal life, which was with the Father and has appeared to us. (1 John 1:1-2)

How come, when God spoke, the heaven and earth came to existence; when Jesus spoke, the sick were healed, and the dead were resurrected; but today, we read Bible in which God speaks to us, and our lives have not been changed? The reason is that, we never see God's face even we read His Word. As long as you see God's face, your life will be changed for sure. Paul is an example (Act 9). How come we don't see God's face? It is because we are not holy, as "without holiness, no one will see the Lord." (Heb. 12:14).

Truth is a Person, a Person whom His disciples had heard, had seen with their eyes, had looked at, and had touched. We still have personal touch with this Person, Son of God, and the Word of Life. The Word of Life is so tangible that we can experience in our daily lives. We can experience Him in every aspect of life (1 John 1:1-2). Especially, we can experience Him in suffering with him, and for Him, and in sharing in His glory (Rom 8:16-17).

Without knowing the risen Lord, we won't be able to understand the Scriptures. Paul was a Pharisee who was well-versed in the Scriptures, but did not know the Lord (Phil. 3:5-6) until he encountered the Risen Lord and was filled with the Holy Spirit (Acts 9).

Reflection: Perhaps one of the most profound names of Jesus Christ in the Scriptures is the "Word of Life", which reveals His divine attribute of life capable of providing eternal life. He is the Word and He gives life – the eternal life. "In him was life." (John 1:4). He is the Word of God incarnate (John 1:14), and the life-giving Spirit (1 Cor. 15:45). He represents the living Word of God. He was the Word of Life even before the creation. He existed from eternity. And He is the eternal life that has no end (John 14:6). Moreover, the Word of God was not only the agent in the creation, but the source of all life. Without the Word of Life, no life would have come into existence. Furthermore, the Word of Life is the only begotten Son, who is in the bosom of the Father (John 1:18). He is always in an intimate relation with the Father. "The 'Word of Life' combines the two truths that (Christ Jesus) is Himself life and that He imparts it, as the life (John 14:6), He is the personal expression of what God is, the interpreter of His nature (John 1:18)" (W.E. Vine). He is the way and the truth and the life. No one comes to the Father except through Him (John 14:6). The Son is the Incarnate Truth, the Incarnate Word of God, and the Word of Life. Experiencing God and encountering the Risen Lord is the key to our spiritual growth. Knowing His Incarnate Word (Jesus Christ) will lead to knowing His written Word (the Scriptures). The Truth can be touched; and we can touch the Truth. Touch the Truth, experience the Truth, know the Truth, and hold firmly to the Word of Life (Phil. 2:16), this is the secret to the spiritual life which is full of blessings. On the other hand, without seeing the risen Lord, and encountering the Word of life, we won't believe that the Promises in the Scriptures are true. God's Written Word won't work in our lives if His Incarnate Word is not accepted by us. God's Written Word and His Incarnate Word work together in our salvation.

January 11

Suffering and Holiness

Therefore, since Christ suffered in his body, arm yourselves also with the same attitude, because he who has suffered in his body is done with sin. (1 Peter 4:1)

Suffering like Christ leads to holiness. "Therefore, since Christ suffered in his body, arm yourselves also with the same attitude, because he who has suffered in his body is done with sin." (1 Pet. 4:1) Suffering is a path to holiness. If we are put in a trial by the Lord, we are so blessed, as the Lord sees precious outcrop of faith in our lives. However, there are still some dross and impurities in our lives. So, the Lord puts us in a refining furnace, and purifies us seven times (Ps. 12:6) until all the dross and impurities are purged away. "I will turn my hand against you; I will thoroughly purge away your dross and remove all your impurities." (Isa. 1:25). After dross and impurities are removed, the Lord will clearly see His own image mirrored in our lives. At this point, we will become Christ-like and be made perfect, as the Scriptures read, "In bringing many sons and daughters to glory, it was fitting that God, for whom and through whom everything exists, should make the pioneer of their salvation perfect through what he suffered." (Heb. 2:10). "Son though he was, he learned obedience from what he suffered and, once made perfect, he became the source of eternal salvation for all who obey him." (Heb. 5:8-9). And we will share in His glory if we share in His sufferings: "Now if we are children, then we are heirs—heirs of God and co-heirs with Christ, if indeed we share in his sufferings in order that we may also share in his glory" (Rom. 8:17).

Reflection: The Scriptures teach us, "Indeed, all who desire to live godly in Christ Jesus will be persecuted" (2 Tim. 3:12). In other words, no one can be holy and not suffer. Suffering persecution for the sake of Christ is a required course in our spiritual journey. Jesus Christ, the Son of God, has suffered for righteousness, and we must follow His steps (1 Pet. 2:20-21), because "a disciple is not above his teacher, nor a slave above his master" (Matt. 10:24). God imparts holiness through suffering and humiliation of His Son. God cannot suffer, but He did suffer with us, in our most human weaknesses, even death (St. Bernard of Clairvaux). We shall fix our eyes on Jesus, the author and perfecter of faith, who for the joy set before Him endured the cross, despising the shame, and has sat down at the right hand of the throne of God (Heb. 12:2). Through suffering, God disciplines us for our good, so that we may share His holiness. All discipline for the moment seems not to be joyful, but sorrowful; yet to those who have been trained by it, afterwards it yields the peaceful fruit of righteousness (Heb. 12:10-11). The Cross is the ladder to God (St. Rose of Lima); and suffering is the way to holiness. Therefore, suffering is necessary for us to grow in holiness, and without holiness, we will never be in union with God. "God causes all things to work together for good to those who love God, to those who are called according to His purpose." (Rom. 8:28). God has a purpose in the sufferings of His people. The purpose is to increase hope and holiness of His people through suffering: "we exult in hope of the glory of God. And not only this, but we also exult in our tribulations, knowing that tribulation brings about perseverance; and perseverance, proven character; and proven character, hope." (Rom. 5:2-4). Suffering is the approach to get done with sin. Suffering is a school of holiness in which we learn from our Lord. The Lord has called us to follow in His steps by suffering for righteousness. We have no shortcut to the goal of holiness but suffering.

January 12

Suffer according to God's will

So then, those who suffer according to God's will should commit themselves to their faithful Creator and continue to do good. (1 Peter 4:19)

Not all the sufferings will lead to blessing. To suffer according to God's will is the key (1 Pet. 4:19). God will let everything work together for the good of those who love Him, who have been called according to His purpose (Rom. 8:28). If we are called according to His purpose, we are called to suffer according to His will. As Christ's disciples, we are called to suffer by the Lord Himself: "Whoever wants to be my disciple must deny themselves and take up their cross and follow me." (Mark 8:34).

The Apostle Peter encourages us, "Dear friends, do not be surprised at the fiery ordeal that has come on you to test you, as though something strange were happening to you. But rejoice inasmuch as you participate in the sufferings of Christ, so that you may be overjoyed when his glory is revealed. If you are insulted because of the name of Christ, you are blessed, for the Spirit of glory and of God rests on you. If you suffer, it should not be as a murderer or thief or any other kind of criminal, or even as a meddler. However, if you suffer as a Christian, do not be ashamed, but praise God that you bear that name." (1 Pet. 4:12-16).

He also exhorts us, "Slaves, in reverent fear of God submit yourselves to your masters, not only to those who are good and considerate, but also to those who are harsh. For it is commendable if someone bears up under the pain of unjust suffering because they are conscious of God. But how is it to your credit if you receive a beating for doing wrong and endure it? But if you suffer for doing good and you endure it, this is commendable before God. To this you were called, because Christ suffered for you, leaving you an example, that you should follow in his steps." (1 Pet. 2:18-21)

Reflection: Those who suffer according to God's will are those who suffer for righteousness. They should have assurance that "the peace of God, which transcends all understanding, will guard your hearts and your minds in Christ Jesus." (Phil. 4:7). Having such assurance, we must commit ourselves to our faithful Creator who creates all things by His Word. The Lord also encourages us: "Be strong and courageous. ... Be strong and very courageous." (Josh. 1:6, 7), as He "will never leave you nor forsake you." (Josh. 1:5). Daniel's three friends: Shadrach, Meschach and Abednego had such experience that a son of the gods was with them while they were put into fiery furnace (Dan. 3:25). To commit ourselves to our faithful Creator in the midst of suffering also means that we trust His righteousness, and we leave everything to His justice. We "do not take revenge... but leave room for God's wrath, for it is written: 'It is mine to avenge; I will repay.'" (Rom. 12:19) and we continue to do good. "Bless those who persecute you" (Rom 12:14), and "Do not repay anyone evil for evil. Be careful to do what is right in the eyes of everybody." (Rom 12:17) "Do not be overcome by evil, but overcome evil with good." (Rom 12:21). Obedience is the highest level of faith. To follow Christ means to obey each and every of His commands. Obedience also suggests confidence - confidence in Christ's Lordship. And this confidence is true faith. Consequently, true faith is obedience. Without obedience, we won't be able to follow Christ. Faith is not only to believe in the person of Christ, but to follow Him, even follow in His step by suffering for righteousness (1 Pet. 2:21).

January 13

Suffering and Comfort

My comfort in my suffering is this: Your promise preserves my life. (Psalm 119:50)

Christ suffered for us, and set us an example (1 Pet. 2:21). Since Christ suffered in his body, we shall arm ourselves with the same attitude (1 Pet. 4:1). The Apostle Peter is convinced that he will share in the glory to be revealed, as a witness of Christ's sufferings (1 Pet. 5:1).

Yes, the Spirit of Christ predicted the sufferings of Christ and the glories that would follow (1 Pet. 1:11). Likewise, we are called to God's glory in Christ (1 Pet. 5:10), if we participate in the sufferings of Christ (1 Pet. 4:13), because if indeed we share in His sufferings, we will share in His glory (Rom. 8:17).

What a comfort to us! We will be overjoyed when the glory of Christ is revealed (1 Pet. 4:13). Let's rejoice in suffering (Col. 1:24). Just as the sufferings of Christ flow over into our lives, our comfort overflows through Christ (2 Cor. 1:5). Thus, we can say to the Lord. "My comfort in my suffering is this: Your promise preserves my life." (Ps. 119:50).

Reflection: God not only created the world with His word, but also sustain the world with his word. Likewise, God not only created us in His own image with His word, but preserves our lives with His word: "My comfort in my suffering is this: your promise preserves my life." (Ps. 119:50). We have His promise to preserves our lives. This is the reason that we have comfort in the midst of suffering. And we have reason to rejoice in the midst of suffering, as the Scriptures promise: "For our light and momentary troubles are achieving for us an eternal glory that far outweighs them all." (2 Cor. 4:17). Suffering is one of the major topics in many religions and philosophies. Human-beings have endeavored to find answer of the reasons and causes of suffering. In fact, faith is not expected to provide the answer of the reasons and causes of suffering, but it is to help us endure the suffering. God never promises that we won't suffer in misery, but He promises that He will comfort us, as the Psalmist declares, "Even though I walk through the darkest valley, I will fear no evil, for you are with me; your rod and your staff, they comfort me." (Ps. 23:4); and as the Lord Jesus Christ promises, "I have told you these things, so that in me you may have peace. In this world you will have trouble. But take heart! I have overcome the world." (John 16:33). Suffering and comfort are a pair of antitheses, however, God can turn our suffering into comfort, as long as we fix our eyes on Jesus, the author and the perfector of faith in the midst of suffering.

January 14

Obedience and Sacrifice

But Samuel replied: "Does the Lord delight in burnt offerings and sacrifices as much as in obeying the Lord? To obey is better than sacrifice, and to heed is better than the fat of rams." (1 Samuel 15:22)

Now it came about after these things, that God tested Abraham, and said to him, "Abraham!" And he said, "Here I am." He said, "Take now your son, your only son, whom you love, Isaac, and go to the land of Moriah, and offer him there as a burnt offering on one of the mountains of which I will tell you." So Abraham rose early in the morning and saddled his donkey, and took two of his young men with him and Isaac his son; and he split wood for the burnt offering, and arose and went to the place of which God had told him. On the third day Abraham raised his eyes and saw the place from a distance. Abraham said to his young men, "Stay here with the donkey, and I and the lad will go over there; and we will worship and return to you." Abraham took the wood of the burnt offering and laid it on Isaac his son, and he took in his hand the fire and the knife. So the two of them walked on together. Isaac spoke to Abraham his father and said, "My father!" And he said, "Here I am, my son." And he said, "Behold, the fire and the wood, but where is the lamb for the burnt offering?" Abraham said, "God will provide for Himself the lamb for the burnt offering, my son." So the two of them walked on together. Then they came to the place of which God had told him; and Abraham built the altar there and arranged the wood, and bound his son Isaac and laid him on the altar, on top of the wood. Abraham stretched out his hand and took the knife to slay his son. But the angel of the Lord called to him from heaven and said, "Abraham, Abraham!" And he said, "Here I am." He said, "Do not stretch out your hand against the lad, and do nothing to him; for now I know that you fear God, since you have not withheld your son, your only son, from Me." Then Abraham raised his eyes and looked, and behold, behind him a ram caught in the thicket by his horns; and Abraham went and took the ram and offered him up for a burnt offering in the place of his son. Abraham called the name of that place The Lord Will Provide, as it is said to this day, "In the mount of the Lord it will be provided." (Gen. 22:1-14).

But Samuel replied: "Does the Lord delight in burnt offerings and sacrifices as much as in obeying the Lord? To obey is better than sacrifice, and to heed is better than the fat of rams" (1 Sam. 15:22).

Reflection: True obedience always involves sacrifice. As the Father of faith, Abraham is a good example of obedience. Actually, faith in God means to believe in God, to trust God, and to obey God. Obedience is faith in action, and is volitional aspect of faith. Abraham not only believed in the Lord, and trusted the Lord, but obeyed the Lord. He obeyed the Lord "When called to a place he would later receive as his inheritance, obeyed and went, even though he did not know where he was going." (Heb. 11:8); He obeyed the Lord when he was commanded to have himself and his household circumcised (Gen. 17:23, 21:4). When he was commanded by the Lord to sacrifice his only son, Isaac as a burnt offering, his faith was tested at the utmost extent, as he had to show his obedience that will sacrifice his only son, the most precious thing to himself, although he reasoned God could raise the dead, his obedience demanded sacrifice (Heb. 11:17-19). This is the highest level of obedience, and the highest level of faith. The highest level of faith is dedication and obedience at the cost of self-sacrifice. True obedience always involves sacrifice. When sacrifice is demanded, our level of obedience is tested, thus the level of our faith is tested. Obedience is the highest level of faith. True faith is demonstrated in obedience. To follow Christ is to follow in His steps in obedience. We all know the reason that God stopped Abraham from slaying Isaac is that Abraham did pass the test of faith by being willing to sacrifice his only son. In my opinion, there is one more reason, which is that the Lord delights in Abraham's obedience more than in burnt offerings and sacrifices he was going to offer, as the Scriptures read, "Does the Lord delight in burnt offerings and sacrifices as much as in obeying the Lord? To obey is better than sacrifice, and to heed is better than the fat of rams." (1 Sam. 15:22).

JANUARY 15

OBEDIENCE THAT IS WORTHWHILE

I swear by myself, declares the Lord, that because you have done this and have not withheld your son, your only son, I will surely bless you and make your descendants as numerous as the stars in the sky and as the sand on the seashore. Your descendants will take possession of the cities of their enemies, and through your offspring all nations on earth will be blessed, because you have obeyed me. (Genesis 22:16-18)

Does the LORD delight in burnt offerings and sacrifices as much as in obeying the voice of the LORD? To obey is better than sacrifice, and to heed is better than the fat of rams. (1 Sam. 15:22)

The angel of the Lord called to Abraham from heaven a second time and said, "I swear by myself, declares the Lord, that because you have done this and have not withheld your son, your only son, I will surely bless you and make your descendants as numerous as the stars in the sky and as the sand on the seashore. Your descendants will take possession of the cities of their enemies, and through your offspring all nations on earth will be blessed, because you have obeyed me." (Gen. 22:15-18).

Reflection: When Abraham obeyed the voice of the Lord, and was ready to sacrifice his only son, Isaac as a burnt offering on one of the mountains in the region of Moriah, the angel of the Lord stopped him (Gen. 22:1-12). The angel said to Abraham: "Now I know that you fear God, because you have not withheld from me your son, your only son." (Gen. 22:12). Why the Lord didn't want Abraham's sacrifice anymore? Not only because Abraham passed a test of faith, more precisely, a test of obedience; but because God delighted in his obedience more than in the burnt offering which he was going to make by sacrificing his only son (1 Sam. 15:22). Abraham's obedience was worthwhile. The Lord provided him a ram by which he sacrificed as a burnt offering instead of his son (Gen. 22:13). And he came to realize that God is the Lord Will Provide (Gen. 22:13-14). Because of his obedience, God revealed to him that He is the Lord Will Provide. Yes, our obedience helps us know God more, and help us receive and understand God's revelation. Furthermore, the Lord promised to Abraham great blessings as a reward to his obedience. The angel spoke on behalf of the Lord: "I swear by myself, declares the Lord, that because you have done this and have not withheld your son, your only son, I will surely bless you and make your descendants as numerous as the stars in the sky and as the sand on the seashore. Your descendants will take possession of the cities of their enemies, and through your offspring all nations on earth will be blessed, because you have obeyed me." (Gen. 22:16-18). Our obedience to God is the key to receiving his abundant blessings. Although Saul offered sacrifice to God, he showed disobedience to God. And God removed him from the throne (1 Sam. 13:8-9, 14). In contrast, when Abraham built an altar, he bound his son Isaac and laid him on it. An altar is a place of worship. He rendered God a true worship which involved sacrifice and obedience, a living sacrifice and true obedience. However, just because he did not withhold his son, his only son, God promised to him: "I will surely bless you and make your descendants as numerous as the stars in the sky and as the sand on the seashore. Your descendants will take possession of the cities of their enemies, and through your offspring all nations on earth will be blessed, because you have obeyed me." (Gen. 22:17-18). Our obedience is what God values the most, and is always worthwhile.

January 16

Obedience in the Midst of Suffering

Son though he was, he learned obedience from what he suffered and, once made perfect, he became the source of eternal salvation for all who obey him. (Hebrews 5:8-9)

Then Jesus came with them to a place called Gethsemane, and said to His disciples, "Sit here while I go over there and pray." And He took with Him Peter and the two sons of Zebedee, and began to be grieved and distressed. Then He said to them, "My soul is deeply grieved, to the point of death; remain here and keep watch with Me." And He went a little beyond them, and fell on His face and prayed, saying, "My Father, if it is possible, let this cup pass from Me; yet not as I will, but as You will." And He came to the disciples and found them sleeping, and said to Peter, "So, you men could not keep watch with Me for one hour? Keep watching and praying that you may not enter into temptation; the spirit is willing, but the flesh is weak."

He went away again a second time and prayed, saying, "My Father, if this cannot pass away unless I drink it, Your will be done." Again He came and found them sleeping, for their eyes were heavy. And He left them again, and went away and prayed a third time, saying the same thing once more (Matt. 26:36-44; also see Mark 14:32-39, Luke 22:39-44).

During the days of Jesus' life on earth, he offered up prayers and petitions with fervent cries and tears to the one who could save him from death, and he was heard because of his reverent submission. Son though he was, he learned obedience from what he suffered and, once made perfect, he became the source of eternal salvation for all who obey him and was designated by God to be high priest in the order of Melchizedek (Heb. 5:7-10).

Reflection: Although He was the Son of God, Jesus Christ was not exempted from suffering. Jesus' suffering has a purpose which is to let him learn obedience. And His obedience made others righteous: "For just as through the disobedience of the one man the many were made sinners, so also through the obedience of the one man the many will be made righteous." (Rom 5:19). And Jesus Himself has been perfected: "In bringing many sons to glory, it was fitting that God, for whom and through whom everything exists, should make the author of their salvation perfect through suffering." (Heb. 2:10). Christ's obedience in the midst of suffering has made it possible that "in all things God works for the good of those who love him, who have been called according to his purpose." (Rom. 8:28). Even in His Son's suffering, God has a good purpose. God's purpose can be understood this way. He let His only-begotten son suffer for righteousness, and learn obedience in the midst of suffering. Christ has thus been perfected. And He also made others who believe in Him righteous. Finally, they are brought to glory. Even the Son of God needed to learn obedience by the things which He suffered. Let alone us. Having been perfected, He became the author of eternal salvation to all who obey Him. Pay attention here, "He became the author of eternal salvation to all who obey Him." Only will those who obey Him receive salvation.

January 17

Trust in the Lord

Trust in the LORD with all your heart and lean not on your own understanding; in all your ways submit to him, and he will make your paths straight. (Proverbs 3:5-6)

I hate those who cling to worthless idols; as for me, I trust in the LORD (Ps. 31:6). The greedy stir up conflict, but those who trust in the LORD will prosper (Prov. 28:25). All you Israelites, trust in the LORD— he is their help and shield. House of Aaron, trust in the LORD— he is their help and shield. You who fear him, trust in the LORD— he is their help and shield (Ps. 115:9-11). Those who trust in the LORD are like Mount Zion, which cannot be shaken but endures forever (Ps. 125:1).

Trust in the LORD with all your heart and lean not on your own understanding; in all your ways submit to him, and he will make your paths straight (Prov. 3:5-6). Trust in the LORD and do good; dwell in the land and enjoy safe pasture (Ps. 37:3). Trust in the LORD forever, for the LORD, the LORD himself, is the Rock eternal (Isa. 26:4). Offer the sacrifices of the righteous and trust in the LORD (Ps. 4:5).

Reflections: Our faith has three realms. The first realm is the rational realm. In this realm, we believe in the Triune God with intellect. The second realm is the emotional realm. In this realm, we trust in the Lord with all our heart. The third realm, which is the highest realm, is the volitional realm. In this realm, we obey the LORD our God and keep His commands and decrees. To trust in the Lord means more than believing in who He is and what He says, it means to place our confidence only in the Lord, to have confidence in Him, and to entrust everything to the Lord: "Commit your way to the LORD; trust in him." (Ps. 37:5); "Commit to the LORD whatever you do, and he will establish your plans." (Prov. 16:3). Without knowing God and knowing God better (Eph. 1:17), we won't be able to trust in the Lord. On the other hand, if we truly know God, we will trust in Him. If we truly know God, we will believe what He says, "For as the heavens are higher than the earth, so are my ways higher than your ways and my thoughts than your thoughts." (Isa. 55:9). We will have confidence in the depth of the riches of the wisdom and knowledge of God, and His unsearchable judgments (Rom. 11:33). If we commit to the LORD whatever we do, we will have assurance that He will establish our plans in the best time, in the best place, and in the best way. Even if sometimes things don't go in a favorable way, God will cause "all things to work together for good of those who love him, who have been called according to his purpose." (Rom. 8:28).

January 18

Jesus Christ is the Goal of Our Spiritual Race

Brothers and sisters, I do not consider myself yet to have taken hold of it. But one thing I do: Forgetting what is behind and straining toward what is ahead, I press on toward the goal to win the prize for which God has called me heavenward in Christ Jesus. (Philippians 3:13-14)

Therefore, since we are surrounded by such a great cloud of witnesses, let us throw off everything that hinders and the sin that so easily entangles. And let us run with perseverance the race marked out for us, fixing our eyes on Jesus, the pioneer and perfecter of faith. For the joy set before him he endured the cross, scorning its shame, and sat down at the right hand of the throne of God (Heb. 12:1-2).

Not that I have already obtained all this, or have already been made perfect, but I press on to take hold of that for which Christ Jesus took hold of me. Brothers, I do not consider myself yet to have taken hold of it. But one thing I do: Forgetting what is behind and straining toward what is ahead, I press on toward the goal to win the prize for which God has called me heavenward in Christ Jesus. Let us therefore, as many as are perfect, have this attitude; and if in anything you have a different attitude, God will reveal that also to you; however, let us keep living by that same standard to which we have attained (Phil. 3:12-16).

Reflection: We all know that Jesus Christ is the object of our faith, but we seem to neglect that He is also the author and perfecter of our faith. We always assume that we are the generator of our faith. In fact, Jesus Christ is not only the object of our faith, but the author of our faith. Without Him, we will have no true faith at all. We won't have the object of faith. Moreover, our faith won't come to existence. Satan attempts to allure us to shift our eyes from the Creator to Creatures, to shift our eyes from the author and perfecter of our faith to everything else. However, we should fix our eyes on Jesus, the author and perfecter of our faith, who is also the goal which we must press on toward in our spiritual race. Christlikeness is the goal of our spiritual race. As long as we focus our eyes on the goal, we will finish the race well, and receive a good prize which is the crown of glory (I Peter 5:4). If we don't fix our eyes on the goal, we won't be able to press on toward it, and won't be able to reach the goal. You go to where you fix your eyes on. If you fix your eyes on the worldly things, you will be tempted by them. If you fix your eyes on difficulties, you will be defeated by them. If you fix your eyes on Jesus, the author and perfecter of our faith, you will come to Jesus. Our spiritual journey is a race which cannot be run without fixing our eyes on Jesus, who is our goal of sanctification.

January 19

The Meaning of Joy

Rejoice always, pray continually, give thanks in all circumstances; for this is God's will for you in Christ Jesus. (1 Thessalonians 5:16-18)

What is joy? Joy is neither gladness nor happiness. Gladness is a mood; and happiness is a feeling. Both of them are dependent on circumstances. Joy is an attitude of heart, and it is not dependent on circumstances. Joy is satisfaction with God, regardless of what circumstances. We cannot be glad or happy in all circumstances, but we can be joyful in all circumstances: "Be joyful always; pray continually; give thanks in all circumstances" (I Thess. 5:16-18).

As long as we see the Lord, we will be filled with joy (John 20:20); even as long as we believe in the Lord, we will be filled with joy (Acts 16:34). Without the Lord, we will have no joy at all, as joy is an attitude by which we enjoy the presence of the Lord in all circumstances, by which we "rejoice in the Lord." (Ps. 33:1; Isa. 41:16; Hab. 3:8; Phil. 3:1, 4:4,10). Joy is to be delighted in the Almighty (Job 22:26).

In fact, the Lord is the source of our joy (Zech. 10:7, Rom. 14:17, 1 Thess. 1:6). Our joy is originated from the joy of the Lord (John 17:13). "And the joy of the Lord is our strength." (Neh. 8:10). "Strength and joy are in His dwelling place" (1 Chron. 16:27). If you want to have true joy, you have to come to the Lord. If you "come near to God and He will come near to you" (James 4:8), as God is the source of our joy, "surely then you will find delight in the Almighty." (Job 22:26).

Reflection: Joy is satisfaction with God, and peace is reconciliation with God. Joy is to enjoy His presence; peace can only be found in our relationship with God. The Lord is the source of our joy. We cannot find joy outside of the Lord. The joy of the Lord is our strength. Let's find strength and joy in His dwelling place. In fact, joy is rejoicing in the Lord (1 Sam. 2:1; Ps. 32:11, 35:9, 64:10, 97:12, 104:34; Isa. 29:19, 41:16; Joel 2:23; Hab. 3:18; Zech. 10:7; Phil. 3:1, 4:4,10). Christian joy is a good feeling in the soul, produced by the Holy Spirit, as He causes us to see the beauty of Christ in the word and in the world (John Piper). In other words, joy is the result of the work of the Holy Spirit. The Holy Spirit opens the eyes of our heart to see the beauty of Christ. As a matter of fact, joy is the fruit of the Holy Spirit. There is only a single fruit of the Holy Spirit, which is "love". If we personify "love", "joy" will be her "smile". Joy is expressed as "smile" of "love". The Holy Spirit bears this fruit by causing us to see the beauty of Jesus Christ. Gladness is a mood, happiness is a feeling, and joy is an attitude, an attitude that rejoices in the Lord regardless of circumstances. It is satisfaction with God, when we are able to behold the glory of Christ in the midst of sufferings, as the Apostle Peter teaches us, "Praise be to the God and Father of our Lord Jesus Christ! In his great mercy he has given us new birth into a living hope through the resurrection of Jesus Christ from the dead, and into an inheritance that can never perish, spoil or fade. This inheritance is kept in heaven for you, who through faith are shielded by God's power until the coming of the salvation that is ready to be revealed in the last time. In all this you greatly rejoice, though now for a little while you may have had to suffer grief in all kinds of trials. These have come so that the proven genuineness of your faith—of greater worth than gold, which perishes even though refined by fire—may result in praise, glory and honor when Jesus Christ is revealed. Though you have not seen him, you love him; and even though you do not see him now, you believe in him and are filled with an inexpressible and glorious joy, for you are receiving the end result of your faith, the salvation of your souls." (1 Pet. 1:3-9)

January 20

The Fullness of Christ

For God was pleased to have all his fullness dwell in him. (Colossians 1:19)

The Word became flesh and made his dwelling among us. We have seen his glory, the glory of the one and only Son, who came from the Father, full of grace and truth. (John testified concerning him. He cried out, saying, "This is the one I spoke about when I said, 'He who comes after me has surpassed me because he was before me.'") Out of his fullness we have all received grace in place of grace already given. For the law was given through Moses; grace and truth came through Jesus Christ (John 1:14-17).

And God placed all things under his feet and appointed him to be head over everything for the church, which is his body, the fullness of him who fills everything in every way (Eph. 1:22-23).

For this reason I kneel before the Father, from whom every family in heaven and on earth derives its name. I pray that out of his glorious riches he may strengthen you with power through his Spirit in your inner being, so that Christ may dwell in your hearts through faith. And I pray that you, being rooted and established in love, may have power, together with all the Lord's holy people, to grasp how wide and long and high and deep is the love of Christ, and to know this love that surpasses knowledge—that you may be filled to the measure of all the fullness of God (Eph. 3:14-19).

He who descended is the very one who ascended higher than all the heavens, in order to fill the whole universe. So Christ himself gave the apostles, the prophets, the evangelists, the pastors and teachers, to equip his people for works of service, so that the body of Christ may be built up until we all reach unity in the faith and in the knowledge of the Son of God and become mature, attaining to the whole measure of the fullness of Christ (Eph. 4:10-13).

And he is the head of the body, the church; he is the beginning and the firstborn from among the dead, so that in everything he might have the supremacy. For God was pleased to have all his fullness dwell in him, and through him to reconcile to himself all things, whether things on earth or things in heaven, by making peace through his blood, shed on the cross (Col. 1:18-20).

For in Christ all the fullness of the Deity lives in bodily form, and you have been given fullness in Christ, who is the head over every power and authority (Col. 2:9-10).

Reflection: God's fullness is manifested in Christ, the Incarnate Word. Through Christ, God's fullness is accessible. Christ not only has all sufficiency in everything, but has supremacy over all things. The fullness of Christ originated from the fullness of the Father, as God was pleased to have all his fullness be dwelt in him. This indicates that the Father and the Son are one in essence (John. 10:33, 17:22). The Son is the image of the invisible God (Col. 1:15), and He is equal to the Father (John 5:18, 10:33; Phil. 2:6). In Christ, all the fullness of the Deity lives in bodily form. "The Word became flesh, and made his dwelling among us. We have seen his glory, the glory of the one and the only." (John 1:14). Thus, the incarnation was to the full extent. The fullness of the Father dwells in Christ. And the fullness of Christ is given to us (Col. 2:9-10). What amazing grace! We are given abundant life (John 10:10)! No wonder Paul claims: "But whatever was to my profit I now consider loss for the sake of Christ. What is more, I consider everything a loss compared to the surpassing greatness of knowing Christ Jesus my Lord, for whose sake I have lost all things. I consider them rubbish, that I may gain Christ." (Phil. 3:7-8). We, Christians, do not pursue the state of emptiness as Buddhists do; instead, we forsake everything which we deem meaningless, in order to gain the fullness of Christ. When we were born again in Christ, we received eternal life, and the abundant life. Christ gives us life, and abundant life. The fullness of Christ guarantees the abundant life He gives us. When the fullness of Christ is given to us, we are given abundant life.

January 21

Obedience and Righteousness

For just as through the disobedience of the one man the many were made sinners, so also through the obedience of the one man the many will be made righteous. (Romans 5:19)

But the gift is not like the trespass. For if the many died by the trespass of the one man, how much more did God's grace and the gift that came by the grace of the one man, Jesus Christ, overflow to the many! Nor can the gift of God be compared with the result of one man's sin: The judgment followed one sin and brought condemnation, but the gift followed many trespasses and brought justification. For if, by the trespass of the one man, death reigned through that one man, how much more will those who receive God's abundant provision of grace and of the gift of righteousness reign in life through the one man, Jesus Christ! Consequently, just as one trespass resulted in condemnation for all people, so also one righteous act resulted in justification and life for all people. For just as through the disobedience of the one man the many were made sinners, so also through the obedience of the one man the many will be made righteous (Rom. 5:15-19).

Don't you know that when you offer yourselves to someone as obedient slaves, you are slaves of the one you obey—whether you are slaves to sin, which leads to death, or to obedience, which leads to righteousness? But thanks be to God that, though you used to be slaves to sin, you have come to obey from your heart the pattern of teaching that has now claimed your allegiance. You have been set free from sin and have become slaves to righteousness (Rom. 6:16-18).

Reflection: Disobedience was the first sin that human beings have ever committed (Gen. 3). Through the disobedience of the First Adam, humankind was condemned. On the other hand, through the obedience of the Last Adam, the effect of sin has been nullified (Rom. 5:19). Again, obedience is the key. Without Christ's obedience, we would not be made righteous. The First Adam's disobedience made us sinful, whereas, the Second Adam's obedience made us righteous. Christ is humble and obedient, humble before men, and obedient to God. And being found in appearance as a man, he humbled himself by becoming obedient to death — even death on a cross! (Phil. 3:8). Christ became obedient because He humbled himself (Phil. 2:8). Obedience is an act, and humbleness is an attitude. Without attitude of humbleness, there is no act of obedience. Obedience is also an attitude resulted by attitude of humbleness (Phil 2:8). If we are not humble, we won't be obedient. Because of Christ's humbleness and obedience we are made righteous (Rom. 5:19). We are not only declared righteous by God (Rom. 3:22-24), but also made righteous by God (2 Cor. 5:21). In other word, in justification, we not only receive imputed righteousness, but also receive imparted righteousness. Because we are made righteous through obedience of Christ, we become partaker of the divine nature (2 Pet. 1:4), and are enabled to strive for holiness and sanctification (Heb. 12:14).

JANUARY 22

THE REVELATION OF THE MYSTERY OF CHRIST

Now to him who is able to establish you in accordance with my gospel, the message I proclaim about Jesus Christ, in keeping with the revelation of the mystery hidden for long ages past. (Romans 16:25)

Now to him who is able to establish you in accordance with my gospel, the message I proclaim about Jesus Christ, in keeping with the revelation of the mystery hidden for long ages past, but now revealed and made known through the prophetic writings by the command of the eternal God, so that all the Gentiles might come to the obedience that comes from faith — to the only wise God be glory forever through Jesus Christ! Amen (Rom. 16:25-27).

For this reason I, Paul, the prisoner of Christ Jesus for the sake of you Gentiles—Surely you have heard about the administration of God's grace that was given to me for you, that is, the mystery made known to me by revelation, as I have already written briefly. In reading this, then, you will be able to understand my insight into the mystery of Christ, which was not made known to people in other generations as it has now been revealed by the Spirit to God's holy apostles and prophets. This mystery is that through the gospel the Gentiles are heirs together with Israel, members together of one body, and sharers together in the promise in Christ Jesus (Eph. 3:1-6).

Reflection: Revelation means to uncover something. In the context of today's Scriptures, "mystery" means something that was hidden, but has now been revealed: "Now to him who is able to establish you in accordance with my gospel, the message I proclaim about Jesus Christ, in keeping with the revelation of the mystery hidden for long ages past, but now revealed and made known through the prophetic writings by the command of the eternal God, so that all the Gentiles might come to the obedience that comes from faith — to the only wise God be glory forever through Jesus Christ! Amen" (Rom. 16:25-27). In fact, in Romans 16:25-27 and in Ephesians 3:1-6 Paul makes it clear that the mystery that has been hidden for long ages past is that through the gospel the Gentiles are heirs together with Israel, members together of one body, and sharers together in the promise in Christ Jesus (Eph. 3:6). And the revelation of the mystery has been hidden since the world began, however, it has been revealed by the prophetic Scriptures to all partakers of God's promise in Christ for the purpose of obedience to the faith. Therefore, the only way to receive and understand the revelation of the mystery of Christ is through faith in Christ. As a matter of fact, if we don't have faith in Christ, we won't be able to understand what God reveals to us in His book, the Holy Scriptures, even though we are well-versed in it. Israelites are not able to understand the revelation of the mystery of Christ due to their disobedience and their unbelief in Christ. "Their minds were made dull, for to this day the same veil remains when the old covenant is read. It has not been removed, because only in Christ is it taken away. Even to this day when Moses is read, a veil covers their hearts." (2 Cor. 3:14-15). However, when we believe in Christ, we will be able to receive and understand the revelation of God. "Whenever anyone turns to the Lord, the veil is taken away. ...and we, who with unveiled face all reflect the Lord's glory, are being transformed into his likeness with ever-increasing glory." (2 Cor. 3:16, 18).

January 23

A Life Hidden with Christ in God

For you died, and your life is now hidden with Christ in God. When Christ, who is your life, appears, then you also will appear with him in glory. (Colossians 3:3-4)

When Christ died, we died (Col. 2:20). However, our life is hidden with Christ in God (Col. 3:3). Our life in Christ is a new creation (2 Cor. 5:17), and it has experienced formation of the life of Christ (Gal. 4:19) as well as transformation (Phil. 3:20-21).

The meaning of the word *"hidden"* connotes indwelling: we remain in the love of Christ just as Christ remains in the love of the Father (John 15:9-10); it also connotes belonging: "You are of Christ, as Christ is of God." (1 Cor. 3:23). The fact that our life is hidden with Christ in God implies that Christ's power rests on us (2 Cor. 12:9). Moreover, it implies that the peace of Christ rules in our hearts (Col. 3:15), peace to all of us who are in Christ (1 Pet. 5:14), and the peace of God will guard our hearts and minds in Christ (Phil. 4:7).

Christ transforms our lowly bodies to be like His glorious body (Phil. 3:21). We are being transformed into His likeness with ever-increasing glory (2 Cor. 3:18). And God brings many sons to glory (Heb. 2:10). Although Christ's glory is hidden, one day, His glory will be revealed (1 Pet. 4:13). And we will see His glorious appearing (Tit. 2:13). When Christ, who is our life, appears, then we also will appear with Him in glory (1 Col. 3:4).

Reflection: Our life is hidden with Christ in God. This means indwelling and belonging. It also means empowering, ruling, and guarding. Our life is hidden with Christ in God. This implies that we are united with Christ in God, and we are covered by Christ. He is our refuge and fortress, and He is our rock, our shield, our stronghold, and our dwelling place. Although Christ's glory is hidden, His glory will be revealed. Since our lives are hidden with Christ in God, we will appear with Him in glory, when Christ, who is our life, appears. As a matter of fact, hiding and revealing are another pair of paradox. When the Word became flesh, Christ has hidden his glory as the Son of God in the very nature of a servant, and in human likeness: "being in very nature God, did not consider equality with God something to be used to his own advantage; rather, he made himself nothing by taking the very nature of a servant, being made in human likeness. And being found in appearance as a man, he humbled himself by becoming obedient to death—even death on a cross!" (Phil. 2:6-8). Christ intentionally hid His glory, by taking the lowliest status of man, and dying the most humiliating death. Nevertheless, "God exalted him to the highest place and gave him the name that is above every name, that at the name of Jesus every knee should bow, in heaven and on earth and under the earth, and every tongue acknowledge that Jesus Christ is Lord, to the glory of God the Father" (Phil. 2:9-11). On the cross, the glory of God the Father has been revealed, and the glory of Christ, the Son of God has been revealed. Likewise, when our old self died, our life is hidden with Christ in God. And when Christ appears, we also will appear with Him in glory (Col. 3:3-4). Humility is one of highest Christian virtues. The glory of God will be revealed through our humble attitudes.

January 24

Faith, Obedience, and Guidance of God

By faith Abraham, when called to go to a place he would later receive as his inheritance, obeyed and went, even though he did not know where he was going. (Hebrews 11:8)

The Lord had said to Abram, "Go from your country, your people and your father's household to the land I will show you. "I will make you into a great nation, and I will bless you; I will make your name great, and you will be a blessing. I will bless those who bless you, and whoever curses you I will curse; and all peoples on earth will be blessed through you." So Abram went, as the Lord had told him; and Lot went with him. Abram was seventy-five years old when he set out from Harran. He took his wife Sarai, his nephew Lot, all the possessions they had accumulated and the people they had acquired in Harran, and they set out for the land of Canaan, and they arrived there (Gen. 12:1-5).

Reflection: The life of Abraham is a good example of faith, obedience and guidance of God. "By faith Abraham, when called to go to a place he would later receive as his inheritance, obeyed and went, even though he did not know where he was going." (Heb. 11:8). Abraham obeyed and went. His faith is demonstrated in his obedience to God's call. True faith is obedience; and obedience is the highest level of faith. As a matter of fact, God's guidance only works on those who show obedience. And only through obedience can we seek God's guidance. Because of his obedience, Abraham was able to take one step a time to follow God's guidance. In fact, the guidance of God works most effectively on a person with a heart of obedience. Sometimes, God's instructions may sound ridiculous (Josh. 6:2-5); sometimes, God's instructions may sound inhuman (Gen. 22:1-2); however, whenever we choose to obey Him, we will see His glory (Josh. 6:30), and we will marvel at His plan and be convinced by His Word: "As the heavens are higher than the earth, so are my ways higher than your ways and my thoughts than your thoughts." (Isa. 55:9). Often, we will not see the logic of God's plan until we have completely obeyed His Word. In fact, reasoning has no place in our journey of faith. In our journey of faith, obedience is the key. Abraham did not argue with God about His calling and His plan. He had no map, no GPS, and even didn't have itinerary of his journey. What he only had was obedience to God and trust in God. Reasoning has nothing to do with faith. Faith is trust and obedience.

January 25

The Fruit of Righteousness and the Tree of Life

The fruit of the righteous is a tree of life, and the one who is wise saves lives. (Proverbs 11:30)

The Lord God made all kinds of trees grow out of the ground—trees that were pleasing to the eye and good for food. In the middle of the garden were the tree of life and the tree of the knowledge of good and evil (Gen. 2:9).

And the Lord God said, "The man has now become like one of us, knowing good and evil. He must not be allowed to reach out his hand and take also from the tree of life and eat, and live forever." So the Lord God banished him from the Garden of Eden to work the ground from which he had been taken. After he drove the man out, he placed on the east side of the Garden of Eden cherubim and a flaming sword flashing back and forth to guard the way to the tree of life (Gen. 3:22-24).

The fruit of the righteous is a tree of life, and the one who is wise saves lives (Prov. 11:30).

Whoever has ears, let them hear what the Spirit says to the churches. To the one who is victorious, I will give the right to eat from the tree of life, which is in the paradise of God (Rev. 2:7).

Then the angel showed me the river of the water of life, as clear as crystal, flowing from the throne of God and of the Lamb down the middle of the great street of the city. On each side of the river stood the tree of life, bearing twelve crops of fruit, yielding its fruit every month (Rev. 22:1-2).

"Blessed are those who wash their robes, that they may have the right to the tree of life and may go through the gates into the city (Rev. 22:14).

And this is my prayer: that your love may abound more and more in knowledge and depth of insight, so that you may be able to discern what is best and may be pure and blameless for the day of Christ, filled with the fruit of righteousness that comes through Jesus Christ—to the glory and praise of God (Phil. 1:9-11).

Reflection: The tree of life first appearing in Genesis (Gen. 2:9) appears again in the New Jerusalem (Rev. 22:1-3). Standing on each side of the water of life, it yields fruit perpetually. This reminds us of Jesus Christ, in whom is the eternal life (1 John 5:11).

Jesus, the Wisdom, is the Tree of Life (Prov. 3:18). In fact, the Tree of Life, which is in the paradise of God (Rev. 2:7), is made available to us. When we are made righteous, we are entitled to accessing to the tree of life (Rev. 22:14). On the other hand, the fruit of righteous is a tree of life (Prov. 11:30). How to gain the fruit of righteousness? The fruit of righteousness comes through Jesus Christ (Phil. 1:11). And Jesus Christ, the Wisdom, is the Tree of Life (Prov. 3:18). Therefore, we can assert that, without the Tree of Life, we cannot bear the fruit of righteousness. Having Jesus Christ, the righteous will have eternal life (1 John 5:12). The righteous are just like a tree planted by streams of water (Ps. 1:3), which is the water of life (Rev. 22:1). The tree yields its fruit, which is the fruit of righteousness, and its leaf does not whither (Ps. 1:3). The righteous will thrive like a green leaf (Prov. 11:28), because the Tree of Life is evergreen (Heb. 13:8). The Tree of Life yields the fruit of righteousness. If Adam and Eve had chosen the Tree of Life other than the tree of the knowledge of good and evil, they would have yielded the fruit of righteousness. Unfortunately, they chose the tree of the knowledge of good and evil, and they sinned. And the price of sin is death. Goethe, the German poet says, "All theory, dear friend, is gray, but the golden tree of life springs ever green."

January 26

God's Grace

The Word became flesh and made his dwelling among us. We have seen his glory, the glory of the one and only Son, who came from the Father, full of grace and truth. (John 1:14)

Through him we received grace and apostleship to call all the Gentiles to the obedience that comes from faith for his name's sake (Rom. 1:5). Out of his fullness we have all received grace in place of grace already given (John 1:16).

However, what kind of grace do we receive from God through Christ? Literally, all grace. We receive all grace from God because He is the God of all grace (1 Pet. 5:10). We receive all grace from God: the grace of election (Rom. 11:5), the grace of calling (Gal. 1:15), the grace of believing (Acts 18:27), the grace of justification (Rom. 3:24; Tit. 3:7), the grace of righteousness (Rom. 5:7), the grace of salvation (Acts 15:11; Tit. 2:11), the grace of redemption (Rom. 3:24), the grace of forgiveness (Eph. 1:7), the grace of adoption (John 1:12; Rom. 8:16-17; Eph. 1:5-6; 1 John 3:1), the grace of all gifts (Rom. 8:32; 12:6, Eph. 4:7-12; Jam. 1:17), the grace of encouragement (2 Thess. 2:16), the grace of help (Heb. 4:16), the grace of sufficiency (2 Cor. 12:9), the grace of hope (2 Thess. 2:16), and the grace of glorification (2 Thess. 1:12).

And, how much God's grace do we receive? As a matter of fact, we are lavished on the riches of God's grace (Eph. 1:7-8), which is indeed incomparable and expressed in His kindness in Christ (Eph. 2:6-7). God's grace is not only sufficient (2 Cor. 12:9), but also bountiful: "And God is able to make all grace abound to you, so that in all things at all times, having all that you need, you will abound in every good work." (2 Cor. 9:8). Especially, when sin increased, God's grace increased all the more (Rom. 5:20). After all, God's grace is glorious grace (Eph. 1:5-6).

Reflection: Although presented in many religions, the concept of grace is a distinctiveness of Christian faith. In the original languages of the Scriptures, the word "grace" is the Hebrew word *"Chanan"* or the Greek word *"charis"*, which means "the state of kindness and favor toward someone, often with a focus on a benefit given to the object." (Strong's Greek 5485). In the Old Testament, the Hebrew word *"chen"* which means *"grace"* appears 68 times; and in the New Testament, the Greek word *"charis"* appears over 140 times. Grace is in essence the free and unmerited favor of God demonstrated in the atonement of Christ for the sins of human-beings. It means: "graciousness (as gratifying), of manner or act (abstract or concrete; literal, figurative or spiritual; especially the divine influence upon the heart, and its reflection in the life; including gratitude." (Strong's Concordance). Graciousness is one of God's attributes, Everything He does demonstrates His grace. Every action of His towards us involves grace. The Apostle Paul uses this word numerous times to explain Christ's gift to people, especially the atonement of Christ. If we explain the concept of grace in our everyday language, we can put it this way, "grace is you get what you don't deserve." While mercy is you don't get what you deserve. You get what you deserve or you don't get what you don't deserve, that is justice and fairness. We Christians are saved in Christ, not because we are better than others by the standard of God's justice and holiness, we are saved in Christ because God loves us, who shows us His grace and mercy: "As for you, you were dead in your transgressions and sins, in which you used to live when you followed the ways of this world and of the ruler of the kingdom of the air, the spirit who is now at work in those who are disobedient. All of us also lived among them at one time, gratifying the cravings of our flesh and following its desires and thoughts. Like the rest, we were by nature deserving of wrath. But because of his great love for us, God, who is rich in mercy, made us alive with Christ even when we were dead in transgressions—it is by grace you have been saved." (Eph. 2:1-5). Love, grace, and mercy, these three attributes of God are closely related, and manifested in the salvation of man. In fact, they are different expressions of the same attribute of God, which is love, because God is love (1 John 4:8). Moreover, through Jesus Christ, we received God's grace. Jesus Christ is the way, the truth, and the life. He is full of grace and truth. Grace and truth go hand in hand, so do love and righteousness. Because He is full of grace, He is love. Because He is full of truth, He is righteousness. Furthermore, grace and truth are incarnated in the Son of God: "The Word became flesh and made his dwelling among us. We have seen his glory, the glory of the one and only Son, who came from the Father, full of grace and truth." (John 1:14).

JANUARY 27

THE FULLNESS OF HIS GRACE

We have seen his glory, the glory of the one and only Son, who came from the Father, full of grace and truth. (John 1:14)

The Word became flesh and made his dwelling among us. We have seen his glory, the glory of the one and only Son, who came from the Father, full of grace and truth. (John testified concerning him. He cried out, saying, "This is the one I spoke about when I said, 'He who comes after me has surpassed me because he was before me.'") Out of his fullness we have all received grace in place of grace already given. For the law was given through Moses; grace and truth came through Jesus Christ. No one has ever seen God, but the one and only Son, who is himself God and is in closest relationship with the Father, has made him known. (John 1:14-18).

Reflection: The reason we have received one blessing after another is that the blessings are from the fullness of the grace of Christ (John 1:16). The grace of Christ is of fullness, without any deficiency, as the psalmist praises: "The Lord is my shepherd, I shall not be in want." (Ps. 23:1). Yes, our Lord is the God of all-sufficiency (2 Cor. 9:8). Moreover, the grace of our Lord is abundant. Paul praises: "the grace of our Lord was poured out on me abundantly, along with the faith and love that are in Christ Jesus." (1 Tim. 1:14). The grace of Christ is so abundant that we may receive His blessings abundantly, for we receive His blessings from the fullness of His grace (John 1:16). Nevertheless, we are not supposed to be a reservoir just to collect and store His abundant grace but to become a channel of grace to impart His abundant grace to others: "And God is able to make all grace abound to you, so that in all things at all times, having all that you need, you will abound in every good work." (2 Cor. 9:8). We receive God's blessings from the fullness of His grace. His grace is abundant. The full measure of His blessings comes from the fullness of His grace. God's blessings are like the Widow's olive oil in 2 Kings 4, will not stop flowing until utensils are run out.

January 28

Call to the Lord

Have mercy on me, Lord, for I call to you all day long. (Psalms 86:3)

(David calls to the Lord:) Answer me when I call to you, my righteous God. Give me relief from my distress; have mercy on me and hear my prayer (Ps. 4:1). Hear my cry for mercy as I call to you for help, as I lift up my hands toward your Most Holy Place (Ps. 28:2). From the ends of the earth I call to you, I call as my heart grows faint; lead me to the rock that is higher than I (Ps. 61:2). Have mercy on me, Lord, for I call to you all day long (Ps. 86:3). When I am in distress, I call to you, because you answer me (Ps. 86:7). I call to you, Lord, every day; I spread out my hands to you (Ps. 88:9). I call to you, Lord, come quickly to me; hear me when I call to you (Ps. 141:1). You, Lord, are forgiving and good, abounding in love to all who call to you (Ps. 86:5).

The Lord hears when I call to him (Ps. 4:3). I call to God, and the Lord saves me (Ps. 55:16). I call out to the Lord, and he answers me from his holy mountain (Ps. 3:4). As He promises: "Call to me and I will answer you and tell you great and unsearchable things you do not know" (Jer. 33:3).

Reflection: The scriptures describe praying as calling upon the name of the Lord (e.g. Gen. 4:26). When David is in distress, he calls to the Lord; when his heart grows faint, he calls to the Lord. He calls to the Lord and asks for His mercy; he calls to the Lord and asks Him to hear his prayer; he calls to the Lord for help. He calls to the Lord every day and all day long, from the ends of the earth, spreading out his hands to Him. He calls to the Lord so earnestly, because he knows the Lord hears, and will answer him, and will answer him from His holy mountain, as He promises: "Call to me and I will answer you and tell you great and unsearchable things you do not know" (Jer. 33:3). David knows the Lord is righteous, forgiving, and good, abounding in love to all who call to Him. When we call to the Lord for His healing, we shall ask Him to have mercy on the patient. The Lord is definitely able to heal any disease, because the name of the Lord is Jehovah Rapha – the Lord who heals. However, He is the sovereign Lord, He heals at His own disposal. So, we shall ask His mercy when we pray for a patient.

January 29

Jesus, the Perfecter

Fixing our eyes on Jesus, the pioneer and perfecter of faith. (Hebrews 12:2)

Day after day every priest stands and performs his religious duties; again and again he offers the same sacrifices, which can never take away sins. But when this priest had offered for all time one sacrifice for sins, he sat down at the right hand of God, and since that time he waits for his enemies to be made his footstool. For by one sacrifice he has made perfect forever those who are being made holy (Heb. 10:11-14).

Therefore, since we are surrounded by such a great cloud of witnesses, let us throw off everything that hinders and the sin that so easily entangles. And let us run with perseverance the race marked out for us, fixing our eyes on Jesus, the pioneer and perfecter of faith. For the joy set before him he endured the cross, scorning its shame, and sat down at the right hand of the throne of God. Consider him who endured such opposition from sinners, so that you will not grow weary and lose heart (Heb. 12:1-3).

Reflection: Jesus Christ is the perfecter of our faith. However, first of all, He is the author of our faith (Heb. 12:2). "For just as through the disobedience of the one man the many were made sinners, so also through the obedience of the one man the many will be made righteous." (Rom. 5:19). Jesus deserves the title of the author of faith, because through His obedience, the effect of sin has been offset. And He was made sacrifice by obedience. Nevertheless, he not only has made us righteous, but also has made us perfect, and perfect forever: "For by one sacrifice he has made perfect forever those who are being made holy" (Heb. 10:14). This scripture claims that the perfection He has made has eternal efficacy. Jesus Christ is the one who makes the perfection possible. "He who began a good work in you will carry it on to completion until the day of Christ Jesus." (Phil. 1:6). He is the sanctifier. He not only makes us righteous, but also sanctifies us until perfection. In other words, our justification, our sanctification, and our perfection all are authored by Him. In the whole process of our salvation, He is Alpha, and He is Omega (Rev. 1:8, 21:6). He is the author and the perfecter of our faith (Heb. 12:2). In the process of our sanctification, He initiates our sanctification, and carries it on to completion. Perfection is not perfection without completion. And, the perfection He has made has eternal efficacy.

January 30

The Full Measure of the Blessing of Christ

I know that when I come to you, I will come in the full measure of the blessing of Christ. (Romans 15:29)

"For this reason I kneel before the Father, from whom his whole family in heaven and on earth derives its name. I pray that out of his glorious riches he may strengthen you with power through his Spirit in your inner being, so that Christ may dwell in your hearts through faith. And I pray that you, being rooted and established in love, may have power, together with all the saints, to grasp how wide and long and high and deep is the love of Christ, and to know this love that surpasses knowledge—that you may be filled to the measure of all the fullness of God." (Eph. 3:14-19).

Reflection: Paul was confident that he would come in the full measure of the blessing of Christ when he came to visit Roman Christians. He had such confidence because he lived in the full measure of the blessing of Christ. He believed "the grace of our Lord was poured out on me abundantly, along with the faith and the love that are in Christ." (1 Tim. 1:14). Do we have such confidence? In fact, the blessing of Christ will be dispensed to us in full measure as long as we earnestly plead for it. Paul not only receives the full measure of the blessing of Christ, but also supplicates it on behalf of Ephesian believers: "For this reason I kneel before the Father, from whom his whole family in heaven and on earth derives its name. I pray that out of his glorious riches he may strengthen you with power through his Spirit in your inner being, so that Christ may dwell in your hearts through faith. And I pray that you, being rooted and established in love, may have power, together with all the saints, to grasp how wide and long and high and deep is the love of Christ, and to know this love that surpasses knowledge—that you may be filled to the measure of all the fullness of God." (Eph. 3:14-19). The full measure of the blessing of Christ is available to us as long as we plead for it, as Christ has made his dwelling among us, who came from the Father, full of grace and truth (John 1:14). And, with the full measure of the blessing of Christ, Christ Himself dwells in our hearts through our faith (Eph. 3:16-17). Full measure of the blessings of Christ is available to us as long as we earnestly plead for it. This is a good news. However, we tend to forget this truth, and don't have sufficient faith to claim the blessings of Christ. Full measure of the blessings of Christ is found in the full measure of all the fullness of God (Eph. 3:19). Our faith is measured by how much we know God. The more we know God, the bigger our faith is. The bigger our faith is, the more blessings we will receive from God.

January 31

Faith, Hope, and Love That Are in Christ

And now these three remain: faith, hope and love. (1 Corinthians 13:13)

We always thank God, the Father of our Lord Jesus Christ, when we pray for you, because we have heard of your faith in Christ Jesus and of the love you have for all God's people— the faith and love that spring from the hope stored up for you in heaven and about which you have already heard in the true message of the gospel that has come to you. In the same way, the gospel is bearing fruit and growing throughout the whole world—just as it has been doing among you since the day you heard it and truly understood God's grace. You learned it from Epaphras, our dear fellow servant, who is a faithful minister of Christ on our behalf, and who also told us of your love in the Spirit. (Col. 1:3-8).

Reflection: Faith, hope and love are all from Christ. Christ is the author and perfecter of our faith. Christ is the hope of glory. Christ is where our love is rooted. Among Jesus' closest disciples, some argue that James represents faith, Peter hope, and John love; while some others insist that Paul represents faith, Peter hope, and John love. No matter which statement is more convincing, faith, hope and love that are three virtues of a believer come with grace of Jesus Christ, as Paul believes: "The grace of our Lord was poured out on me abundantly, along with the faith and love that are in Christ Jesus." (1 Tim. 1:14). And Paul also believes that Christ is the hope of glory: "To them God has chosen to make known among the Gentiles the glorious riches of this mystery, which is Christ in you, the hope of glory." (Col. 1:27). Apart from Christ, there is no true faith, no true hope, and no true love, because Christ is the author and perfecter of our faith (Heb. 12:2); Christ Himself is our hope (Col. 1:27; 1 Tim. 1:1); and we are rooted and grounded in Christ's love (Eph. 3:17-19). Furthermore, as Christ dwells in our hearts, we are rooted and established in love (Eph. 3:17). The true faith is in Christ, and the true love is what we have for all the saints. Both the faith and love spring from the hope that is stored up for us in heaven (Col. 1:4-5). The Apostle Paul writes to the Thessalonian Christians, "We always thank God for all of you and continually mention you in our prayers. We remember before our God and Father your work produced by faith, your labor prompted by love, and your endurance inspired by hope in our Lord Jesus Christ." (1 Thess. 1:2-3). In 1 Corinthians, Paul sums up, "And now these three remain: faith, hope and love. But the greatest of these is love." (1 Cor. 13:13). In a word, faith, hope and love are three highest Christian virtues.

Pearls of Wisdom VOLUME 1

February 1

True Assurance (I)

And the peace of God, which transcends all understanding, will guard your hearts and your minds in Christ Jesus. (Philippians 4:7)

Rejoice in the Lord always. I will say it again: Rejoice! Let your gentleness be evident to all. The Lord is near. Do not be anxious about anything, but in every situation, by prayer and petition, with thanksgiving, present your requests to God. And the peace of God, which transcends all understanding, will guard your hearts and your minds in Christ Jesus. Finally, brothers and sisters, whatever is true, whatever is noble, whatever is right, whatever is pure, whatever is lovely, whatever is admirable—if anything is excellent or praiseworthy—think about such things. Whatever you have learned or received or heard from me, or seen in me—put it into practice. And the God of peace will be with you (Phil. 4:4-9).

Reflection: This is a true assurance of God recorded in the Scriptures. This is the first true assurance, the assurance of peace. In this passage, the word "peace" appears two times. This peace is from God. As a matter of fact, God is the best "insurance provider" in the world. With Him, we are offered full coverage, and don't have to pay any premium, and are not subject to any liability or premium increase, which is indeed a penalty incurred by an accident. He Himself will never go bankrupt as any insurance provider may do. Strictly speaking, He provides us assurance rather than insurance. Indeed, He provides us true assurance. His true assurance is anchored on His promises. And His promises never fail. "For no matter how many promises God has made, they are 'Yes' in Christ." (2 Cor. 1:20). And this scripture itself is also a true assurance. His true assurance is built on His faithfulness. The reason that His promises never fail is that "for he who promised is faithful." (Heb. 10:23). His true assurance is also built on His immutability: "Jesus Christ is the same yesterday and today and forever." (Heb. 13:8). All of these determine that in Jesus Christ, we will have true assurance, because "the peace of God, which transcends all understanding, will guard your hearts and your minds in Christ Jesus." (Phil. 4:7). In other words, God provides us true peace of mind. God is the best "insurance provider" in the world. He provides us an absolute assurance. His promises never fail. "God is not human, that he should lie, not a human being, that he should change his mind. Does he speak and then not act? Does he promise and not fulfill?" (Num. 23:19).

Pearls of Wisdom VOLUME 1

February 2

True Assurance (II)

And my God will meet all your needs according to the riches of his glory in Christ Jesus. (Philippians 4:19)

I rejoiced greatly in the Lord that at last you renewed your concern for me. Indeed, you were concerned, but you had no opportunity to show it. I am not saying this because I am in need, for I have learned to be content whatever the circumstances. I know what it is to be in need, and I know what it is to have plenty. I have learned the secret of being content in any and every situation, whether well fed or hungry, whether living in plenty or in want. I can do all this through him who gives me strength. Yet it was good of you to share in my troubles. Moreover, as you Philippians know, in the early days of your acquaintance with the gospel, when I set out from Macedonia, not one church shared with me in the matter of giving and receiving, except you only; for even when I was in Thessalonica, you sent me aid more than once when I was in need. Not that I desire your gifts; what I desire is that more be credited to your account. I have received full payment and have more than enough. I am amply supplied, now that I have received from Epaphroditus the gifts you sent. They are a fragrant offering, an acceptable sacrifice, pleasing to God. And my God will meet all your needs according to the riches of his glory in Christ Jesus. To our God and Father be glory for ever and ever. Amen (Phil. 4:10-20).

Reflection: This is another true assurance of God recorded in the Scriptures. This is the second true assurance, the assurance of providence. In this passage, the word "need" appears four times. God will always provide what we "need", not what we "want". Unfortunately, we are always unable to tell the difference between what we need and what we want, and always assume what we want is actually what we need. And this is the trick from Satan, who seduces us to greed, which is a sin of excessive desire. He deceives us so that we may justify what we want as what we need, and ignore our sins of excessive desire that are grave indeed. Thomas Aquinas maintains, "Greed is a sin against God, just as all mortal sins, in as much as man condemns things eternal for the sake of temporal things." As a matter of fact, God will always provide what we need. He always knows what we need. And He will never mix up what we need with what we want. He will faithfully and generously provide what we need as long as we are faithful and generous in giving as Philippian Christians, who used the resources they had according to His purposes, and became channels of blessing. This is assurance of providence. In fact, it is also a promise. This promise is also recorded in the Old Testament: "Honor the Lord with your wealth, with the first-fruits of all your crops; then your barns will be filled to overflowing, and your vats will brim over with new wine (Prov. 3:9-10). Charles H. Spurgeon compares this promise of God to a bank draft: "my God" is the name of the banker; "meet all your needs" is the promise of payment, "all your needs" is the amount of payment; "the riches of His glory" is the assets of the bank. "glory" is the address of the bank; "in Christ Jesus" is the signature on the bank draft. Without the signature of Christ Jesus, the manager of the bank, the bank draft won't be valid.

February 3

True Assurance (III)

Now to Him who is able to do immeasurably more than all we ask or imagine, according to his power that is at work within us. (Ephesians 3:20)

For this reason I kneel before the Father, from whom every family in heaven and on earth derives its name. I pray that out of his glorious riches he may strengthen you with power through his Spirit in your inner being, so that Christ may dwell in your hearts through faith. And I pray that you, being rooted and established in love, may have power, together with all the Lord's holy people, to grasp how wide and long and high and deep is the love of Christ, and to know this love that surpasses knowledge—that you may be filled to the measure of all the fullness of God. Now to him who is able to do immeasurably more than all we ask or imagine, according to his power that is at work within us, to him be glory in the church and in Christ Jesus throughout all generations, for ever and ever! Amen (Eph. 3:14-21).

Reflection: This is one more true assurance of God recorded in the Scriptures. This is the third true assurance of God, the assurance of power. The word "power" appears three times in this passage. God is able. In the original language, the word "able" has the same root as the word "power" does. In other words, God is "powerful"; and He is omnipotent. Moreover, our God is able to do exceedingly abundantly above all that we ask or think. What do we ask or think? We always ask the Providence to provide us what we need to sustain ourselves on the earth. As our Lord is God-Will-Provide, he will definitely provide us all we need (Gen. 22:14). However, the way He provides may not be what we expect, because God's ways are higher than ours and God's thoughts are higher than ours (Isa. 55:9). In fact, God is able to do way more than what we ask or think. God was pleased to have all his fullness dwell in Christ (Col. 1:19). For in Christ all the fullness of the Deity lives in bodily form, and we have been given fullness in Christ, who is the head over every power and authority (Col. 2:9-10). What God is able to do is based on the fullness of Christ.

He blesses us with "the full measure of the blessing of Christ" (Rom. 15:29). Out of His glorious riches He strengthens us with power through his Spirit in our inner being (Eph. 3:16). As a matter of fact, the Holy Spirit is the power of God. In the Scriptures, the Holy Spirit is described as God's divine power (Mic. 3:8). God does everything with the power of the Holy Spirit and with the fullness of Christ. He does this out of His glorious riches, exceedingly abundantly above all that we ask or think, according to the power that works within us, so that we won't be able to grasp how wide and long and high and deep is the love of Christ without the power of the Holy Spirit. Apparently, three persons of the Triune Godhead work together to bless us so abundantly that we may be filled to the measure of all the fullness of God. God is able! God is powerful! God is omnipotent! This is a true assurance of God, the assurance of power.

February 4

Suffering and Perfection

In bringing many sons and daughters to glory, it was fitting that God, for whom and through whom everything exists, should make the pioneer of their salvation perfect through what he suffered. (Hebrews 2:10)

Not only so, but we also glory in our sufferings, because we know that suffering produces perseverance; perseverance, character; and character, hope (Rom. 5:3-4).

I want to know Christ—yes, to know the power of his resurrection and participation in his sufferings, becoming like him in his death, and so, somehow, attaining to the resurrection from the dead (Phil. 3:10-11).

Now I rejoice in what I am suffering for you, and I fill up in my flesh what is still lacking in regard to Christ's afflictions, for the sake of his body, which is the church (Col. 1:24).

But we do see Jesus, who was made lower than the angels for a little while, now crowned with glory and honor because he suffered death, so that by the grace of God he might taste death for everyone. In bringing many sons and daughters to glory, it was fitting that God, for whom and through whom everything exists, should make the pioneer of their salvation perfect through what he suffered (Heb. 2:9-10).

Therefore, since Christ suffered in his body, arm yourselves also with the same attitude, because whoever suffers in the body is done with sin (1 Pet. 4:1).

Reflection: Christ, the author of our salvation, was made perfect through suffering. Thus, we can say suffering is one of spiritual disciplines that bring us to Christian perfection.

Even Christ Himself was made perfect through suffering; let alone ourselves. However, suffering won't automatically produce perfection, if we don't learn obedience from what we suffer. In other words, obedience learned from suffering will make us perfect. If we don't learn obedience from what we suffer, we will suffer in vain. This is the reason that many of us have been suffered, but not all of us have been made perfect. Even Christ Himself learned obedience from what He suffered, and thus was made perfect (Heb. 5:7-9). So, we can say that obedience is the key to perfection. We are called by Christ to perfection (Matt. 5:48). How to attain perfection? Through suffering. Therefore, we are called to suffer for righteousness. As Peter says: "But if you suffer from doing good and you endure it, this is commendable before God. To this you were called, because Christ suffered for you, leaving you an example, that you should follow in his steps." (1 Pet. 2:20-21). Jesus also calls us to follow Him, by denying ourselves, and going through the way of cross (Luke 9:23-24). We are confident that the end of the way of cross is perfection and glory.

February 5

The Supremacy of Christ

And he is the head of the body, the church; he is the beginning and the firstborn from among the dead, so that in everything he might have the supremacy. (Colossians 1:18)

He is the image of the invisible God, the firstborn over all creation. For by him all things were created: things in heaven and on earth, visible and invisible, whether thrones or powers or rulers or authorities; all things were created by him and for him. He is before all things, and in him all things hold together. And he is the head of the body, the church; he is the beginning and the firstborn from among the dead, so that in everything he might have the supremacy. For God was pleased to have all his fullness dwell in him, and through him to reconcile to himself all things, whether things on earth or things in heaven, by making peace through his blood, shed on the cross (Col. 1:15-20).

Who, being in very nature God, did not consider equality with God something to be grasped, but made himself nothing, taking the very nature of a servant, being made in human likeness. And being found in appearance as a man, he humbled himself and became obedient to death— even death on a cross! Therefore, God exalted him to the highest place and gave him the name that is above every name, that at the name of Jesus every knee should bow, in heaven and on earth and under the earth, and every tongue acknowledge that Jesus Christ is Lord, to the glory of God the Father (Phil. 2:6-11).

Reflection: The supremacy of Christ lies in His divine nature. He is the firstborn over all creation that was created by Him and for Him. He is before all things, and in Him all things hold together (Col. 1:17). In His relationship with creation, we can see His supremacy. Moreover, we can see His supremacy in His work of redemption in which His supremacy is reinforced. He is the head of the body, the church, and the beginning and the first born from among the dead. Therefore, He has supremacy in everything (Col. 1:18). In fact, in His work of redemption, He ignored His own supremacy (Phil. 2:6), humbled Himself (Phil. 2:7-8), and became obedient to death - even death on a cross (Phil. 2:8). However, His supremacy was reaffirmed by the Father who exalted Him to the highest place (Phil. 2:9). This testifies His own teaching: "For whoever exalts himself will be humbled, and whoever humbles himself will be exalted." (Matt. 23:12). The supremacy of Christ is manifested not only in His relationship with creation, but also in His work of redemption. And in the Bible, His supremacy is often mentioned together with His fullness of Deity (Col. 1:9, 2:10). The supremacy of Christ demonstrates His fullness of Deity. However, Christ ignored His own supremacy, humbled Himself. Paradoxically, God exalted Him to the highest place. And His supremacy has thus been reinforced.

February 6

Christ and All Creation

The Son is the image of the invisible God, the firstborn over all creation. For in Him all things were created. (Colossians 1:15-16)

Through Him all things were made; without Him nothing was made that has been made (John 1:3). All things have been created through Him and for Him (Col. 1:16). Through Him God made the universe (Heb. 1:2).

In everything He might have the supremacy (Col. 1:18). He is before all things (Col. 1:17). God appointed Him heir of all things (Heb. 1:2), sustaining all things by His powerful word (Heb. 1:3). In Him all things hold together (Col. 1:17). God was pleased to have His fullness dwell in Him, and through Him to reconcile to Himself all things, whether things on earth or things in heaven, by making peace through His blood, shed on the cross (Col. 1:19). Neither height nor depth, not anything else in all creation, will be able to separate us from the love of God that is in Christ Jesus our Lord (Rom. 8:39).

When Christ came as high priest of the good things that are now already here, He went through the greater and more perfect tabernacle that is not made with human hands, that is to say, is not a part of this creation (Heb. 9:11). For Christ did not enter a sanctuary made with human hands that was only a copy of the true one; he entered heaven itself, now to appear for us in God's presence. Nor did he enter heaven to offer himself again and again, the way the high priest enters the Most Holy Place every year with blood that is not his own. Otherwise Christ would have had to suffer many times since the creation of the world. But he has appeared once for all at the culmination of the ages to do away with sin by the sacrifice of Himself (Heb. 9:24-26).

Reflection: Christ is the Word (*Logos*) of God, who is self-existent. He is the only-begotten Son of God, begotten of the father before creation. He was not made, but by whom all things were made. Christ is the firstborn over all creation (Col. 1:15). Through Him, all creation was made, sustained and reconciled to Himself. He has supremacy over all creation. He was appointed heir of all things. He was not only involved in creation, along with the father and the Spirit, but sustains all creation by His powerful word. Moreover, He brings all creation reconciliation to the Father and Himself. And He accomplishes redemption of all creation, including human-beings who are created in the image and the likeness of God, with His precious blood on the cross. In a word, Christ plays a key role not only in creation but in redemption. With His precious blood shed on the cross, He has liberated the creation from its bondage to decay. And He has made peace between God and His creation. Moreover, He has gone through the greater and more perfect tabernacle that is not made with human hands, that is to say, is not a part of this creation (Heb. 9:11). He has entered the true sanctuary, which is heaven itself (Heb. 9:24). And His resurrection ushers the new creation. The true sanctuary is a part of the new creation. The resurrected Lord has entered this heavenly tabernacle which is a part of the new creation. Thus, the resurrection of Christ ushers the new creation. If someone is born again, he is a new creation in Christ: "If anyone is in Christ, the new creation has come." (1 Cor. 5:17). We have to be born again in Christ to be a new creation.

February 7

Fix Our Eyes on Jesus

And let us run with perseverance the race marked out for us, fixing our eyes on Jesus, the pioneer and perfecter of faith. (Hebrews 12:1-2)

Therefore, since we are surrounded by such a great cloud of witnesses, let us throw off everything that hinders and the sin that so easily entangles. And let us run with perseverance the race marked out for us, fixing our eyes on Jesus, the pioneer and perfecter of faith. For the joy set before him he endured the cross, scorning its shame, and sat down at the right hand of the throne of God. Consider him who endured such opposition from sinners, so that you will not grow weary and lose heart (Heb. 12:1-3).

Reflection: Every time when we read these verses of the Scriptures, a question may come to our mind: "How to fix our eyes on Jesus?" First of all, in order to fix our eyes on Jesus, we must look to Him (Ps. 34:5; 145:15; Isa. 17:7; 22:11; 31:1; Zech. 12:10; John 11:37), or watch Him (Prov. 8:34; Micah 7:7; Zech. 11:7), or put our eyes on Him (2 Chron. 20:12; Ps. 25:15; Heb. 12:2). However, to "fix our eyes on Jesus" means more than this. To "fix our eyes on Jesus" also means to turn to Him (Isa. 45:22). We turn our heart to our Savior. And this is the beginning of our salvation. In our further relationship with Jesus, to "fix our eyes on Jesus" means to lift up our souls to Him (Ps. 25:1; 86:4; 143:8); and to put our hope in Him (Ps. 31:24; 33:22; 42:5; 43:5; 52:9; 119:74,81; 130:5,7; 131:3; 146:5; Matt. 12:21; Rom. 15:112). Furthermore, to "fix our eyes on Jesus" means to trust Him (Ps. 78:7), and to wait upon Him (Ps. 38:15; 106:13; 119:116; Lam. 3:26; Jude 21). The author of the Epistle to the Hebrews exhorts us to "fix our eyes on Jesus". It seems he knows our problem. One of our problems is that we are unable to fix our eyes on Jesus, and yet we look to him occasionally. To "fix our eyes on Jesus" implies that we must look to Him, watch Him, put our eyes on Him, turn to Him, lift up our souls to Him, put hope in Him, trust Him, and wait upon Him with attentiveness, constancy and perseverance. This is a good reminder to us. These verses also remind us that we ought to look to our Maker and turn our eyes to the Holy One of Israel (Isa. 17:7). If we turn our eyes to something other than God, woe will be to us (Isa. 31:1). Even if we fix our eyes on blessings of God rather than God of blessings – in fact, we always desire blessings of God rather than God of blessings (Isa. 22:11), even though we are seldom aware – we will not be blessed, as blessed are those whose hope is in the Lord his God (Ps. 146:5) and who watches daily at His doors (Prov. 8:34). And if we put our trust in God, remember His deeds, and keep His commands (Ps. 78:7), we will be so blessed to have radiance of Christ (Ps. 34:5), to reflect the Lord's glory, and to be transformed into His likeness with ever-increasing glory (2 Cor. 3:18). The secret to receiving God's blessings is to fix our eyes on Jesus, the author and perfecter of our faith. Jesus is the God of blessings. The secret is to focus our eyes on the God of blessings instead of the blessings of God. When we fix our eyes on the God of blessings, the blessings of God will be given to us by the God of blessings. If we fix our eyes on the blessings of God rather than the God of blessings, we won't experience God and thus won't be able to receive His blessings.

February 8

Christ, the Hope of Glory

To them God has chosen to make known among the Gentiles the glorious riches of this mystery, which is Christ in you, the hope of glory. (Colossians 1:27)

Now I rejoice in what I am suffering for you, and I fill up in my flesh what is still lacking in regard to Christ's afflictions, for the sake of his body, which is the church. I have become its servant by the commission God gave me to present to you the word of God in its fullness— the mystery that has been kept hidden for ages and generations, but is now disclosed to the Lord's people. To them God has chosen to make known among the Gentiles the glorious riches of this mystery, which is Christ in you, the hope of glory (Col. 1:24-27).

Therefore, since we have been justified through faith, we have peace with God through our Lord Jesus Christ, through whom we have gained access by faith into this grace in which we now stand. And we boast in the hope of the glory of God. Not only so, but we also glory in our sufferings, because we know that suffering produces perseverance; perseverance, character; and character, hope. And hope does not put us to shame, because God's love has been poured out into our hearts through the Holy Spirit, who has been given to us (Rom. 5:1-5)

Reflection: Christ is our hope of glory. In fact, we tend to overlook this fact. We all know that Christ is the author and perfecter of our faith (Heb. 12:2), and we cannot be separated from the love of Christ (Rom. 8:35); but we seldom bear in mind that Christ is our hope of glory. "Faith is being sure of what we hope for…" (Heb. 11:1). We can also say that faith is being sure of our hope, our hope of glory, which is Jesus Christ. In other words, faith is being sure of Christ, who is our hope of glory. Likewise, joy is being rejoicing in Christ, who is the hope of the glory of God (Rom. 5:2). To rejoice in the hope of the glory of God is the true meaning of joy. Thus, we can say: our faith, hope, love, and joy all find true meaning in Christ. We, who are the first to hope in Christ, may be for the praise of His glory (Eph. 1:12). Hope in Christ will bring us glory and the riches of His glorious inheritance in the saints (Eph. 1:18). And the glory of God is what we hope for (Rom. 5:2; Col. 1:27). However, without Christ, both hope and glory will be in vain, for Christ is the hope of glory (Col. 1:27).

February 9

The Glorious Riches of This Mystery

The mystery that has been kept hidden for ages and generations, but is now disclosed to the Lord's people. To them God has chosen to make known among the Gentiles the glorious riches of this mystery, which is Christ in you, the hope of glory. (Colossians 1:26-27)

That Christ in us is our hope of glory is a mystery, a mystery full of glorious riches, it has been hidden in God for ages and generations (Rom. 16:25; Eph. 3:9; Col. 1:26-27) until God reveals it through Christ. Upon our repentance, Christ has first regenerated our spirit (John 3:6); and now is transforming our soul (Rom. 12:2); and will consummately transfigure our body (1 Cor. 15:51-54). The ultimate consummation of God's salvation plan will be reached when these three steps have been completed. Christ in us will accomplish salvation of us. Thus, we say that Christ in us is our hope of glory. Moreover, the Holy Spirit seals us for the day of redemption (Eph. 4:30). The seal of the Holy Spirit guarantees our ultimate salvation. "And you also were included in Christ when you heard the message of truth, the gospel of your salvation. When you believed, you were marked in him with a seal, the promised Holy Spirit, who is a deposit guaranteeing our inheritance until the redemption of those who are God's possession—to the praise of his glory." (Eph. 1:13-14). God will continue to work in us until He is finished perfecting us (Phil. 1:6). This forward-looking guarantee of perfection is what is meant by "Christ in you, the hope of glory." Furthermore, the ultimate salvation will be consummated upon the second coming of Christ, when all creation will be restored (Rom. 8:19-21; 1 Pet. 5:10). Our heavenly inheritance is a sure and certain hope, the hope of glory, although at present, it is an unseen hope, looked for by faith. This hope of glory is a future blessing that has been guaranteed by the seal of the Holy Spirit, and will be fully realized upon the second coming of Christ. And this hope of glory gives us joy, which is being rejoicing in Christ, who is the hope of the glory of God (Rom. 5:2), even in the midst of suffering and adversity.

Reflection: In the New Testament usage, the word "mystery" means a spiritual truth that has been hidden for ages and generations but has been finally revealed by God to His chosen people. The word "mystery" appears twenty-one times in the Pauline epistles, denoting a spiritual truth that has been revealed by God through divine inspiration. Unlike the pagan mysteries that are imparted only to the initiated few, the mysteries of God are initiated to all of God's chosen people (2 Corinthians 4:3). And unlike the modern usage of the word "mystery" which means something hidden and impossible to fully understand, the mystery of God in the New Testament usage denotes the word of God in its fullness — the mystery that has been kept hidden for ages and generations, but is now disclosed to the Lord's people (Col. 1:25-26). This mystery is that through the gospel the Gentiles are heirs together with Israel, members together of one body, and sharers together in the promise in Christ Jesus (Eph. 3:6). In other words, 'church' is the mystery. In this mystery, God's wisdom has been hidden. Moreover, this mystery is Christ Himself. He is the mystery of God, in whom are hidden all the treasures of wisdom and knowledge (Col. 2:2-3). Christ is the mystery that has been kept hidden for ages and generations (1 Cor. 2:7; Eph. 3:9; Col. 1:26). His pre-existence, His virgin birth, His Incarnation, His crucifixion, and His resurrection, and His ascension are the mystery in which God's manifold wisdom has been hidden.

FEBRUARY 10

CHRIST AND THE MYSTERY OF GOD

My goal is that they may be encouraged in heart and united in love, so that they may have the full riches of complete understanding, in order that they may know the mystery of God, namely, Christ, in whom are hidden all the treasures of wisdom and knowledge. (Colossians. 2:2-3)

Paul was eager to proclaim the mystery of Christ, although he was jailed for this cause: "And I pray for us, too, that God may open a door for our message, so that we may proclaim the mystery of Christ, for which I am in chains." (Colossians. 4:3)

What is the mystery of Christ? As the prisoner of Christ for the sake of Gentiles, Paul, like other holy apostles and prophets, was revealed this mystery (Eph 3:1, 3, 5), which was kept hidden in God for ages and generations (Eph. 3:5, 9; Col. 1:26). Paul's insight into the mystery of Christ (Eph.3:4) is: "This mystery is that through the gospel the gentiles are heirs together with Israel, members together of one body, and sharers together in the promise in Christ Jesus." (Eph. 3:6).

This mystery has glorious riches. And God has made known among Gentiles the glorious riches of this mystery in His day through the life, death, and resurrection of Jesus Christ (Col. 1:27). Moreover, the mystery of God is Christ (Col. 1:27; 2:2), which needs full riches of complete understanding in order to comprehend (Col. 2:2). Furthermore, in this mystery of God are hidden all the treasures of wisdom and knowledge (Col. 2:2-3).

This mystery of God is actually the wisdom of God (Eph. 3:10), the secret wisdom of God, a wisdom that has been hidden and that God destined for our glory before time began (1 Cor. 2:7). And this mystery of God is Christ (Col. 1:27; 2:2). Therefore, Christ is the wisdom of God (1 Cor. 1:24, 30).

Reflection: Christ is the mystery of God, and Christ is the wisdom of God. This mystery has glorious riches. All the treasures of wisdom and knowledge are hidden in this mystery. Christ is the power of God and the wisdom of God. This mystery has glorious riches. The glorious riches guarantee the full measure of the blessings of Christ. Witness Lee maintains, "Of all the mysteries in God's New Testament economy, the first of them is the mystery of God." And he elaborates, "Concerning God's mystery, Christ, I have listed six points. First, Christ is the mysterious Word of God. Second, the Word became flesh. Third, He passed through human living. Fourth, He was crucified. Fifth, He resurrected. Sixth, He ascended. All these items that Christ has passed through are the mystery of God. Christ is the Word of God, and the Word is God Himself." (Excerpted from "The mysteries in God's New Testament economy" by Witness Lee). Moreover, the mystery of God is the consummation of God's plan in bringing His kingdom in Christ to fulfillment. Christ is the mystery of God; He is the mystery of God revealed. In fact, the mystery of Christ is the revelation of Christ. The mystery of God is Christ in us, the hope of glory (Col. 1:27).

February 11

The Boundless Riches of Christ

Although I am less than the least of all the Lord's people, this grace was given me: to preach to the Gentiles the boundless riches of Christ. (Ephesians 3:8)

Although the riches of Christ are boundless, we do know the aspects in which the riches of Christ are manifested, for the riches of Christ were made known: "To them God has chosen to make known among the Gentiles the glorious riches of this mystery, which is Christ in you, the hope of glory." (Col. 1:27).

In what aspects are the riches of Christ manifested? Firstly, the riches of Christ are manifested in power through Spirit: "I pray that out of his glorious riches he may strengthen you with power through his Spirit in your inner being" (Eph. 3:16). Secondly, the riches of Christ are manifested in His providence: "And my God will meet all your needs according to his glorious riches in Christ Jesus." (Phil. 4:19). Thirdly, the riches of Christ are manifested in His glory: "What if he did this to make the riches of his glory known to the objects of his mercy, whom he prepared in advance for glory." (Rom. 9:23). Finally, the riches of Christ are manifested in His glorious inheritance in the saints: "I pray also that the eyes of your heart may be enlightened in order that you may know the hope to which he has called you, the riches of his glorious inheritance in the saints." (Eph. 1:18).

Reflection: In the Scriptures, "riches" refers to true, lasting, eternal spiritual blessings that we have in Jesus Christ. Paul describes these blessings as the "boundless riches of Christ" (Eph. 3:8) which implies that believers' blessings in Christ are too deep to be measured, and not to be tracked out. The boundless riches of Christ are exclusively offered to sinners who repent their sins and call upon Him. The boundless riches of Christ center on the person of Jesus Christ who possesses in Himself boundless riches and gives them to all who call upon Him. Consequently, He is able and willing to supply every of our spiritual and personal need. And He has reserved for us many of these blessings, such as peace, provision, and providence. The mystery of God not only has glorious riches, but has boundless riches. The boundless riches of Christ make possible that "the peace of God, which transcends all understanding, will guard your hearts and your minds in Christ Jesus." (Phil. 4:7). The boundless riches of Christ make God Himself the best and the largest "insurance provider" in the world. The boundless riches of Christ also make possible that "my God will meet all your needs according to the riches of his glory in Christ Jesus." (Phil. 4:19). The boundless riches of Christ make God Himself the best and largest "bank" in the world.

February 12

Devotedness in Prayer

Devote yourselves to prayer, being watchful and thankful. (Colossians 4:2)

(Jesus Prays on the Mount of Olives) Jesus went out as usual to the Mount of Olives, and his disciples followed him. On reaching the place, he said to them, "Pray that you will not fall into temptation." He withdrew about a stone's throw beyond them, knelt down and prayed, "Father, if you are willing, take this cup from me; yet not my will, but yours be done." An angel from heaven appeared to him and strengthened him. And being in anguish, he prayed more earnestly, and his sweat was like drops of blood falling to the ground. When he rose from prayer and went back to the disciples, he found them asleep, exhausted from sorrow. "Why are you sleeping?" he asked them. "Get up and pray so that you will not fall into temptation." (Luke 22:39-46). Devote yourselves to prayer, being watchful and thankful. (Colossians 4:2)

Reflection: How to devote ourselves to prayer? First of all, let's look at the meaning of devotedness. Firstly, devotedness means faithfulness. Paul teaches us to be "faithful in prayer" (Rom. 12:12). Second, devotedness means constancy. "They all joined together constantly in prayer." (Acts 1:14). Finally, devotedness means earnestness. "And being in anguish, he (Jesus) prayed more earnestly, and his sweat was like drops of blood falling to the ground." (Luke 22:44). In other words, a faithful prayer demands not only perseverance, but also earnestness. Moreover, today's scripture reminds us that, in order to devote ourselves to prayer, we need being watchful and thankful. Thanksgiving is a component of a prayer; and thankfulness is an attitude a prayer ought to have. A prayer not only ought to be thankful, but also ought to be watchful. How to be watchful? "Fix our eyes on Jesus, the author and perfecter of our faith." (Heb. 12:2). Watch Jesus. Look attentively at Him. We will go to where we fix our eyes on. If we focus our attentions on the problems, we will end up with being trapped by problems; while if we constantly fix our eyes on Jesus, we will end up with being blessed (Prov. 8:34). Be watchful in prayers, otherwise, God's blessings may slip away. Being watchful in prayer is like struggling with God as Jacob's. Jacob said to God, "I will not let you go unless you bless me." Let's say this as Jacob did in our watchful prayers.

FEBRUARY 13

AN AROMA PLEASING TO THE LORD

You are to wash the internal organs and the legs with water, and the priest is to burn all of it on the altar. It is a burnt offering, a food offering, an aroma pleasing to the Lord. (Leviticus 1:9)

An aroma pleasing to the Lord is always associated with offerings: the burnt offering (Gen. 8:20-21; Exod. 29:18; Lev. 1:9; 8:28; 23:18; Num. 28:27), the grain offering (Lev. 2:9, 12; 6:15; Ezek. 16:19), or the fellowship offering (Lev. 3:5). When the Lord smells the pleasing aroma, He will accept the offering (Gen. 8:21); on the other hand, when the Lord takes no delight in the pleasing aroma of the offering, He will turn His back on the offering giver (Lev. 26:31). The offerings with a pleasing aroma that are accepted by the Lord are the offerings from a willing heart. And the Lord is more pleased with a repentant heart (Ps. 51:16-17).

The aroma of Christ (2 Cor. 2:14-16) is pleased to the Lord, because Christ makes Himself a fragrant offering and sacrifice to God (Eph. 5:2). He was willing to sacrifice Himself on the cross to fulfill God's salvation plan. And His sacrifice was atoning sacrifice (1 John 2:2; 4:10).

As imitators of Christ, we will become a fragrant offering and sacrifice to God (2 Cor. 2:14-16). When we offer our bodies as living sacrifices, we are holy and pleasing to God (Rom. 12:1). Our living sacrifices have an aroma pleasing to the Lord. And He will accept our spiritual act of worship for He delights in the pleasing aroma of our living sacrifices (Rom. 12:1).

Reflection: In the Old Testament, the scent of burnt offerings was described as "an aroma pleasing to the Lord" (Gen. 8:20-21; Exod. 29:18; Lev. 1:9; 8:28; 23:18; Num. 28:27); so was the grain offering (Lev. 2:9, 12; 6:15; Ezek. 16:19), or the fellowship offering (Lev. 3:5). Nevertheless, an aroma is pleasing to the Lord associated with offerings is not because of the offerings themselves, but because of the atonement of sins that offerings stand for. In other words, the aroma pleasing to the Lord is not because of the smell, but because of what the smell represents, the atonement for sins. In the Old Testament, when the Israelites made sacrifices and offerings, their atonement of sins was made, and their fellowship with the Lord was restored. Likewise, in the New Testament, when Jesus Christ, the ultimate propitiation, sacrificed Himself on the cross, the atonement of sins was made, and our relationship with God was restored. Offerings without an aroma pleasing to the Lord won't be accepted by God. When we offer ourselves to God as living sacrifices, we are not only priests, but sacrifices themselves, just as Jesus Christ Himself. However, we won't be accepted by God if we don't have the aroma of Christ in our lives. When our living sacrifices have an aroma pleasing to the Lord, that aroma is the aroma of Christ. In other words, we must have the aroma of Christ in our lives so that our living sacrifice may be accepted by God. The aroma pleasing to the Lord is the aroma of our prayers, the aroma of our repentance, the aroma of our witness, and the aroma of our love. The aroma pleasing to the Lord is not what we do, but who we are. Our Christ-centered life is the aroma pleasing to the Lord.

February 14

Death and Baptism

Or don't you know that all of us who were baptized into Christ Jesus were baptized into his death? We were therefore buried with him through baptism into death in order that, just as Christ was raised from the dead through the glory of the Father, we too may live a new life. (Romans 6:3-4)

Christ loved us so much that He died for us (Gal. 2:20). And He died to sin (Rom. 6:10). We were baptized into Christ by being baptized into his death (Rom. 6:3). We died to law through the body of Christ (Rom. 7:4), died with Christ to the basic principles of this world

(Col. 2:20). If we were justified by law, we would have been alienated from Christ (Gal. 5:4).

We have fallen asleep in Christ (1 Cor. 15:18, 20), died to Christ (Rom. 6:8), buried with Christ through baptism into death (Rom. 6:4). As Christ was raised from the dead (Rom. 6:4, 9; Rom. 7:4; 1 Cor. 15:20) through the glory of the Father (Rom.6:4), He became the first-fruits of those who have fallen asleep in Him (1 Cor. 15:20). We were baptized into Christ, and have therefore clothed ourselves with Christ (Gal. 3:27).

God has reconciled us by Christ's physical body through death (Col. 1:22). As a result, we died with Christ, we will live with Him (Rom. 6:8), who died to sin, but lives to God (Rom. 6:10). And we belong to Christ (Rom. 7:4). Being crucified with Him, we no longer live, but Christ lives in us (Gal. 2:20). We live a new life (Rom. 6:4), a life we live by faith in Christ (Gal.2:20).

Reflection: Baptism symbolizes death, burial, and resurrection with Christ. Baptism is full of mysteries. When we were baptized into Christ, we were baptized into His death. And we were buried with Him through baptism into death. And we were raised from the death through the glory of the Father as Christ did. This is a secret. In the physical realm, life comes first, then does death. In the spiritual realm, death comes first, then does life. In other words, in the physical realm, we live before me die; whereas in the spiritual realm, we die before we live. Or put it this way, in the Old Creation, life comes before death. In the New Creation, death comes before life: "The spiritual did not come first, but the natural, and after that the spiritual." (1 Cor. 15:46). In addition, baptism interestingly symbolizes paradoxical transformation from sinful nature to spiritual nature, from mortal life inherited from Adam to eternal life imparted from Christ, from the life of a living being to the life of a life-giving spirit, from the life of the first man of the dust of the earth to the life of second man of heaven, from the perishable to the imperishable, from dishonor to glory, from weakness to power, from mortality to immortality (1 Cor. 15:35-54); from the life pleasing the flesh to the life pleasing the Spirit, from destruction to eternal life (Gal. 6:8); from being the slave to sin to being slave to righteousness, from impurity to holiness, from receiving the wages of sin which is death to receiving the gift of God which is eternal life (Rom. 6:15-23); from death with Christ to the basic principles of this world (Col. 2:20) to being born again in Christ through the law of the Spirit who gives life (Rom. 8:2); from death to law to life with grace (Rom. 7:4); from being died to sin to being live to God (Rom. 6:10).

FEBRUARY 15

LIFE AND CHRIST

I have been crucified with Christ and I no longer live, but Christ lives in me. The life I live in the body, I live by faith in the Son of God, who loved me and gave himself for me. (Galatians 2:20)

Our life is closely related with Christ. Because He laid down His life for us (Gal. 2:20; 1 John 3:16), Christ brought us to eternal life (2 Tim. 1:10; Jude 1:20), and the eternal life was brought to us through Christ (Rom. 5:21; 8:1-2).

By faith in Christ, we have eternal life (John 20:31; Gal. 2:20), an eternal life in Christ (Rom. 6:23; 2 Tim. 1:1; 3:12). Our old life died, and our new life is now hidden with Christ in God (Col. 3:3). As Christ was raised to life, we may live a new life, which is eternal life ((Rom. 6:4; 8:11, 34; 14:9).

But what is eternal life? Eternal life is knowing Christ: "Now this is eternal life: that they may know you, the only true God, and Jesus Christ, who you have sent." (John 7:13). Indeed, Christ is our life (Col. 3:4). Not only Christ has the words of eternal life (John 6:68), but He Himself is the Word of Life (1 John 1:1) and the eternal life (John 14:6; 1 John 5:20).

When we are in Christ, we are a new creation (2 Cor. 5:17), in which Christ is formed (Gal. 4:19). And Christ will transform our lowly bodies to be like His glorious body (Phil. 3:21). We are being transformed into His likeness with ever-increasing glory (2 Cor. 3:18). As we have been united with Him in His death, we will certainly also be united with Him in His resurrection (Rom. 6:5). Therefore, we ought to exalt Christ in our life (Phil 1:20), so that we, who receive God's abundant provision of grace and of gift of righteousness may reign in life through Christ (Rom. 5:17). And in the Millennium, we will come to life and reign with Christ for a thousand years (Rev. 20:4).

Reflection: When God created Adam, He created him in His image and likeness. However, He did not impart him eternal life in this "old creation". Instead, He gave him two choices: the tree of life and the tree of knowledge of good and evil. If he had chosen the tree of life, he would have had been imparted eternal life. Unfortunately, he chose the tree of the knowledge of good and evil, and sinned. Therefore, he was not able to receive eternal life. In other words, in the old creation, God's image and likeness were given to Adam, but the eternal life was not. Adam was created from the dust of the earth, and the dust of the earth implied the frailty and transience of life. The cross of Christ is the tree of life. To Jews, "cursed is everyone that hangs on a tree." (Gal. 3:13). Nevertheless, Christ turned the cursed tree into the tree of life when He shed His blood on the cross. We cannot partake the fruit of the tree of life without coming to the cross of Christ. The cross of Christ is where the new creation takes place: "if anyone is in Christ, the new creation has come: The old has gone, the new is here!" (2 Cor. 5:17). The first man Adam became a living being; the last Adam, a life-giving spirit (1 Cor. 15:45). In Christ was life (John 1:4). Christ is the way, the truth, and the life (John 14:6). When we are in union with Christ, when we are in Christ, and Chrit is in us, we have eternal life. The old creation was done through Christ; whereas the new creation was done in Christ. As the new creation was done in Christ, our new life began in Christ. Without Christ, there would be no new life. The new creation cut us off from the genetic lineage of Adam, which is the genetic lineage of sin. Our new life was formed in Christ, thus it is in the genetic lineage of righteousness and holiness. Eternal life is the life of righteousness and holiness.

February 16

The Treasures of Wisdom and Knowledge

My purpose is that they may be encouraged in heart and united in love, so that they may have the full riches of complete understanding, in order that they may know the mystery of God, namely, Christ, in whom are hidden all the treasures of wisdom and knowledge. (Colossians 2:2-3)

Wisdom and knowledge are always mentioned together in the Scriptures (2 Chron. 1:10-12; Prov. 2:6, 10; 30:3; Eccles. 1:16, 18; 2:21, 26; 9:10; Isa. 47:10; Dan. 2:21). Solomon knows wisdom is more precious than jewels (Prov. 8:11), so that he asked from God wisdom and knowledge only. However, God granted him not only wisdom and knowledge, but wealth, riches and honor (2 Chron. 1:10-12).

The Apostle Paul is in awe of the depth of the riches of the wisdom and knowledge of God (Rom. 11:33-34); however, he knows that all the treasures of wisdom of knowledge are hidden in Christ (Col. 2:2-3). The Prophet Isaiah realizes that the key to the treasure of wisdom and knowledge is the fear of the Lord (Isa. 33:6). Yes, the fear of the Lord is the beginning of wisdom (Ps. 111:10; Prov. 9:10), as well as the beginning of knowledge (Prov. 1:7; 2:5). No wonder the Apostle Paul claims: "What is more, I consider everything a loss compared to the surpassing greatness of knowing Christ Jesus my Lord, for whose sake I have lost all things. I consider them rubbish, that I may gain Christ." (Phil. 3:8). Apostle Paul does know the secret to the treasures of wisdom and knowledge.

Reflection: When we think about wisdom, we tend to think it is a matter of rationality and intellectuality; it is something related to the faculties of intellect. It is "the ability to discern or judge what is true, right, or lasting; insight." (The American Heritage Dictionary). We always think someone who has high intelligence quotient is a man of wisdom. When we think about knowledge, we tend to think it is what we know, it is a matter of learning and scholarship. It is "information gained through experience, reasoning, or acquaintance." We always think a scholar is a man of knowledge. Nevertheless, in the Scriptures, both wisdom and knowledge are matters of spirituality. They are human-beings' spiritual properties. Both are all about knowing God. "The fear of the Lord is the beginning of wisdom, and knowledge of the Holy One is understanding." (Prov. 9 :10). "The fear of the Lord is the beginning of knowledge" (Prov. 1 :7). In other words, wisdom and knowledge are fear of God and knowing God. Christ is the mystery of God. All the treasures of wisdom and knowledge are hidden in Him, in the mystery of God. If you want to seek the treasures of wisdom and knowledge of God, you must seek Christ. No wisdom and knowledge of God is apart from Christ. The Apostle Paul does know the secret to the treasures of wisdom and knowledge. He considers wisdom and knowledge of knowing Christ as his spiritual treasures for which he is willing to abandon everything, just like the treasure hunter and the pearl seeker in Matthew 13. He claims, "whatever were gains to me I now consider loss for the sake of Christ. What is more, I consider everything a loss because of the surpassing worth of knowing Christ Jesus my Lord, for whose sake I have lost all things. I consider them garbage, that I may gain Christ" (Phil. 3:7-8).

FEBRUARY 17

SUFFERING AND GLORY

Now if we are children, then we are heirs-heirs of God and co-heirs with Christ, if indeed we share in his sufferings in order that we may also share in his glory. (Romans 8:17)

The Spirit of Christ predicted the sufferings of Christ and the glories that would follow (1 Pet. 1:11). Isaiah 52:13 talks about the suffering and glory of the servant: "See, my servant will act wisely; he will be raised and lifted up and highly exalted." God's servant, Jesus Christ, died on the cross after enormous suffering. "Therefore God exalted him to the highest place and gave him the name that is above every name" (Phil. 2:9). Christ did not take upon Himself the glory of becoming a high priest; instead, God called him his Son (Heb. 5:5). And Christ entered His glory after his suffering (Luke 24:46). He was crowned with glory and honor because He suffered death (Heb. 2:9). And glory is not only to Christ, but also to God the Father (Phil. 2:11). In other words, Christ shares glory with God the Father.

As heirs of God and co-heirs with Christ, we may also share in His glory if we share in his suffering (Rom. 8:17), and we may attain to the resurrection from the dead after our sharing in His suffering and becoming like Him in His death (Phil. 3:10). In fact, God called us to share in the glory of Christ (2 Thess. 2:14; 1 Pet. 5:10). In bringing us to glory, God makes Christ perfect through suffering (Heb. 2:10). Therefore, if we participate in the suffering of Christ, we may be overjoyed when His glory is revealed (1 Pet. 4:13). When Christ appears, we also will appear with Him in glory (Col 3:4). We, who are the first to hope in Christ, may be for the praise of His glory (Eph. 1:12). With such hope, we have no reason not to consider that our present sufferings are not worth comparing with the glory that will be revealed in us (Rom.8:18). As witness of Christ's suffering, Peter is sure that he will share in the glory to be revealed (1 Pet. 5:1).

Reflection: How to deal the issue of suffering is the touchstone of religious faith. Buddhism attempts to eliminate it; Christian Science denies it; Islam accepts it. Only does Christian faith transforms it, turning suffering for Christ into spiritual growth, into spiritual blessings, and into heavenly glory and rewards. When He returns, Christ will bring to those who suffer for righteousness glory and rewards, as He promises in the Beatitudes: "Blessed are those who are persecuted because of righteousness, for theirs is the kingdom of heaven. Blessed are you when people insult you, persecute you and falsely say all kinds of evil against you because of me. Rejoice and be glad, because great is your reward in heaven, for in the same way they persecuted the prophets who were before you." (Matt. 5 :10-12). The Lord Jesus Christ is the first person who has fulfilled this promise when He goes to the cross: "The hour has come for the Son of Man to be glorified. Very truly I tell you, unless a kernel of wheat falls to the ground and dies, it remains only a single seed. But if it dies, it produces many seeds." (John 12 :23-24). Stephen is the second person on whom this promise has been fulfilled: "But Stephen, full of the Holy Spirit, looked up to heaven and saw the glory of God, and Jesus standing at the right hand of God. 'Look,' he said, 'I see heaven open and the Son of Man standing at the right hand of God.'" (Acts 7 :55-56). And this promise will be fulfilled on all the children of God: "The Spirit himself testifies with our spirit that we are God's children. Now if we are children, then we are heirs—heirs of God and co-heirs with Christ, if indeed we share in his sufferings in order that we may also share in his glory." (Rom. 8:16-17). And, "our light and momentary troubles are achieving for us an eternal glory that far outweighs them all." (2 Cor. 4 :17). Suffering for Christ will lead us into His glory. If we share in His suffering, we will share in His glory. When we partake the Lord's Supper, symbolically, we are participating in His suffering on the cross. The Lord's Supper serves as a reminder that we shall participate in the suffering of Christ, and we shall suffer for righteousness in our real life.

February 18

The Knowledge of God

Oh, the depth of the riches of the wisdom and knowledge of God! How unsearchable his judgments, and his paths beyond tracing out! (Romans 11:33)

The arrogant and the wicked doubt the knowledge of God (Ps. 73:11), and belittle the knowledge of God (Rom. 1:28). The wise know that God gives knowledge to the man who pleases him (Prov. 2:6; Eccles. 2:26; Luke. 8:10); and that the eyes of the Lord keep watch over knowledge (Prov. 22:12); and that no one can teach knowledge to God (Job. 21:22); and that no one can comprehend the depth of the riches of the wisdom and knowledge of God (Rom. 11:33). For the earth will be filled with the knowledge of the Lord as the waters cover the sea (Isa. 11:9).

The fear of the Lord is the beginning of knowledge (Prov. 1:7; 2:5-6). Those who hate knowledge do not choose to fear the Lord (Prov. 1:29). The knowledge of God is understanding (Prov. 9:10). With fear of the Lord, we are given the light of the knowledge of the glory of God in the face of Christ (2 Cor. 4:6); and we may be able to demolish arguments and every pretension that sets itself up against the knowledge of God (2 Cor. 10:5); and we may spread the fragrance of the knowledge of God in triumphal procession in Christ (2 Cor. 2:14).

If we live a life worthy of the Lord in the knowledge and please him in every way, we will grow in the knowledge of God (1 Col. 1:10; 2 Pet. 3:18); and grace and peace will be ours in abundance through the knowledge of God and of Jesus Christ our Lord (2 Pet. 1:2); and we will be effective and productive in our knowledge of our Lord Jesus Christ (2 Pet. 1:8).

Reflection: "Knowledge is a familiarity, awareness, or understanding of someone or something, such as fact (propositional knowledge), skills (procedural knowledge), or objects (acquaintance knowledge). ... The term 'knowledge' can refer to a theoretical or practical understanding of a subject" (Wikipedia). The Greek philosopher, Plato defines knowledge as "justified true belief". When we talk about the knowledge of God, we tend to think it is learning about God, which can be acquired by intellectual faculties; and it belongs to sphere of epistemology. From human perspective, there are three paths to acquire the knowledge of God, intuition, reason, and five senses. By reasoning, philosophers have come up with five philosophical arguments: cosmological argument, teleological argument, anthropological argument, moral argument, and ontological argument. Nevertheless, the knowledge of God cannot be acquired by any human efforts. The knowledge of God can only be acquired by faith from divine revelation: including general revelation, which God reveals Himself through creation, providence, and human conscience; and special revelation, which God reveals Himself through Scriptures (the Written Word), and Christ (the Incarnate Word). As a matter of fact, the incarnation of Christ is the ultimate revelation of God. Knowledge of God cannot be acquired without faith in Christ, God's Incarnate Word. Unlike knowledge of the physical matters which can be acquired by reasoning, knowledge of God can only be acquired by faith alone, the faith in Christ. In fact, true knowledge is the knowledge of God. The fear of the Lord is the beginning of knowledge (Prov. 1:7). When we know Christ, we will know God, because with fear of the Lord, we are given the light of the knowledge of the glory of God in the face of Christ (2 Cor. 4:6). Just as Jesus said, "When you see me, you see the Father." (John 14:9).

FEBRUARY 19

CHRIST AND THE GLORY OF GOD

It is for God's glory so that God's Son may be glorified through it. (John 11:4)

From the Scriptures, we can always see Christ, the Son, is closely related to the glory of God. As Christ Himself prophesies, the Son is going to come in the Father's glory (Matt. 8:38; 16:27; Luke 9:26). No wonder Steven saw Jesus standing at the right hand of God when he saw the glory of God (Acts 7:55). As a matter of fact, the glory of God is seen in the face of Christ (2 Cor. 4:6); and the Son is the radiance of God's glory (Heb. 1:3). In the New Jerusalem, the glory of God gives it light, and Christ is its lamp (Rev. 21:23).

The Father and the Son glorify each other. The Father glorifies the Son (John 8:54). Christ receives glory from the Father (2 Pet. 1:17). It is for God's glory so that God's Son may be glorified through it (John 11:4). And the Son considers His self-glory meaningless without the Father's glorification (John 8:54). Furthermore, the Son of God may be glorified through whatever is for the glory of God (John 11:4), and for the service of God and Father (Rev. 1:6)

The Son also glorifies the Father (John 14:13; Phil. 2:11). And the Father is glorified through the Son (Rom. 16:27; Heb. 13:21; Jude 1:25), and in Christ (Eph. 3:21). And in all things, God the Father is glorified though Christ (1 Pet. 4:11). And everybody worships Christ, to the glory of God the Father (Phil. 2:10-11).

In His glory, the Father witnessed the Son; and the Son received honor and glory from God the Father when the voice came to him from the Majestic Glory, saying, "This is my Son, whom I love; with him I am well pleased." (2 Pet. 1:17). And we have seen His glory, the glory of the One and Only, who came from the Father, full of grace and truth (John 1:14). And the Father calls us to His eternal glory in the Son (1 Pet. 5:10), who is the hope of glory (Col. 1:27).

Reflection: In the Hebrew Old Testament, *shekinah* is the word to describe the glory of God. Literally, *shekinah* is a radiant cloud or brilliant light within a cloud that signals the immediate presence of God. Figuratively, it means the visible manifestation of the invisible God. In the New Testament, the glory of God is ascribed to Christ, and Christ is identified with *shekinah*, the glory of God: "The Son is the radiance of God's glory and the exact representation of his being" (Heb. 1:3). How to understand "The Son is the radiance of God's glory"? The Bible gives us a hint: "In the New Jerusalem, the glory of God gives it light, and Christ is the lamp." Oh, because God is the light, and Christ is the lamp, the Son is the radiance of God's glory. The glory of God is seen in the face of Christ, who is the exact presentation of His being. Jesus Christ, as the ultimate revelation of God, reveals the glory of God. In essence, the revelation of Christ is the revelation of the glory of God. However, if glory is defined as blindingly pure light in a literal sense, on the days when Jesus was taking human flesh on the earth, the glory of God was largely veiled in Him, except on the mount of transfiguration. If glory is defined as the summation of His attributes, Christ revealed the glory of God when exercising His divine attributes in the miracles He performed. Although not seeing the glory of God manifested in Jesus Christ with our physical eyes as His disciples did, we do catch a glimpse of the glory of God manifested in Christ with our spiritual eyes when we read the Scriptures and experience Him day by day. Moreover, we will definitely see the fullness of God in Christ when we meet Him face-to-face. And the revelation of God will reach its fullness when we meet Christ in person.

February 20

Christ and the Image of God

The Son is the image of the invisible God, the firstborn over all creation. (Colossians 1:15)

Christ bears the image of God. Firstly, God is revealed through Christ. God's Only Begotten Son has made the Father known (John 1:15). Whoever sees the Son sees the Father (John 12:45, 14:9). Secondly, Christ is indeed the image of God (2 Cor. 4:4). He is the image of the invisible God (Col. 1:15), and the exact representation of His being (Heb. 1:3). Finally, Christ has God's glory. The glory of God is seen in the face of Christ (2 Cor. 4:6); and He is the radiance of God's glory (Heb. 1:3). We have seen His glory, the glory of the One and Only, who came from the Father, full of grace and truth (John 1:14).

We human beings were made in the image and likeness of God (Gen. 1:26-27, 5:1; 1 Cor. 11:7). Unfortunately, the image of God was marred in our lives due to sin (Rom. 3:23). However, through His redemption, Christ helps us recover the image of God by confirming us to the likeness of Himself (Rom. 8:29), and by transforming us into His likeness with ever-increasing glory (2 Cor. 3:18), so that we may be put on the new self, created to be like God in true righteousness and holiness (Eph. 4:24), and renewed in knowledge in the image of God (Col. 3:10), until one day, we are recovered to God's image and likeness completely (1 Cor. 15:49; 1 John 3:2).

Reflection: "Man is not created to be the image of God but — as is said in vv. 26 and 27, but also Genesis 5:1 (and again in the command not to shed human blood, Genesis 9:6) — he is created in correspondence with the image of God." (Karl Barth). In terms of the image of God, there is a significant difference between Christ and man. Man was created in the image of God, whereas Christ is the image of God (2 Cor. 4 :4); "He is the image of the invisible God, the firstborn over all creation. (Col. 1:15). Among God's creation, only man was created in the image of God. Man, both physically and spiritually, was created in the image of God. Man is said to be after the image of God, because he excels all the other creatures by his reason and intelligence. The image of God in man consisted primarily in man's rational and moral characteristics, and in his capacity for holiness. In contrast, Christ is the image of the invisible God, the exact representation of His being. We cannot know God without knowing Christ. It is the purpose of incarnation to make the invisible God visible. He was with the Father and has appeared to us. This makes Him to be qualified as our Mediator. The meaning of "the image of God" in Genesis differs the meaning of "the image of God in the New Testament, especially in the Pauline epistles. In the Old Creation, man was created in the image of God. It was done in one step. In the New Creation, man is in the process of being conformed to the image of God, which actually is the image of Christ. In fact, this process is the process of salvation, including regeneration, sanctification, and glorification. Man won't be conformed to the image of Christ until glorification is attained, and the process of salvation is completed. In short, man was made in the image of God in creation, and he is conformed to the image of Christ by redemption. In this process of redemption, man is to put off his old self, which is being corrupted by its deceitful desires; to be made new in the attitude of his minds; and to put on the new self, created to be like God in true righteousness and holiness. (Eph. 4:22-24). True righteousness and holiness are the eternal life; and eternal life is the life of true righteousness and holiness.

February 21

Blessings of God and God of Blessings

Your father's blessings are greater than the blessings of the ancient mountains, than the bounty of the age-old hills. (Genesis 49:26)

Jacob's blessings of Joseph: "Joseph is a fruitful vine, a fruitful vine near a spring, whose branches climb over a wall. With bitterness archers attacked him; they shot at him with hostility. But his bow remained steady, his strong arms stayed limber, because of the hand of the Mighty One of Jacob, because of the Shepherd, the Rock of Israel, because of your father's God, who helps you, because of the Almighty, who blesses you with blessings of the skies above, blessings of the deep springs below, blessings of the breast and womb. Your father's blessings are greater than the blessings of the ancient mountains, than the bounty of the age-old hills. Let all these rest on the head of Joseph, on the brow of the prince among his brothers (Gen. 49:22-26).

But he (Joseph) refused. "With me in charge," he told her (Potiphar's wife), "my master does not concern himself with anything in the house; everything he owns he has entrusted to my care. No one is greater in this house than I am. My master has withheld nothing from me except you, because you are his wife. How then could I do such a wicked thing and sin against God?" (Gen. 39:8-9).

But while Joseph was there in the prison, the Lord was with him; he showed him kindness and granted him favor in the eyes of the prison warden. So the warden put Joseph in charge of all those held in the prison, and he was made responsible for all that was done there. The warden paid no attention to anything under Joseph's care, because the Lord was with Joseph and gave him success in whatever he did (Gen. 39:20-23).

Reflection: Satan's trick is to instigate us to seek blessings of God at the cost of drifting apart from the God of blessings. When we focus ourselves on the blessings of God, we may inadvertently substitute God of blessings with blessings of God in our lives. When we do so, we commit the sin of idol worship, as we allow blessings of God to usurp the throne of God of blessings in our lives. Joseph received abundant blessings from God because he feared and loved the God of blessings. He dared not to sin against God (Gen. 39:9), the Lord was with Joseph and gave him success in whatever he did (Gen. 39:23). He valued his personal relationship with God. Likewise, Jesus valued His personal relationship with the Father. He showed His humble attitude and relied on the Father always even after he had performed one of His greatest miracles in his lifetime (Mark 6:46). We, His followers should imitate Him. Sometimes, when we achieve success, or when we are blessed by the Lord in other aspects, we put too much attention to our success or blessings received from the Lord. We shift focus from God of blessings to blessings of God. Day after day, our relationship with the Lord becomes weaker and weaker. And we let these things take place of God in the throne of our lives. Finally, we turn our blessings into stumbling block in our relationship with God. When we turn our blessings to stumbling block in our relationship with God, God may take back His blessings from us, in order to remind us to rely on Himself. Every time when we enjoy the blessings of God rather than the God of blessings, alarm will ring in our life. However, God is so gracious, He always takes away from us the second best, that is the blessings of God, and give us the best, that is Himself, the God of blessings.

February 22

Death and Life

We always carry around in our body the death of Jesus, so that the life of Jesus may also be revealed in our body. For we who are alive are always being given over to death for Jesus' sake, so that his life may also be revealed in our mortal body. (2 Corinthians 4:10-11)

Jesus teaches His disciples, "I tell you the truth, unless a kernel of wheat falls to the ground and dies, it remains only a single seed. But if it dies, it produces many seeds." (John 12:24). Jesus' discourse reveals the spiritual truth of death and life.

Death came through Adam in whom all die, and the resurrection of the dead comes through Christ in whom all will be made alive (1 Cor. 15:21-22). We died to sin, but we are alive to God in Christ (Rom. 6:11), who also died to sin once for all, but lives to God (Rom. 6:10). God made us alive in Christ (Eph. 2:5, 13), who was put to death in the body, but made alive by the Spirit (1 Pet. 3:18), even when we were dead in transgressions (Eph. 2:5), in our sins and in the circumcision of our sinful nature (Col. 2:13). When our old self was crucified with Christ, the body of sin might be done away with, and we have been freed from sin (Rom. 6:6-7). If we live according to the sinful nature, we will die; but if by the Spirit we put to death the misdeeds of the body, we will live (Rom. 8:13). Actually, we no longer live, but Christ lives in us (Gal. 2:20). Because, if we always carry around in our body the death of Christ, His life will be revealed in our body; and if we who are alive are always being given over to His death, His life will be revealed in our mortal body (2 Cor. 4:10-11). If Christ is in us, our body is dead because of sin, yet our spirit is alive because of righteousness (Rom. 8:10).

Reflection: In the physical realm, life comes before death. In the spiritual realm, death comes before life. Our sinful nature has to die before we are born again in Christ. Our new life cannot be born until after our old life is crucified with Christ. Life and death, a pair of antitheses as everybody understands, is also a pair of paradoxes. And this is one of the most important pairs of paradoxes in the biblical teachings. Life is transferrable to death; and death is transferrable to life. Oswald Chambers says that every believer's life is a "Bethlehem" where a "new life in Christ" was born. However, our new life cannot be born until after our old life is crucified with Christ in Golgotha. For physical life, there is life first, then there is death; but for spiritual life, there is death first, then there is life (Rom. 6:8, 10-11, 8:13; 1 Cor. 15:46). Death and life constitute an eternal predicament of choice, which must be made in front of the cross. The paradoxical transformation of death and life takes place on the cross (Gal. 2:20). Jesus said to his disciples, "Whoever wants to be my disciple must deny themselves and take up their cross and follow me. For whoever wants to save their life will lose it, but whoever loses their life for me will find it." (Matt. 16:24-25; also see Mark 8:34-35; Luke 9:23-24). He also teaches his disciples: "Very truly I tell you, unless a kernel of wheat falls to the ground and dies, it remains only a single seed. But if it dies, it produces many seeds. Anyone who loves their life will lose it, while anyone who hates their life in this world will keep it for eternal life." (John 12:24-25).

February 23

The Glory of God

The heavens declare the glory of God. (Psalm 19:1)

Glory belongs to God (Rev. 19:1). God is awesome in glory (Exod. 15:11). The heavens declare the glory of God. (Ps. 19:1). The glory of God covered heavens (Hab. 3:3), and filled the temple of God (2 Chron. 5:14; Rev. 15:8). It moves (Ezek. 9:3, 43:2), and is above all things (Ps. 57:5, 108:5; Ezek. 10:19, 11:22). God of glory thunders (Ps. 29:3).

Unfortunately, men defile the glory of God (Rom. 1:23), and fall short of it (Rom. 3:23). However, God calls us by His own glory (2 Pet. 1:3), and into His glory (1 Thess. 2:12).

God helps us for His glory (Ps. 79:9). Grace causes thanksgiving to overflow to the glory of God (2 Cor. 4:15). Our redemption is to the praise of the glory of God (Eph. 1:13-14). And our sanctification is to the glory and praise of God (Phil 1:11). And judgment is for the glory of God (Rev. 14:7). God will be our glory (Isa. 60:19).

Although it is glory of God to conceal a matter (Prob. 25:2), God shows us glory (Deut. 5:24). The glory of God appeared before men (Ezek. 8:4; Acts 7:2), and will be seen (Isa. 35:2). With faith, we will see the glory of God (John 11:40). And by suffering for Christ, we will see His glory (Acts 7:55), because God made his light shine in our hearts to give us the light of the knowledge of the glory of God in the face of Christ (2 Cor. 4:6).

God is worthy to receive glory (Rev. 4:11). By faith, we give glory to God (Rom. 4:20). We rejoice in the hope of the glory of God (Rom. 5:2). We do everything for the glory of God (1 Cor. 10:31). We speak "Amen" to the glory of God (2 Cor. 1:20). We give glory in His praise (Ps. 106:47); we give glory to God in the highest (Luke 2:14); we give glory to God through Christ (Jude 1:25); and we give glory to God and Father forever and ever (Phil. 4:20, 1 Tim. 1:17, Rev. 7:12). The Holy City will shine with the glory of God (Rev. 21:10-12); and glory of God will give light to the New Jerusalem (Rev. 21:23).

Reflection: The glory of God is the beauty of His spirit, or the essence of Who He Is. The glory of God is the manifest beauty of His holiness: "Holy, holy, holy is the Lord Almighty; the whole earth is full of his glory." (Isa. 6 :3). If there is an evident theme throughout the Holy Scriptures, it is "the glory of God.". Holiness is an intrinsic attribute of God, and the glory of God is the brilliance of His holiness. "The glory of God is the holiness of God made manifest……So to see, to apprehend, and to reckon with his holiness (and, in some sense, to perceive it) is to see glory and, thus, to glorify him." (John Piper). "Holiness is God's hidden glory: glory is God's all-present holiness," (A. Motyer). "The Lord is majestic in holiness and awesome in glory" (Exod. 15:11). No wonder the Scriptures claim: "All have sinned and fall short of the glory of God." (Rom. 3 :23). It means that when we commit sin, which is an offense against the holiness of God, we fall short of the glory of God. The holiness of God and the glory of God go hand and hand, and cannot be separated from each other. In the process of salvation, which includes regeneration, sanctification, and glorification, holiness is the ultimate goal. In the phase of regeneration, holiness is imputed to us; in the phase of sanctification, holiness is imparted to us; and in the phase of glorification, holiness is consummated in us. "The vindication of God's glory is the ground of our salvation, and the exaltation of God's glory is the goal of our salvation." (John Piper). Nevertheless, glory belongs to God only, and it does not belong to anyone else. God is worthy to receive glory, and no one else is. The secret to blessings is to ascribe glory to God. Whenever we try to steal God's glory, curse will be upon us. Humble attitude is of wisdom because it recognizes the glory of God. The humble are wise, because they ascribe glory to God, and God gives them blessings in return. When we "ascribe to the Lord the glory due His name, worship the Lord in the splendor of his holiness." (Ps. 29:2), peace will be upon us: "Glory to God in the highest heaven, and on earth peace to those on whom his favor rests." (Luke 2:14). This is one of the golden promises of God recorded in the Scriptures.

FEBRUARY 24

THE MAJESTY OF THE LORD

The Lord reigns, he is robed in majesty; the Lord is robed in majesty and armed with strength. (Psalm 93:1)

The majesty is the Lord's, for everything in heaven and earth is His. The kingdom is His; He is exalted as head over all (1 Chron. 29:11). His majesty is over Israel (Ps. 68:34). And His name is majestic in all the earth (Ps. 8:1). The Lord has shown us His glory and His majesty (Deut. 5:24). God comes in awesome majesty (Job 37:22). He rides on the clouds in His majesty (Deut. 33:26). The Lord reigns, He is robed in majesty (Ps. 93:1), and clothed with splendor and majesty (Ps. 104:1).

The Israelites had ever seen the majesty of the Lord (Deut. 11:2). And they acclaimed His majesty (Isa. 24:14). On the other hand, the wicked hide in the ground from dread of the Lord and the splendor of His majesty (Isa. 2:10, 19, 21), for the Lord is majestic in holiness and awesome in glory (Exod. 15:11). The wicked do not learn righteousness; they go on doing evil and regard not the majesty of the Lord (Isa. 26:10). However, they will be punished and chastised with everlasting destruction and shut from the presence of the Lord and the majesty of His power on the day He comes to be glorified in His holy people, and to be marveled at among all those who have believed (2 Thess. 1:9).

Reflection: Influenced by a popular hymn, Christians nowadays tend to consider Jesus as our friend. Although Jesus Himself calls us His friend, He does this because He is humble. We cannot forget or ignore the fact that He is the King of kings, and the Lord of lords. He is robed in majesty, and clothed with splendor and majesty. We cannot reduce the Lord to our human level, and fail to acknowledge His majesty. In the ancient China, all the subjects must bow down to the emperor and kneel before him. Our Lord is the King of kings, and the ruler of the kings of the earth. He absolutely deserves our worship. The psalmist sings, "Come, let us bow down in worship, let us kneel before the

LORD our Maker." (Ps. 95:6). This is the proper attitude and posture when we come before Him. In fact, the Psalms are full of awes to the majesty of the Lord: "Lord, our Lord, how majestic is your name in all the earth! You have set your glory in the heavens." (Ps. 8:1). Psalms reveal to us that the majesty of the Lord is closely related to His glory and His holy name, Yahweh, which is translated as the word "LORD". This is a name to which we must yield reverent obedience. The Jewish scribes must wipe the pen and wash their entire body every time before writing this holy name. The name Yahweh, which means "I am who I am" indicates that our Lord is the self-existent and sovereign God, to whom all creation owes its existence. He is the God of holiness, and He displays glory in both creation and redemption. He is the God the Creator and the Lord the Redeemer. He is the majestic Lord because of His holiness and glory. He is the God of holiness and glory; and He is the Lord of glory and majesty.

FEBRUARY 25

CHRIST HAS THE MAJESTY OF GOD

For we did not follow cleverly devised stories when we told you about the coming of our Lord Jesus Christ in power, but we were eyewitnesses of his majesty. (2 Peter 1:16)

The apostles witnessed Christ's majesty when He received honor and glory from God the Father (2 Pet. 1:16-17). As a matter of fact, Christ has the same majesty as God the Father does. Just as God is clothed with majesty (Ps. 93:1, 104:1), Christ will be clothed with majesty and will sit and rule on His throne (Zech. 6:13); Just as God rides on the clouds (Deut. 33:26), Christ is coming with the clouds (Rev. 1:7); Just like God whose majesty is over Israel (Ps. 68:34), Christ is the King of Israel (John 12:13) and the ruler over Israel (Mic. 5:2).

Christ will stand and shepherd His flock in the majesty of the name of the Lord His God (Mic. 5:4). Meanwhile, Christ sits down at the right hand of the Majesty in heaven (Heb. 1:3). He will be worshiped by His people (Dan. 7:14; Rev. 4:8-11), for He is King of kings (Rev. 17:14, 19:16) and the ruler of the kings of the earth (Rev. 1:5). And the scepter will not depart from Judah (Gen. 49:10). He reigns on David's throne and over his kingdom, whose house and kingdom will endure forever, and whose throne will be established forever (2 Sam. 7:16).

Reflection: Not only does the Father have majesty, but also the Son has majesty. Christ has the same majesty as God the Father does. That is why Jesus says, "When you see me, you see the Father." The reason that Christ has the same majesty as God the Father does is that the Son is the image of the invisible God, and the Son is the radiance of God's glory and the exact representation of His being. Christ is equal with the Father in essence. He is one with the Father in essence, nature, power, action, and will. Although He existed in the very nature of God, Christ chose not to "consider equality with God something to be used to his own advantage; rather, he made himself nothing by taking the very nature of a servant, being made in human likeness. And being found in appearance as a man, he humbled himself by becoming obedient to death—even death on a cross!" (Phil. 2:6-8). Although He shared majesty with the Father from eternity, Christ humbled Himself, and voluntarily forsook His divine privileges, including majesty, and became a humble servant and died on the cross. However, just because of His humility, "God exalted him to the highest place and gave him the name that is above every name, that at the name of Jesus every knee should bow, in heaven and on earth and under the earth, and every tongue acknowledge that Jesus Christ is Lord, to the glory of God the Father." (Phil. 2:9-11). Paradoxically, Christ's majesty has not been gravitated, but augmented. This is one of the spiritual paradoxes recorded in the Scriptures. Now, Christ sits down at the right hand of the Majesty in heaven (Heb. 1:3). And, He reigns on David's throne and over his kingdom, whose house and kingdom will endure forever, and whose throne will be established forever (2 Sam. 7:16). When He returns, He is coming with the clouds (Rev. 1:7), and will sit on the throne to judge all the humanity. Christ has the majesty of God as the Creator, as the Redeemer, and as the Judge in the Final Judgment.

FEBRUARY 26

SPLENDOR AND MAJESTY

Praise the Lord, my soul, Lord my God, you are very great; you are clothed with splendor and majesty. (Psalm 104:1)

Yours, Lord, is the greatness and the power and the glory and the majesty and the splendor, for everything in heaven and earth is yours. Yours, Lord, is the kingdom, you are exalted as head over all (1 Chron. 29:11). They speak of the glorious splendor of your majesty – and I will meditate on your wonderful works (Ps. 145:5).

Splendor and majesty are before Him; strength and joy are in his dwelling place (1 Chron. 16:27). Splendor and majesty are before Him; strength and glory are in His sanctuary (Ps. 96:6). Out of the north He comes in golden splendor; God comes in awesome majesty (Job 37:22).

People will flee to caves in the rocks and to holes in the ground from the fearful presence of the Lord and the splendor of his majesty, when he rises to shake the earth (Isa. 2:19). They will flee to caverns in the rocks and to the overhanging crags from the fearful presence of the Lord and the splendor of his majesty, when he rises to shake the earth (Isa. 2:21). Go into the rocks, hide in the ground from the fearful presence of the Lord and the splendor of his majesty! (Isa. 2:10).

Gird your sword on your side, you mighty one; clothe yourself with splendor and majesty (Ps. 45:3). Then adorn yourself with glory and splendor, and clothe yourself in honor and majesty (Job 40:10). Which of the trees of Eden can be compared with you in splendor and majesty? (Ezek. 31:18).

Reflection: The Hebrew Scriptures describe Yahweh as the sovereign King of creation who clothes himself with glorious splendor and majesty (Ps. 96:6; 104:1-2; 145:1-2, 5, 12-13). The Hebrew Scriptures also state that Messiah shares God's splendor and majesty. The Messiah, the anointed King, is crowned with splendor and majesty of God Himself. Splendor and majesty describe God's royal presence. They are aspects of His glory. True splendor and majesty belong to God only, as glory is His nature, essence and attribute. He is clothed with splendor and majesty, and is awe-inspiring. He deserves an awe-inspiring worship and praise. He is the King of kings, and the Lord of lords. Splendor and majesty are His royal attire. He is clothed with splendor and majesty. Allan Poe sings, "To the glory that was Greece, And the grandeur that was Rome." However, where are the empires now? Splendor and majesty only belong to God, the King of kings, and the Lord of the lords. In history, empires rise and fall, only does the Kingdom of God endure forever and ever. He is the Creator of universe, and Redeemer of the cosmos. By creation and redemption, God deserves all the praise, honor, glory and power. Although at His first coming, Jesus Christ came in a very humble fashion, when He comes back, He will come with splendor and majesty: "When the Son of Man comes in his glory, and all the angels with him, he will sit on his glorious throne." (Matt. 25:31). At the end time, in the New Heaven and the New Earth, God's splendor and majesty will reach their apex. The New Jerusalem will shine with the glory of God (Rev. 21:11), for the glory of God gives it light, and the Lamb is its lamp (Rev. 21:23). A great multitude in heaven are shouting: "Hallelujah! Salvation and glory and power belong to our God." (Rev. 19:1).

February 27

The Glorious Splendor of the Kingdom

They will tell of the glory of your kingdom and speak of your might, so that all men may know of your mighty acts and the glorious splendor of your kingdom. (Psalm 145:11-12)

For a full 180 days King Xerxes displayed the vast wealth of his kingdom and the splendor and glory of his majesty (Esth. 1:4). Where did the splendor of his kingdom come from? Daniel knew that King Nebuchadnezzar's dominion, power, might, and glory came from the God of heaven (Dan. 2:37). And King Nebuchadnezzar praised and exalted and glorified the King of heaven (Dan. 4:37) after his honor and splendor were returned to him for the glory of his kingdom (Dan. 4:36). Daniel reminded King Belshazzar that the Most High God gave his father Nebuchadnezzar sovereignty and greatness and glory and splendor (Dan. 5:18). Likewise, the Lord highly exalted Solomon in the sight of all Israel and bestowed on him royal splendor such as no king over Israel ever had before (1 Chron. 29:25). On the other hand, God is able to take away glorious splendor of any kingdom. For instance, God overthrew Babylon, the jewel of kingdoms, the glory of the Babylonians' pride (Isa. 13:19). Nevertheless, they (His faithful people) will tell of the glory of His kingdom and speak of His might, so that all men may know of His mighty acts and the glorious splendor of His kingdom. (Ps. 145:11-12)

Reflection: Babylon, the jewel of kingdoms, the glory of the Babylonians' pride, has been overthrown by God. The most powerful kingdom in the history has vanished. Even King Nebuchadnezzar praised and exalted and glorified the King of heaven. This foretells that the kingdom of this world will become the kingdom of our Lord and of His Christ, and He will reign for ever and ever (Rev. 11:15). No wonder all kings will see the glory of the Lord (Isa. 62:2); and all kings of the earth will revere His glory (Ps. 102:15), although, ironically, the devil took Jesus to a very high mountain and showed him all the kingdoms of the world and their splendor (Matt. 4:8). Jesus said to Pilate, "My kingdom is not of this world. If it were, my servants would fight to prevent my arrest by the Jews. But now my kingdom is from another place." (John 18:36). Nevertheless, the kingdom of the world will become the kingdom of our Lord and of His Christ, and He will reign for ever and ever (Rev. 11:15), as Christ is given authority, glory and sovereign power (Dan. 7:14). All peoples, nations and men of every language will worship him (Dan. 7:14); and His faithful people will extol Him. They tell of the glory of His kingdom and speak of His might, so that all people may know of His mighty acts and the glorious splendor of His kingdom. His kingdom is an everlasting kingdom, and His dominion endures through all generations (Ps. 145:10-13).

February 28

The Eternal Kingdom

How great are his signs, how mighty his wonders! His kingdom is an eternal kingdom; his dominion endures from generation to generation. (Daniel 4:3)

The Prophet Daniel prophesied that the God of heaven would set up a kingdom that would never be destroyed, nor would it be left to another people; and it would crush all those kingdoms and bring them to an end, but it would itself endure forever (Dan. 2:44). How come that kingdom can endure forever? It is because the God of heaven who would set up the kingdom lives forever (Dan. 4:34); it is because He is the living God, and He endures forever (Dan. 6:26); and it is because His signs are great and His wonders are mighty (Dan. 4:3).

God of heaven promised to David an eternal kingdom, and He would establish the throne of Solomon's kingdom over Israel forever (2 Sam. 7:13, 16; 1 Chron. 17:14, 22:10, 28:7). As a prophet, David knew that God had promised him on oath that he would place one of his descendants on his throne, who is Jesus Christ (Acts 2:30). It was also prophesied that Jesus Christ would reign on David's throne and over his kingdom (Isa. 9:7), and would reign over the house of Jacob forever (Luke 1:33), being given authority, glory and sovereign power (Dan. 7:14); and His kingdom will never end (Dan. 7:14; Isa. 9:7; Luke 1:33).

Besides, the sovereignty, power, and greatness of the kingdoms under the whole heaven will be handed over to the saints of the Most High (Dan. 7:27), who will receive the eternal kingdom and will possess it forever (Dan. 7:18). As the saints of the Most High, we are welcome into the eternal kingdom of our Lord and Savior Jesus Christ (2 Pet. 1:11); and we will inherit the Kingdom God promised (James 2:5). As the Lord is faithful to all His promises, His kingdom is everlasting kingdom, and His dominion endures through all generations (Ps. 145:13).

Reflection: In Daniel's statue prophecy, the statue's head of pure gold symbolizes the Babylonian Empire; the chest and arms of silver the Medes and Persian Empire; the belly and thighs of bronze the Greek Empire; and the statue's legs and iron and feet partly of iron and partly of baked clay the Roman Empire. These were the only four world kingdoms in the ancient history. They rose and fell one after another. The stone which destroys the statue symbolizes the eternal kingdom of Christ. In the Book of Revelation, the kingdom of this world will become the kingdom of our Lord and of His Christ, and He will reign for ever and ever. The kingdom of Christ will crush all those kingdoms and bring them to an end, but it would itself endure forever. The statue prophecy in the Book of Daniel will be fully fulfilled at the end of time. It proves again that prophecies are virtually God's promises, as the psalmist sings, "Your kingdom is an everlasting kingdom, and your dominion endures through all generations. The Lord is trustworthy in all he promises and faithful in all he does." (Ps. 145:13). The kingdom of Christ is an eternal kingdom because Christ is the eternal king, who has fulfilled God's promises included in the Abrahamic covenant (Gen. 17:6, 15-16; 35:11), as well the promises included in the Davidic covenant (2 Sam. 7:13, 16; 1 Chron. 17:14, 22:10, 28:7). God's kingdom promise is a twofold promise, a promise of a physical kingdom, and a promise of spiritual kingdom. When David was ordained by the Lord as the king of Israel, the kingdom promise starts to be fulfilled partly. Nevertheless, due to the sins of David and Solomon, the Davidic kingdom was divided. Due to sins of the kings of both the kingdom of Judah and the kingdom of Israel, both kingdoms vanished. However, the kingdom of Christ will last forever. Christ is the one of David's descendants who will sit on his throne forever and ever. God's kingdom promise will be finally fulfilled in both spiritual and physical spheres when Christ comes back and ushers in the New Heavens and the New Earth. His eternal kingdom will endure beyond the end of the world, and stand in the New Heavens and the New Earth without end.

MARCH 1

HE WHO PROMISED IS FAITHFUL

Let us hold unswervingly to the hope we profess, for he who promised is faithful. (Hebrews. 10:23)

"Has his promise failed for all time?" (Ps. 77:6). Absolutely not! Every good promise of the Lord has come true (Josh. 23:15). The history has witnessed that not one of all the Lord's good promises to the house of Israel failed; and every one was fulfilled (Josh. 21:45, 23:14; 1 Kings 8:56).

Regarding God's promises to Abraham, Abraham considered the Lord faithful who had made His promise that He would give him a son by Sarah (Heb. 11:11), and He would make his offspring countless (Gen. 13:16). In fact, the history has testified that as the time drew near for God to fulfill his promise to Abraham, the number of his descendants greatly increased (Acts. 7:17).

In God's promise to David, the Lord promised David that his descendants should never fail to have a man on the throne of Israel (1 Kings 9:5), which David believed that would be fulfilled (Acts 3:13); that his kingdom is an everlasting kingdom, and his dominion endures through all generations (Ps. 145:13). And the Lord reaffirmed this covenant with people of Israel (Isa. 55:3). The Lord declared that He would fulfill the gracious promise He made to the house of Israel and to the house of Judah (Jer. 33:14); and He would fulfill His gracious promise to bring people of Israel back to the Promised Land (Jer. 29:10).

God never changes His mind, and always fulfills what He promises (Num. 23:19). He is faithful to all His promises (Ps. 145:13). No matter how many promises God has made, they are "Yes" in Christ (2 Cor. 1:20). As to His promises regarding end-days, the Lord is not slow in keeping His promise (2 Pet. 3:9), because He who promised is faithful (Heb. 10:23).

Reflection: According to the dictionary, faithfulness is being firm in adherence to promises or in observance of duty (Merriam-Webster Dictionary). Faithfulness is not what God does, but who He is. It is one of His exclusive moral attributes. The faithfulness of God is His trustworthiness, expressed in His commitment to keeping His covenants and promises to His chosen people. Although Israel has broken His covenants again and again, God has always faithfully kept His covenants. Our Lord is the God of covenants. He has initiated covenants with His people, and committed Himself in a covenantal relationship with them. Anything may change, but God never changes. In our real life, we may experience unfaithfulness even betrayal from the people who are closely related to us, but God will never let us down. "God is not human, that he should lie, not a human being, that he should change his mind. Does he speak and then not act? Does he promise and not fulfill?" (Num. 23:19). In fact, the history has witnessed that not one of all the Lord's good promises to the house of Israel failed; and every one was fulfilled. This is the reason why all the Bible prophecies have been fulfilled except few that are to be fulfilled at the end of time. God never changes His mind, and always fulfills what He promises. He is faithful to all His promises. Just as He faithfully kept His covenants with Abraham and David, God is and will always be faithful to His promises He has made to us through His Son Jesus Christ. As a matter of fact, His promises to us are true assurances, including the assurance of peace: "And the peace of God, which transcends all understanding, will guard your hearts and your minds in Christ Jesus." (Phil. 4:7); the assurance of providence: "And my God will meet all your needs according to the riches of his glory in Christ Jesus." (Phil. 4:19); the assurance of power: God "is able to do immeasurably more than all we ask or imagine, according to his power that is at work within us." (Eph. 3:20), and many other true assurances recorded in the Scriptures. He who promised is faithful, "for no matter how many promises God has made, they are 'Yes' in Christ." (2 Cor. 1:20).

MARCH 2

THE COVENANTS OF THE PROMISE

Remember that at that time you were separate from Christ, excluded from citizenship in Israel and foreigners to the covenants of the promise, without hope and without God in the world. (Ephesians 2:12)

All of God's covenants with us are covenants of the promise (Eph. 2:12). When the Lord found his heart faithful to Him, He made a covenant with Abraham to give to his descendants the Promised Land (Neh. 9:8). And the Lord chose Abraham, so that he would direct his children and his household after him to keep the way of the Lord by doing what was right and just, so that the Lord would bring about for Abraham what He had promised him (Gen. 18:19).

Through His covenant with Abraham, the Lord made promises of land, of descendants, and of blessings (Gen. 12:1-3). The Lord promised the Israelites prosperity after their turning to the Lord, which is especially a promise of the land. And this promise is dependent on the Israelites' obedience (Deut. 30:1-10). Continuing His covenant with Abraham, the Lord made a covenant with David with His promise to perpetuate his kingdom (2 Sam. 7:12-16). Finally, the Lord made the new covenant with the house of Israel and with the house of Judah, with promises of putting His law in their minds and writing it on their hearts and of being their God (Jer. 31:31-33). The Lord made this everlasting covenant with them, which was His faithful love promised to David (Isa. 55:3). In conclusion, all of God's covenants are covenants of the promise (Eph. 2:12).

Reflection: Why God's promises never fail? Because all of His promises to His chosen people come with covenants, and all of God's covenants with us are covenants of the promise. The purpose of God's covenants of promise is to bring blessings to His chosen people. God's covenants of promise are only dependent on the obedience of His chosen people. This is why if we are obedient, we will be blessed for sure. As soon as Abraham showed his obedience to God by being willing to sacrifice his only son, Isaac, the Lord renewed His covenant with Abraham (Gen. 22:15-18). Each and every covenant God made with people in the Old Testament encompasses God's promises. For instance, in the Adamic Covenant, God's promise to Adam is that the offspring of the woman will crush the head of serpent (Gen. 3:15), which prophesizes the virgin birth of Jesus and the coming of Messiah. In the Noahic Covenant, God's promise to Noah is to bless Noah and his sons so that they will be fruitful and increase in number and fill the earth (Gen. 9:1); manage over all creature (Gen. 9:2); and He promises that He will never destroy the earth and life on it with a flood, and He sets His rainbow in the cloud as the sign of the covenant (Gen. 9:13). In the Abrahamic Covenant, God's promise to Abraham is: "I will make you into a great nation, and I will bless you; I will make your name great, and you will be a blessing. I will bless those who bless you, and whoever curses you I will curse; and all peoples on earth will be blessed through you." (Gen. 12:1-3). In this covenant, God also promises to give Abraham and his descendants everlasting possession of Promised Land (Gen. 12:7, 17:8); give Abraham countless offspring (Gen. 15:5); and make him very fruitful; make nations of him, and kings will come from him (Gen. 17:6). In the Mosaic Covenant, God's promise is that Israel will be His treasured possession, a kingdom of priests and a holy nation (Exod. 19:5-6). In the Palestinian Covenant, God's promise is that He will bring His chosen people back to the Promised Land (Deut. 30:2-5a), make them more prosperous and numerous than their fathers (Deut. 30:5b), circumcise their hearts and the hearts of their descendants (Deut. 30:6), put all the curses on their enemies who hate and persecute them (Deut. 30:7), and they will again obey the Lord and follow His commands (Deut. 30:8), and they will be most prosperous (Deut. 30:9-10). In the Davidic Covenant, God's promise to David is that David will be ruler over His people Israel (2 Sam. 7:8), He will cut off all his enemies from before him, make his name great (2 Sam. 7:9), provide a place for His people Israel free from disturbance (2 Sam. 7:10), establish a house for him (2 Sam. 7:11), raise up his offspring to succeed him, and establish the throne of his kingdom forever (2 Sam. 7:12-13), His love will never be taken away from him (2 Sam. 7:15), and David's house and his kingdom will endure forever before Him; his throne will be established forever (2 Sam. 7:16). In the New Covenant, God's promise to the people of Israel and the people of Judah is that He will put His law in their minds and write it on their hearts; He will be their God, and they will be His people (Jer. 31:33), He will forgive their wickedness and will remember their sins no more (Jer. 31:34). As a matter of fact, all the promises encompassed in the covenants have been fulfilled in the physical dimension, and they will be fulfilled in the spiritual dimension in Christ, and only in Christ eventually.

March 3

Precepts and Promises

As for this temple you are building, if you follow my decrees, carry out my regulations and keep all my commands and obey them, I will fulfill through you the promise I gave to David your father. (1 Kings 6:12)

The covenants of God are covenants of the promise (Eph. 2:12). However, a covenant consists of two parts: precepts and promises. The intent of God's covenant is to bring about us blessings (Neh. 9:8). Nevertheless, in order for God to fulfill His promises, we must follow His precepts.

The Lord expects Abraham to lead his children and his household to keep the way of the Lord by doing what is right and just, so that the Lord may fulfill His promises to Abraham (Gen. 18:19). Moses affirms that the Lord will fulfill His promises to the house of Israel by establishing them as His holy people provided that they keep His commands (Deut. 26:18, 28:9). The Lord promises David to establish Solomon's kingdom forever if he is unswerving in carrying out His commands and laws (1 Chron. 28:7). The Lord reaffirms with Solomon that if he follows His precepts, He will fulfill His promises He gave to David his father (1 Kings 6:12, 9:4-5). Even David exhorts Solomon to observe God's precepts in order that the Lord may keep His promise to him (1 Kings 2:3-4).

Reflection: In contrast to a contract, which is an agreement creating and defining the obligations between two or more parties, in which terms and conditions define the rights and responsibilities of each party, a covenant is a one-way agreement whereby the covenanter, God is the only party bound by the promise. Nevertheless, a covenant, which is a formal agreement made by God with His people, may have conditions and prerequisites that qualify the undertaking, that are precepts the people of God need to observe. On God's part, promises are what He intends to fulfill in order to bring about blessings to His people. On people's part, precepts are what His people must observe in order to receive God's blessings. Promises and precepts are two indispensable components of God's covenants with His people. They go hand in hand. On one side, God is bound by His promises; on the other side, His people must observe His precepts. God's blessings come with His covenants. That is why when we obey, we will be blessed. When we observe His precepts, God will fulfill His promises. Without our observance of God's precepts, God will not fulfill His promises He made to us. If His people do not remain faithful to His covenant, He will turn away from them (Heb. 8:9). In fact, in all of the holy covenants in the Old Testament, the Adamic Covenant, the Noahic Covenant, the Abrahamic Covenant, the Mosaic Covenant, the Palestinian Covenant, the Davidic Covenant, and the New Covenant, there are both promises and precepts encompassed in each covenant. Whenever His people observe His precepts, God will fulfill His promises, and bring about to His people blessings.

MARCH 4

THE OFFER OF LIFE AND DEATH

This day I call heaven and earth as witness against you that I have set before you life and death, blessings and curses. Now choose life, so that you and your children may live. (Deuteronomy 30:19)

The intent of God's covenant with His people is to bring about blessings to His people (Neh. 9:8). However, whether or not keep the commands entailed by the covenant will result in either life and prosperity or death and destruction (Deut. 30:15). The Lord solemnly set before His people life and death, blessings and curses – blessings for obedience (Deut. 28:1-14), and curses for disobedience (Deut. 28:15-68).

With His people's obedience, the Lord will fulfill His promises of land, descendants, and blessings (Deut. 30:16). And blessings will come upon them and accompany them (Deut. 28:1-2, 9, 29:12-13). The Lord will bring them back to the Promised Land (Deut. 30:3-5), and bless them in that land (Deut. 28:8, 11, 30:20). And the Lord will make them prosperous and numerous than their fathers (Deut. 28:11, 30:5). Furthermore, the Lord will bestow to them abundant blessings (Deut. 28:3-14, 30:6-7, 9-10).

With His people's disobedience, curses will come upon them and overtake them (Deut. 28:15, 29:20-21, 27-28, 30:18). They will be afflicted with diseases (Deut. 28:21, 28, 34), displaced and dispersed (Deut. 28:64-65), and uprooted from the Promised Land

(Deut. 29:28, 30:18). Their descendants will be cursed (Deut. 28:18, 32, 41, 51-59, 62-63). And numerous curses will come upon them (Deut. 28:16-68).

The offer of life and death (Deut. 30:11-20) was set again before Solomon (1 Kings 9:4-5), and other descendants of Abraham. Unfortunately, the history witnessed that the Lord turned away from Israelites when they did not remain faithful to His covenant (Heb. 8:9). The offer of life and death (Deut. 30:11-20) is still set before us today. The same Lord who fulfills His good promises may bring on us all the evil He has threatened if we do not keep His commands (Josh. 23:15). Nevertheless, all the ways of the Lord are loving and faithful for those who keep the demands of His covenant (Ps. 25:10). And prosperity will come upon us after we turn to the Lord (Deut. 30:1-10).

Reflection: The offer of life or death is called Deuteronomy theology. As a matter of fact, the offer of life or death is found in God's covenants with His people. We are bound by God's precepts entailed by the covenant; whereas God is bound by His promises entailed by the covenant. When we obey His precepts, God will fulfill His promises that are promises of blessings; when we disobey His precepts, curse will be upon us and overtake us. This is the mechanics how offer of life and death works. In a word, obedience leads to life; and disobedience leads to death, this is the theme of the Deuteronomy theology. In fact, in Garden of Eden, Adam and Eve was given two options, choosing the Tree of Life would lead to life; or choosing the Tree of Knowledge of the Good and Evil would lead to death. In other words, the Deuteronomy theology was even working on Adam and Eve, in the first covenant God made with people. Unfortunately, as the federal head of mankind, Adam failed. His disobedience led to his death, the physical, spiritual and eternal death. In the Old Testament era, God gave the law to Israel, His chosen people through Moses, the mediator of the Old Covenant. Israel's obedience to the law was demanded. Her obedience to the law would lead to life and blessings, whereas her disobedience to the law would lead to death and curse. This is the Deuteronomy theology, especially expressed in Deuteronomy Chapters 28 to 30. In the New Testament era, God bestowed grace to people He favored through Christ, the mediator of the New Covenant. Our obedience to the Holy Spirit is demanded: "Whoever sows to please their flesh, from the flesh will reap destruction; whoever sows to please the Spirit, from the Spirit will reap eternal life." (Gal. 6:8). In conclusion, obedience leads to life; and disobedience leads to death, this theme of the Deuteronomy theology is actually valid throughout the entire Scriptures.

Pearls of Wisdom VOLUME 1

MARCH 5

A COVENANT SEALED WITH AN OATH

You are standing here in order to enter into a covenant with the Lord your God, a covenant the Lord is making with you this day and sealing with an oath. (Deuteronomy 29:12)

God made a covenant with His people, and sealed the covenant with an oath (Deut. 29:12). He gave His people His solemn oath and entered into a covenant with them (Ezek. 16:8). Moreover, He remembers His covenant forever - the covenant He made with Abraham, the oath He swore to Isaac. He confirms it to Jacob as a decree, to Israel as an everlasting covenant (1 Chron. 16:15-17; Ps. 105:8-10).

Unfortunately, His people were not faithful to His covenant (Ps. 78:37). They have despised His oath by breaking the covenant (Ezek. 16:59). As they did not remain faithful to His covenant, the Lord turned away from them (Heb. 8:9), and promised to bring down on their head His oath that they despised and His covenant that they broke (Ezek. 17:19).

However, because of Abraham's faithfulness, the Lord made covenant with him, which was the covenant of the promise (Eph. 2:12). The Lord is a merciful God; He will not abandon or destroy His people or forget the covenant with their forefathers, which He confirmed to them by oath (Deut. 4:31). Instead, He will make an everlasting covenant with His people, a better covenant of which Jesus has become the guarantee because of the oath with which He became a priest (Heb. 7:21-22).

Reflection: God deals with His people in terms of covenants. He does everything to His people with covenants; and he doesn't do anything with His people without covenants. Covenant is an "agreement enacted between two parties in which one or both make promises under oath to perform or refrain from certain actions." (The Anchor Yale Bible Dictionary). In the ancient Near East context, animals were often slaughtered as part of a covenant ceremony, with the purpose of affirming their pledges between two parties. Nevertheless, the biblical covenants are not made by equal parties. In the Scriptures, God imposed the covenants on His people. He made a covenant of pieces with Abraham, in which He revealed Himself to Abraham and made a covenant with him, in the manner of covenant ratification ceremony according to the ancient Near East ritual. In Genesis 15, when God made a covenant with Abraham encompassed with His promises to give him land, descendants and blessing, Go had various animals cut in half, and He passed between the pieces of the animals. He was virtually making a statement: "Let this done to me if I violate this covenant." By placing Himself face the consequences of violation of the covenant, God showed Abraham how faithful He was to His covenant. This is a covenant sealed with an oath. In God's covenant He made with His people, God is bound by His promises, because He sealed the covenant with an oath. Just because He sealed the covenant with an oath, God will never abandon or destroy His people or forget the covenant with their forefathers. Although bound by His precepts in the covenant, His people sometimes did not remain to His covenant. However, God will never change although His people may change. God has made covenants with Israel's forefathers, and sealed them with an oath. That is why in the Scriptures, God is always called the God of Abraham, the God of Isaac, and the God of Jacob. And Israel was reminded: "You are standing here in order to enter into a covenant with the Lord your God, a covenant the Lord is making with you this day and sealing with an oath." (Deut. 29:12)

MARCH 6

COVENANT OF LOVE

Give ear and come to me; listen, that you may live. I will make an everlasting covenant with you, my faithful love promised to David. (Isaiah 55:3)

The Lord's covenant with His people is indeed a covenant of love. The Lord declares, "I will make an everlasting covenant with you, my faithful love promised to David." (Isa. 55:3). The appositive here indicates that the everlasting covenant the Lord will make with His people is His faithful love promised to David. His everlasting covenant is not only a covenant of promise, but also a covenant of love. The Lord also declares, "I will maintain my love to him (David) forever, and my covenant with him will never fail." (Ps. 89:28), and "for their (the Israelites') sake he remembered his covenant and out of his great love he relented." (Ps. 106:45). These psalms reinforce that the Lord's covenant is the covenant of love.

The Lord keeps His covenant of love with those who love Him and obey His commands (Neh. 1:5; Dan. 9:4), and with His servants who continue wholeheartedly in His way (1 Kings 8:23; 2 Chron. 6:14). The Lord is the faithful God. He keeps His covenant of love to a thousand generations of those who love Him and keep His commands (Deut. 7:9), as He swore to the patriarchs (Deut. 7:12).

Reflection: The intent of God's covenant is to bring about blessings to his people, because His covenant is indeed the covenant of love. God's covenant is not only a covenant of promise, but also a covenant of love. His covenant is actually His faithful love. God is love, and God is the God of covenant. Therefore, God's covenant is the covenant of love. God has made covenants with His people out of love, with motive of love. He desires to be an intimate friend with His people. He craves to build a permanent relationship based on love with His people and draw them close to His heart. He loves His people so much that He even has sacrificed His only-begotten Son as a price paid for their sins. God's covenant comes at price that costs His beloved Son. As a covenant in the ancient Near East culture often involved blood sacrifice, the Lord Jesus has made His New Covenant with the Church with His own precious blood (Luke 22:20; 1 Cor. 11:25). This New Covenant is a covenant of grace, and a covenant of love. God's covenant of love is the covenant of sacrificial love. In fact, not only did the Father show us His sacrificial love by sacrificing His only begotten Son, but also the Son showed us His sacrificial love by making atonement for our sins on the cross. God's covenant of love is the covenant of the unconditional love: "God demonstrates his own love for us in this: While we were still sinners, Christ died for us." (Rom. 5:8). God's love is the "Agape" love, an unconditional love. God's covenant of love is the covenant of steadfast love: "The steadfast love of the Lord never ceases; his mercies never come to an end; they are new every morning; great is your faithfulness." (Lam. 3:22-23, ESV version). And God's covenant of love is the covenant of everlasting love: "I have loved you with an everlasting love; I have drawn you with unfailing kindness." (Jer. 31:3). In conclusion, God's covenant of love is the covenant of sacrificial love, of unconditional love, of steadfast love, and of everlasting love.

MARCH 7

CHRIST AND THE PROMISES OF GOD

For no matter how many promises God has made, they are "Yes" in Christ. And so through him the "Amen" is spoken by us to the glory of God. (2 Corinthians 1:20)

In the Scriptures, there are some promises of God that were made about Christ: the promise that Christ will defeat Satan (Gen. 3:15), the promise that the scepter will not depart from Judah (Gen. 49:10), the promise that a star will come out of Jacob (Num. 24:17), the promise that a prophet will be raised up, the promise that a virgin will give birth to a son (Isa. 7:14), and the promise that the son will be born in Bethlehem (Mic. 5:2-4), etc.

In the Scriptures, there are many other promises that were made to us (2 Pet. 1:4). However, these promises of God will be invalid without Christ, for the promises of God are given through Christ (Gal. 3:22), and we receive the promises of God through Christ (Gal. 3:14). In a word, the promises of God are in Christ (2 Tim. 1:1). Through the gospel, we are the sharers in the promise in Christ (Eph. 3:6). If we are separate from Christ, we will have no part with the covenant of the promise (Eph. 2:12). On the other hand, if we belong to Christ, we are Abraham's seed, and heirs according to the promise (Gal. 3:29). The promises of God will never fail in Christ (2 Cor. 1:20), for Christ Himself confirms the promises of God (Rom. 15:8).

Reflection: As a matter of fact, no promise of God will be valid without Christ. All the promises of God are given through Christ, and have been or will be fulfilled in Christ. The word promise appears more than 100 times in the Scriptures. Hundreds of promises are contained in the Scriptures. There are seven covenants recorded in the Scripture that were made between God and people. Among them, six covenants along with the attached promises have been fulfilled in Christ. In the Covenant with Adam, the promise has been fulfilled in Christ that a Son of Adam would crush the head of Satan. In the Covenant with Noah, the promise has been fulfilled in Christ that mankind would be preserved and protected. In the Covenant with Abraham, the promise of land has been fulfilled in Christ as Christ is our dwelling place. He is our promised land. The promise of seed has been fulfilled in Christ, as He is the ultimate Seed who would make every promise come true (Gal. 3:16). The promise of blessing has been fulfilled in Christ, as in Christ we have every spiritual blessing (Eph. 1:3). In the Covenant with Moses, the promise has been fulfilled in Christ that He is the sacrifice that has been made atonement for mankind, and the Law has been fulfilled in Him. In the Covenant with David, the promise has been fulfilled that the everlasting King would come from the line of David, and sit on the throne of David forever and ever. In the New Covenant, the promise has been fulfilled in Christ that all who call upon His name would be redeemed and made God's chosen people. In fact, the birth, life, ministry, death, and resurrection of Christ have fulfilled Messianic promises. And at the end day, all the promises of God will be fulfilled in Christ.

March 8

Everlasting Covenant

Whenever the rainbow appears in the clouds, I will see it and remember the everlasting covenant between God and all living creatures of every kind on the earth. (Genesis 9:16)

God's covenant is not only a covenant of Love, but an everlasting covenant. When God made his covenant with Noah, He sealed it with a rainbow, and promised no more devastating flood to destroy all life. He stated that it was a covenant for all generations to come (Gen. 9:9-17).

The Lord promised to establish His covenant as an everlasting covenant with Abraham and his descendants to be their God (Gen. 17:7). That was the covenant of circumcision, an everlasting covenant in their flesh (Gen. 7:13). The Lord also promised Abraham to establish an everlasting covenant with his son, Isaac for his descendants after him (Gen. 17:19). The Lord made an everlasting covenant of salt for Aaron and his sons and daughters to bestow them perpetual share from the holy offerings the Israelites presented to the Lord (Num. 18:19).

Although David recognized God's everlasting covenant (2 Sam. 23:5; 1 Chron. 16:17; Ps. 105:10), Israelites broke His everlasting covenant again and again (Isa. 24:5). However, God's everlasting covenant is His faithful love. His everlasting covenant is indeed the covenant of love (Isa. 55:3). The Lord solemnly declared to make an everlasting covenant with His people (Isa. 61:8; Jer. 32:40). The Lord promised to establish an everlasting covenant with the unfaithful Jerusalem (Ezek. 16:60), which was a covenant of peace (Ezek. 37:26).

Reflection: The phrase "everlasting covenant" appears 17 times in the Scriptures, including 16 times in the Old Testament, and 1 time in the New Testament. It refers to God's covenant of promises, the covenant God has made out of love and made in grace. When God made His covenant with Noah, the covenant was an everlasting covenant: "I will remember my covenant between me and you and all living creatures of every kind. Never again will the waters become a flood to destroy all life. Whenever the rainbow appears in the clouds, I will see it and remember the everlasting covenant between God and all living creatures of every kind on the earth." (Gen. 9 :15-16). God sealed this covenant with the sign of rainbow. When God made a covenant with Abraham encompassed with promises, the covenant was made an everlasting covenant: "I will establish my covenant as an everlasting covenant between me and you and your descendants after you for the generations to come, to be your God and the God of your descendants after you." (Gen. 17 :7, 13, 19). The seal of the covenant was the rite of circumcision (Gen. 17 :13). God made the covenant of Sabbath with Israel which was also to be an everlasting covenant: "The Israelites are to observe the Sabbath, celebrating it for the generations to come as a lasting covenant. It will be a sign between me and the Israelites forever, for in six days the Lord made the heavens and the earth, and on the seventh day he rested and was refreshed." (Exod. 31 :16-17). The seal of the covenant is Sabbath. God made an everlasting covenant of salt with his chosen people Israel: "Whatever is set aside from the holy offerings the Israelites present to the Lord I give to you and your sons and daughters as your perpetual share. It is an everlasting covenant of salt before the Lord for both you and your offspring." (Num. 18 :19). Salt symbolizes the long endurance of the covenant. God reaffirms His everlasting covenant with His people from generation to generation, from Noah to Moses, from Moses to David. Finally, God's everlasting covenant with His people will be fulfilled in Jesus Christ: "Now may the God of peace, who through the blood of the eternal covenant brought back from the dead our Lord Jesus, that great Shepherd of the sheep, equip you with everything good for doing his will, and may he work in us what is pleasing to him, through Jesus Christ, to whom be glory for ever and ever. Amen". (Heb. 13 :20-21). God's covenant is not only the covenant of promise, but also the covenant of love. God's covenant is not only the covenant of love, but also the everlasting covenant. He has sealed His covenant with an oath. He even promised to establish an everlasting covenant with the unfaithful Israel. He is so faithful that He will never abandon His covenant with His people. The rainbow is a living example of His faithfulness to His covenant with His people.

March 9

Sign of Covenant

I have set my rainbow in the clouds, and it will be the sign of the covenant between me and the earth. (Genesis. 9:13)

Many of the Old Testament covenants were attached with signs. We can numerate some signs of covenant in the Old Testament. For instance, when the Lord made His everlasting covenant with Noah and every living creature, He set His rainbow in the clouds, as the sign of the covenant between Himself and the earth. God said to Noah, "This is the sign of the covenant I have established between me and all life on the earth." (Gen. 9:12-13, 17).

When the Lord made His covenant of circumcision with Abraham and his descendants after him, the Lord declared circumcision as the sign of the covenant (Gen. 17:11).

And in the Old Testament, a pillar of stones was sometimes used as a sign of covenant between the two parties of the covenant (Gen. 28:18, 22, 31:45; Exod. 24:4). Right after his dream in which the Lord appeared to him at Bethel, Jacob set up a stone as a pillar and poured oil on top of it (Gen. 28:18) and made his commitment to tithing (Gen. 28:22). After Jacob returned to Bethel, and built an altar to God over there, the Lord appeared to him again. The Lord gave Jacob His promise to continue on him His covenant with Abraham and Isaac. Then Jacob set up a stone pillar on which he poured a drink offering and oil (Gen. 35:14).

Today, in the New Testament era, the Lord's Supper acts as the sign of the New Covenant (Jer. 31:31; Heb. 8:8), which is the confirmation of the New Testament. Lord Jesus made drinking of the cup representing the Blood of the Covenant a sign of our acceptance of the New Covenant (Matt. 26:27-28; Luke. 22:20; 1 Cor. 11:25).

Reflection: Sign of covenant! God is so faithful that He has attached signs to the covenants He has made with His people. In each and every covenant He made with His people, God used certain real object as a sign to help His people understand and observe the covenant, and wait upon Him to fulfill His promises. When there is a sign, it is easy to remember the covenant. Whenever we see a rainbow in the sky, does it come to our mind that this is the sign of the covenant God made with Noah and people on the earth? When we partake the Lord's Supper, does it come to our mind that we are bound by the New Covenant our Lord Jesus Christ made with His church? In fact, there is a sign of covenant in each of the covenant God made with His people in the Old Testament. For instance, in the Adamic Covenant, the Tree of the Knowledge of Good and Evil is the sign of covenant. In this covenant, Adam was required to take care of the Garden of Eden and refrain from eating from the Tree of the Knowledge of Good and Evil. As long as he obeyed the covenant requirements, he would live. But if he were to disobey the covenant requirements, he would die (Gen. 2:15-17). In the Noahic Covenant, rainbow is the sign of covenant. It serves as reminder of the everlasting covenant between God and all living creatures of every kind on the earth (Gen. 9:13, 15-16). Because, when the sunlight strikes raindrops in the air, they act like a prism and form a rainbow, rainbow symbolizes God's common grace which is represented by the sunlight, the air, and the raindrops. Thus, the covenant of rainbow is also called the covenant of grace. In the Abrahamic Covenant, circumcision is the sign of covenant. God's covenant in the flesh of the Israeli males is to be an everlasting covenant (Gen. 17:13). It also symbolizes our spiritual circumcision which is the seal of the Holy Spirit (Eph. 1:13-14). In the Mosaic Covenant, Sabbath is the sign of covenant. It serves as a perpetual sign between God and the people of Israel to remind them of their covenant relationship and God's creation of the heavens and the earth. In the Palestinian Covenant, the Promised Land is the sign of covenant. The Promised Land is actually part of God's promises to Abraham and his descendants. It symbolizes that we will inherit the earth (Matt. 5:5). In the Davidic Covenant, which is also called the covenant of kingdom, "throne" is the sign of covenant. David's house and his kingdom will endure forever before Him; his throne will be established forever (2 Sam. 7:16). It symbolizes that Christ, the King of kings, the Lord of lords, will sit on David's throne forever and ever. In the New Covenant, the law written on the hearts is the sign of covenant. The New Covenant is a better covenant than the old covenant, and

Christ is the mediator of this new covenant (Heb. 9:15). He made this new covenant with us with his precious blood (1 Cor. 11:25).

MARCH 10

TERMS OF THE COVENANT

The LORD said to me, "Proclaim all these words in the towns of Judah and in the streets of Jerusalem: 'Listen to the terms of this covenant and follow them.'" (Jeremiah 11:6)

These are the terms of the covenant the LORD commanded Moses to make with the Israelites in Moab, in addition to the covenant he had made with them at Horeb (Deut. 29:1). Carefully follow the terms of this covenant, so that you may prosper in everything you do (Deut. 29:9). This is the word that came to Jeremiah from the LORD: "Listen to the terms of this covenant and tell them to the people of Judah and to those who live in Jerusalem. Tell them that this is what the LORD, the God of Israel, says: 'Cursed is the one who does not obey the terms of this covenant - the terms I commanded your ancestors when I brought them out of Egypt, out of the iron-smelting furnace.' I said, 'Obey me and do everything I command you, and you will be my people, and I will be your God. Then I will fulfill the oath I swore to your ancestors, to give them a land flowing with milk and honey'—the land you possess today." The LORD said to me, "Proclaim all these words in the towns of Judah and in the streets of Jerusalem: 'Listen to the terms of this covenant and follow them'" (Jer. 11:1-6). Those who have violated my covenant and have not fulfilled the terms of the covenant they made before me, I will treat like the calf they cut in two and then walked between its pieces (Jer. 34:18).

Reflection: The covenant is an organizing principle in the Scriptures. In the Old Testament, the Hebrew word we translate as "covenant" is *berith*. In the New Testament, the Greek word *diathēkē*, which means "testament" in Greek culture, is used to convey the concept of "covenant." Nevertheless, in Greek culture, a *diathēkē*—a testament—could be changed at any time by the testator while the testator was still alive; whereas, in Biblical sense, *berith*—a covenant—which is made by the Lord on His own initiative with His chosen people, Israel, will never be broken by the Lord Himself. When Israel breaks the covenant, the Lord will punish her, but He Himself will never cancel the promises that are entailed in the covenant. In a covenant the Lord makes with His chosen people, Israel, terms of the covenant serve like terms and conditions in a contract, or an agreement. On Israel's side, they need to follow the commands, decrees, and laws that are entailed by the covenant. On the Lord's side, as long as Israel follow the terms of the covenant, He will fulfill His promises attached to the covenant. On the other hand, the Lord demands Israel's loyalty, her commitment to obey His law. His expectation is for Israel to be faithful to the terms of the covenant. For instance, the Mosaic covenant is a conditional covenant between the Lord and Israel. The Ten Commandments serve as the terms of the covenant which demands Israel's obedience. If Israel carefully follow the terms of this covenant, they will prosper in everything they do. If they do not obey the terms of this covenant, they will be cursed. And this is called "Deuteronomy theology". If they obey Him and do everything He commands them, they will be His people, and He will be their God. Then He will fulfill the oath He swore to their ancestors, to give them a land flowing with milk and honey (Palestinian Covenant). Those who have violated His covenant and have not fulfilled the terms of the covenant they made before Him, He will treat like the calf they cut in two and then walked between its pieces, as a common practice in those days, which was called, "cutting the covenant".

MARCH 11

LOOKING FOR HIS PROMISES

My eyes fail, looking for your promise: I say, "When will you comfort me?" (Psalm 119:82)

Standing before the altar of the Lord in front of the whole assembly of Israel, Solomon supplicated the Lord: "Now Lord, the God of Israel, keep for your servant David my father the promises you made to him when you said, 'you shall never fail to have a man to sit before me on the throne of Israel, if only your sons are careful in all they do to walk before me as you have done.' And now, God of Israel, let your word that you promised your servant David my father come true." (1 Kings 8:25-26; 2 Chron. 6:16-17). The Lord appeared to Solomon a second time and reaffirmed to him that He would establish his royal throne over Israel forever as He promised David his father (1 Kings 9:4-5). Solomon, as David did, looked for His promise (Ps. 119:82, 123).

Paul was aware that it was because of his hope in what God has promised the forefathers that he was on trial. And that was the promise the twelve tribes were hoping to see fulfilled as they earnestly served God day and night (Act. 26:6-7). Although the heroes of faith mentioned in Hebrews 11 were still living by faith when they died, and did not receive the things promised (Heb. 11: 13), the author of the Hebrews exhorts us to hold unswervingly to the hope we profess, for He who promised is faithful (Heb. 10:23). And in keeping with His promise we are looking forward to a new heaven and a new earth, the home of righteousness (2 Pet. 3:13).

Reflection: The secret of the life of faith is to look for God's promises. Look for His promises, and don't look at our problems. If you look at our problems, you won't find God, because God is not a God of problems. Instead, when you look for His promises, you will find God, because He is God of promises. There is one thing in common for the heroes of faith in the Bible: they all look for His promises, no matter Abraham, David, or other heroes of faith mentioned in Hebrew 11. The heroes of faith mentioned in Hebrew 11 were still living by faith when they died, and did not receive the things promised. They are heroes of faith because they looked for His promises. True faith is anchored on God's promises, and sustained by God's promises. It is looking upon Lord Jesus Christ, the God of promises with our spiritual eyes. As a matter of fact, our journey of faith is in essence the process during which we focus our spiritual eyes on the promises of God attentively, constantly, and unswervingly.

March 12

The Lord Remembers His Covenant

He remembers his covenant forever, the promise he made, for a thousand generations. (1 Chronicles 16:15; Psalms 105:8)

The Lord remembers His covenant. When the Lord made His covenant with Noah, His first covenant with His people, He promised to remember His covenant sealed with the rainbow, and He promised that never again would the waters become a flood to destroy all life, which was the everlasting covenant between God and all living creatures of every kind on the earth (Gen. 9:15-16).

And when the Lord heard the groaning of the Israelites, whom the Egyptians were enslaving, He remembered His covenant with Abraham, with Isaac and with Jacob (Exod. 2:24, 6:5). When the Lord affirmed His laws and His decrees to the Israelites, He promised that He would remember His covenant with Jacob and His covenant with Isaac and His covenant with Abraham (Lev. 26:42,45). And the Lord gave the Israelites the ability to produce wealth, and so confirmed His covenant, which He swore to their forefathers (Deut. 8:18). And for their sake, He remembered the covenant with their ancestors (Lev. 26:45; Ps. 106:45). The Israelites supplicated the Lord to remember His covenant with them (Jer. 14:21). And the Lord reaffirmed that He would remember His covenant, and promised that He would establish an everlasting covenant with them (Ezek. 16:60). The history testifies that the Lord remembers His covenant forever, the promise he made, for a thousand generations (1 Chron. 16:15; Ps. 105:8). He remembers His holy covenant (Luke 1:72). And he remembers His covenant forever (Ps. 111:5).

Reflection: True wisdom comes from knowing God. If you really know God, you will know that He will remember His covenant. True faith is anchored on God's promise. And true wisdom is to look for His promises, because He remembers His covenant. We know that all of God's covenants are covenants of promise. God remembers His covenant thus all the promises attached to His covenant will be fulfilled for sure. In other words, because the Lord remembers His covenant, it is wise for us to look for His promises. When God made covenant with Noah, He set a rainbow in the clouds as the sign of covenant. Whenever He sees it, He remembers His covenant. The history of Israel is the history of God's covenants with His chosen people. The Lord God made covenants with the patriarchs of Israel, and he remembered His covenants and kept His promises encompassed in the covenants, although Israel broke the covenants again and again. Today, God is faithful to His promises which are "Yes" in Jesus Christ. And, Jesus Christ is the same yesterday and today and forever. God will never break His covenant, and He will always keep His promises. He is so faithful that He will never fail us. When we partake the Lord's Supper, we are eating the bread and drinking the cup of the Lord in remembrance of Christ. And, we must bear in mind that Christ will remember the New Covenant He made with the church with His blood. Just as the Lord remembered His covenant He made with Israel, His firstborn son, Christ will remember His covenant He made with the church, His bride.

March 13

God's Unfailing Love

The Lord loves righteousness and justice, the earth is full of his unfailing love. (Psalm 33:5)

Though He brings grief, He will show compassion, so great is His unfailing love (Lam. 3:32). The Lord's unfailing love surrounds the man who trusts in him (Ps. 32:10).

The Psalmist pleads with the Lord to have mercy on him according to His unfailing love (Ps. 51:5), to save him in His unfailing love (Ps. 6:4, 31:16), to silence his enemies, and destroy all his foes in His unfailing love (Ps. 143:12), to be his comfort (Ps. 119:76), to redeem us because of His unfailing love (Ps. 44:26), to show us His unfailing love (Ps. 85:7), and to satisfy us with His unfailing love (Ps. 90:14). The psalmist trusts in God's unfailing love (Ps. 13:5, 21:7, 52:8). He says to the Lord, "Let the morning bring me word of your unfailing love, for I have put my trust in you" (Ps. 143:8). The psalmist trusts the Lord that He will lead the people He has redeemed in His unfailing love (Exod. 15:13).

We wish God's unfailing love come to us (Ps. 119:41), and rest upon us even as we put our hope in Him (Ps. 33:22). In fact, the eyes of the Lord are on those who fear him, on those whose hope is in His unfailing love (Ps. 33:18). Furthermore, the Lord delights in those who fear Him, who put their hope in His unfailing love (Ps. 147:11).

What a man desires is unfailing love (Prov. 19:22), and many a man claims to have unfailing love, but a faithful man who can find? (Prov. 20:6). And unfailing love is with the Lord (Ps. 130:7). We ought to sow ourselves righteousness, and reap the fruit of unfailing love (Hos. 10:12). How priceless is God's unfailing love (Ps. 36:7)! We should meditate on His unfailing love (Ps. 48:9), and give thanks to the Lord for His unfailing love (Ps. 107:8, 15, 21, 31). And God's unfailing love will not be shaken (Isa. 54:10), and will never vanish (Ps. 77:8).

Reflection: God has shown His unfailing love to Israel generation after generation. His unfailing love is bound with His covenants, because His covenants are covenants of love. God's unfailing love is more awesome than His justice. When we are a new Christian, we fear God's justice. When we grow up spiritually, we fear God's love, His unfailing love. This is similar to our relationship with our fathers on the earth. When we were a child, we feared our father because we were afraid that our father might punish us. When we grow up, we will fear our father's love other than his punishment, and not dare to hurt our father's heart. When we grow up spiritually, we fear God's love, His unfailing love, and not dare to hurt His heart, our Heavenly Father's heart. As a matter of fact, God's love is more awe-inspiring than His justice. When you realize this truth, you have grown spiritually. You have started to fear the Lord not because of His justice, but because of His love, His unfailing love. In fact, just as the cross is a sign of reconciliation, God's love and His justice have been reconciled on the cross. His love and His justice are no longer a pair of antitheses, but a pair of antinomies. Because of the cross, God's love and His justice don't contradict with each other anymore, because the cross has fulfilled both His love and His justice. God has applied justice in love, and showed love with justice on the cross, when Jesus Christ has fulfilled both His love and His justice by shedding blood on the cross.

MARCH 14

TRUTH AND LOVE

To the lady chosen by God and to her children, whom I love in the truth—and not I only, but also all who know the truth— because of the truth, which lives in us and will be with us forever: Grace, mercy and peace from God the Father and from Jesus Christ, the Father's Son, will be with us in truth and love. (2 John 1:1-3)

Truth and love always go hand in hand. In the Psalms, the psalmist says, "for your (the Lord's) love is ever before me, and I walk continually in your truth." (Ps. 26:3). The Psalmist entreats the Lord not to conceal His love and His truth (Ps. 40:10), and to protect him with His love and His truth (Ps. 40:11). And in his benediction to his readers, John wishes that grace, mercy and peace from the Father and the Son be with them in truth and love (2 John 1:1-3).

Paul exhorts us to speak the truth in love (Eph. 4:15). And this is one of principles of Christian living. However, we seem to neglect another principle of Christian living, which is to love in the truth (2 John 1:1; 3 John 1:1). John sets us a good example of practicing this principle (2 John 1:1; 3 John 1:1). If we have purified ourselves by obeying the truth, we will have sincere love for our brothers (1 Pet. 1:22). And love does not delight in evil but rejoices with the truth (1 Cor. 13:6).

Reflection: Truth and love are a pair of spiritual antinomies. However, they always go hand in hand. This pair of antinomies make our spiritual life complete. God is love (1 John 4:8); and Jesus Christ is the truth (John 14:6). Our Lord is the God of justice and love. He applies justice with love, and shows love in justice. Justice and love are symbolized in the cross, with the horizontal bar symbolizing justice, and the vertical bar love, where Jesus Christ died on to fulfill the requirements of God's justice and to demonstrate His love that is wide and long and high and deep (Eph. 3:18). Truth and love are in perfect harmony in God and His Son Jesus Christ. Both of them are indispensable in the attributes of God. As Bible says, we ought to speak the truth in love, and to love in the truth at the same time. Without truth, love is foolish sentiment. Without love, truth is icy indifference. David knows His truth and His love; Paul knows that truth and love cannot be separated; Peter knows that love is the natural result of obeying the truth; and John not only teaches about truth and love, but also exemplifies them. If we know God, we will not only know that He is truth, but also know that He is love. If we have experienced God, we will have not only experienced that He is truth, but also experienced that He is love. Therefore, if we want that grace, mercy and peace from God the Father and from Jesus Christ, the Father's Son, will be with us in truth and love (2 John 1:1-3), we ought to not only speak truth in love (Eph. 4:15), but also love in the truth (2 John 1:1; 3 John 1:1).

March 15

Paul and Christ (I)

As a result, it has become clear throughout the whole palace guard and to everyone else that I am in chains for Christ. (Philippians 1:13)

Paul claims himself a prisoner of Christ (Eph. 3:1, 4:1; Phile. 1:1, 9). He says he is in chain for Christ (Phil. 1:13), for the reason of proclaiming the mystery of Christ (Col. 4:3), and for the sake of Gentiles (Eph. 3:1). However, through Christ the law of the Spirit of life set Paul free from the law of sin and death (Rom. 8:2). Christ displays His unlimited patience in Paul, who claims to be the worst of sinners (1 Tim. 1:16).

As a servant of Christ (Gal. 1:10), Paul was called to be an apostle of Christ (1 Cor. 1:1). Christ considered him faithful, and appointed him to His service (1 Tim. 1:12). Christ did not send him to baptize, but to preach the gospel (1 Cor. 1:17). Paul preached Christ (2 Cor. 1:19). He has fully proclaimed the gospel of Christ (Rom. 15:19). And it has always been Paul's ambition to preach the gospel where Christ was not known (Rom. 15:20). Paul was given the grace to preach to the Gentiles the unsearchable riches of Christ (Eph. 3:8). When Paul went to Troas to preach the gospel of Christ, the Lord had opened a door for him (2 Cor. 2:12).

Paul was ever demanded proof that Christ was speaking through him (2 Cor. 13:3). Paul asserted that the truth of Christ was in him (2 Cor. 11:10). And he received it by revelation from Christ (Gal. 1:12).

Paul exhorts the Corinthian Christians to follow his example, as he follows the example of Christ (1 Cor. 11:1). And Christ has accomplished through him in leading the Gentiles to obey God by what he has said and done (Rom. 15:18). However, Paul never boasts except in the cross of our Lord Jesus Christ (Gal. 6:14).

Reflection: Paul is in chain for Christ, yet through whom the law of the Spirit of life sets him free from the law of sin and death. This is a spiritual paradox, paradox of freedom and bondage. If we seek the freedom out of Christ, we will be put under bondage of sin. If we are bound for Christ, we will be set free by the law of the Spirit. True freedom can only be found in Christ. When you try to seek freedom out of Christ, you will be snared by sin, because the sting of death is sin, and the power of sin is the law (1Cor. 15:56), the law of sin and death. Nevertheless, Jesus Christ has conquered death, and removed the law of sin and death. "Death has been swallowed up in victory." (1Cor. 15:54), and God gives us the victory through our Lord Jesus Christ (1Cor. 15:57). Paul knows this spiritual paradox very well. He claims himself a prisoner of Christ, who is in chain for Christ. He knows Christ is the truth (John 14:6), and the truth sets him free (John 8:32). He knows when he becomes a bondservant of His Master, Jesus Christ, he will have freedom in Christ, freedom not to sin, and freedom from being bound by the law of sin and death. Do we realize this spiritual paradox? When we use freedom to sin, we will actually end up in the bondage of sin. When we are bound by the life-giving law, we will in the end have true freedom in Christ.

March 16

Paul and Christ (II)

For to me, to live is Christ and to die is gain. (Philippians 1:21)

Paul considers whatever was to his profit loss for the sake of Christ. And he considers everything a loss compared to the surpassing greatness of knowing Christ, for whose sake he has lost all things. He considers them rubbish, that he may gain Christ and be found in Him, having a righteousness which is through faith in Christ (Phil. 3:7-9). To Paul, to live is Christ and to die is gain (Phil. 1:21). Paul pressed on to take hold of that for which Christ took hold of him (Phil. 3:12). Although he did not consider himself yet to have taken hold of it, he presses on toward the goal to win the prize for which God has called him heavenward in Christ (Phil. 3:13-14).

Paul also wants to know Christ and the power of His resurrection, and the fellowship of sharing in His sufferings, becoming like him in his death (Phil. 3:10). Christ said to Paul, "My grace is sufficient for you, for my power is made perfect in weakness." (2 Cor. 12:9). Indeed, Christ gave him strength (1 Tim. 1:12). And Paul would boast all the more gladly about his weaknesses, so that Christ's power might rest on him (2 Cor. 12:9).

Paul resolved to know nothing except Jesus Christ and Him crucified (1 Cor. 2:2). Paul says, "I have been crucified with Christ and I no longer live, but Christ lives in me. The life I live in the body, I live by faith in the Son of God, who loved me and gave himself for me." (Gal. 2:20). He hopes Christ will be exalted in his body, whether by life or by death (Phil. 1:20).

Reflection: From today's reading, we can see three of the spiritual paradoxes in the Scriptures. The first one is the paradox of loss and gain; the second one is the paradox of weakness and strength; and the last one is the paradox of life and death. Paul knows the paradox of loss and gain. He knows the divine wisdom and the secrets of the Kingdom of Heaven. He knows loss is gain, and gain is loss. Loss for the sake of Christ is actually gain; and gain is actually loss for the sake of Christ. He resolves to forsake all things in order to gain the abundance of Christ; and he presses on toward the goal to win the prize for which God has called him heavenward in Christ. Likewise, we Christians do not pursue the state of emptiness as Buddhists do; instead, we forsake everything which we deem meaningless, in order to gain the fullness of Christ, which is in essence the abundant life. We forsake everything in order to gain the abundance of Christ, who has the supremacy in everything. We press on toward the goal to win the prize for which God has called us heavenward in Christ. This is the paradox of loss and gain. Moreover, Paul knows the paradox of weakness and strength. He knows the power of Christ is made perfect in weakness (2 Cor. 12:9). Indeed, Christ gave him strength (1 Tim. 1:12). And Paul would boast all the more gladly about his weaknesses, so that Christ's power might rest on him (2 Cor. 12:9). Furthermore, Paul also knows the paradox of life and death. He knows that, to him, to live is Christ and to die is gain (Phil. 1:21). He knows that he has been crucified with Christ and he no longer lives, but Christ lives in him (Gal. 2:20). Do you know these spiritual paradoxes? If you do, you are blessed.

MARCH 17

PROPHECIES AND PROMISES

You have kept your promise to your servant David my father; with your mouth you have promised and with your hand you have fulfilled it—as it is today. Now, Lord, the God of Israel, keep for your servant David my father the promises you made to him when you said, "You shall never fail to have a successor to sit before me on the throne of Israel, if only your descendants are careful in all they do to walk before me according to my law, as you have done." (2 Chronicles 6:15-16)

In the Scriptures, there are numerous prophecies. All prophecies are from God (2 Pet. 1:21). When prophecies are spoken by men from God, they are carried along by the Holy Spirit who is God Himself (2 Pet. 1:21). In other words, prophecies are originated from God, and men are merely God's messengers to speak out prophecies (2 Pet. 1:21). In fact, all prophecies from God are virtually the promises of God.

Let's examine some examples of the Messianic prophecies. It is a prophecy that Christ will crush Satan's head (Gen. 3:15); in fact, this is also God's promise made for Christ and for His kingdom. It is a prophecy that a virgin will give birth to a Son (Isa. 7:14); in fact, this is also God's promise made for Christ and for His kingdom. It is a prophecy that a Ruler will be born in Bethlehem (Mic. 5:2-4); in fact, this is also God's promise made for Christ and for His kingdom.

On the other hand, God promised that Christ would crush Satan's head; and this was the first Messianic prophecy (Gen. 3:15). God promised that a virgin would give birth to a Son; and this was the prophecy of Virgin Birth (Isa. 7:14). God promised that a Ruler would be born in Bethlehem; and this was a prophecy of the Nativity (Mic. 5:2-4). God promises that Jesus Christ, Son of God, also the seed of David will sit on the throne of Isreal forever and ever; and this was a throne prophecy (2 Chron. 6:15-16; Luke 1:32-33).

Reflection: Although with the help from the evil spirits, fortune tellers or witches may be able to foresee the future, they are not able to control the future. They cannot make things happen or prevent anything from occurring. "He spoke, and it came to be; he commanded, and it stood firm." Only can He do! With His mouth God has promised and with His hand He has fulfilled it. As a matter of fact, all prophecies from God are virtually the promises of God. God makes promises, and He fulfills them (1 Kings 8:15, 24; 2 Chron. 6:4, 15). As He is not bound by space and time, He actually does not have to prophesy. Everything to Him is present; and everything comes to existence by His decree. He is omniscient (Ps. 117:5); He is omnipresent (Ps. 139:7-18); and He is omnipotent (Gen. 18:14; Job 42:2; Matt. 19:26; Mark 10:27; Luke 18:27). He promises, and He ordains all things to happen. And everything happens according to His promise and His decree (Ps. 33:9, 11; Isa. 46:9-11, 48:3). He has kept His promises; with His mouth He has promised and with His hand He has fulfilled it (1 Kings 8:24; 2 Chron. 6:15). In other words, with His own hand He has fulfilled what He promised with His own mouth (1 Kings 8:15; 2 Chron. 6:4).

March 18

Loss or Gain

But whatever were gains to me I now consider loss for the sake of Christ. What is more, I consider everything a loss because of the surpassing worth of knowing Christ Jesus my Lord, for whose sake I have lost all things. I consider them garbage, that I may gain Christ. (Philippians 3:7-8)

Paul knows what is loss or what is gain. He considers whatever was to his gain loss for the sake of Christ. Furthermore, he considers everything a loss compared to the surpassing greatness of knowing Christ. And for Christ's sake, he has lost all things (Phil. 3:7-8).

Jesus teaches that whoever finds their life will lose it, and whoever loses their life for His sake will find it (Matt. 10:39); whoever wants to save their life will lose it, but whoever loses their life for Him will save it (Matt. 16:25; Mark. 8:35; Luke. 9:24); whoever tries to keep their life will lose it, and whoever loses their life will preserve it (Luke 17:33); and whoever loves their life will lose it, while whoever hates their life in this world will keep it for eternal life (John. 12:25).

Jesus also teaches that whoever has left houses or brothers or sisters or father or mother or children or fields for His sake will receive a hundred times as much and will inherit eternal life (Matt. 19:29; Make. 10:29-30; Luke 18:29-30).

Moreover, Jesus points out that if you sell your possessions and give to the poor, you will have treasure in leaven (Matt. 19:21; Mark. 10:21; Luke. 12:33, 18:22).

Reflection: From today's reading, we can see three of the spiritual paradoxes in the Scriptures; the paradox of loss and gain, the paradox of life and death, and the paradox of giving and receiving. After we were born again, what was our gain we will consider loss for the sake of Christ. If we hold on to life, we will lose it. If we are willing to give away our physical possessions, we will receive abundant spiritual blessings. These spiritual paradoxes are the secrets of the Kingdom of Heaven, as well as the spiritual principles of Christian living. Paul does know these secrets of the Kingdom of Heaven. And Jesus reveals these secrets of the Kingdom of Heaven in His teachings. What are the secrets of the Kingdom of Heaven that are revealed to children according to Jesus (Matt. 11:25)? Spiritual paradoxes are some of them, including the paradox of loss and gain, paradox of life and death, and paradox of giving and receiving. If you know these spiritual paradoxes, you will know some of the secrets of the Kingdom of Heaven. If you don't know these spiritual paradoxes, you are actually far from the Kingdom of Heaven; in fact, you don't have true knowledge of God and His Son Jesus Christ.

MARCH 19

THE TRINITY (I)

As soon as Jesus was baptized, he went up out of the water. At that moment heaven was opened, and he saw the Spirit of God descending like a dove and alighting on him. And a voice from heaven said, "This is my Son, whom I love; with him I am well pleased." (Matthew 3:16-17)

When we think about the trinity, a scene always comes to our mind, in which all the three Persons of the triune God are present: when Jesus was baptized, the Holy Spirit was descending like a dove and alighting on Him. And God the Father testified Christ with a voice from heaven, saying, "This is my Son, whom I love; with him I am well pleased."

(Matt. 3:16-17; Mark 1:10-11; Luke 3:22). Both the Father and the Spirit are the witnesses of the Son; and according to the law, the testimony of two men is valid (John 8:17).

Likewise, the three Persons of the triune God are all involved in the baptism of a disciple, as Christ commands: "Therefore go and make disciples of all nations, baptizing them in the name of the Father and of the Son and of the Holy Spirit." (Matt. 28:19).

However, we always neglect the fact that all the three Persons of the triune God were present at the birth of Christ. The angel reaffirmed to Mary regarding the birth of Christ, saying, "The Holy Spirit will come on you, and the power of the Most High will overshadow you. So the holy one to be born will be called the Son of God." (Luke 1:35).

Another scene which we tend to overlook is the one in which all the three Persons of the triune God were present was happening when Stephen was martyred: "But Stephen, full of the Holy Spirit, looked up to the heaven and saw the glory of God, and Jesus standing at the right hand of God." (Acts. 7:55).

Reflection: A few scenes can be numerated when all of the three Persons of the triune God appear. The scene of Jesus' baptism is well-known. The baptism of the believers is sometimes mentioned as a proof of trinity. However, another scene is always overlooked: when Stephen was martyred, all of the three Persons of the triune God were present. Being full of the Holy Spirit, Stephen saw "the glory of God, and the Son of Man standing at the right hand of God." (Acts 7:55). In Acts 7:2, Stephen mentioned that the glory of God appeared to Abraham, and in this verse, Stephen himself saw the glory of God with his own eyes. Seeing the glory of God was a powerful encouragement to the one who was suffering for the sake of the kingdom. And this is also a powerful encouragement to all of us. And he saw "heaven open and the Son of Man standing at the right hand of God." (Acts 7:56). The fact that heaven opened for him testifies what Jesus promised in the Beatitude: "Blessed are those who are persecuted because of righteousness, for theirs is the kingdom of heaven." (Matt. 5:10). As a matter of fact, the Lord in ascension is usually referred as sitting at the right hand of God (Matt. 26:64; Heb. 1:3, 13). This is the only time in the Scriptures that Jesus was standing at the right hand of God, rather than sitting at the right hand of God. In my opinion, Jesus was standing because He was greeting to Stephen, and doing honor to the first martyr of Christianity when Stephen was entering the heaven. What an incredible reward Stephen received from our Lord Jesus Christ!

March 20

The Trinity (II)

"When the Advocate comes, whom I will send to you from the Father—the Spirit of truth who goes out from the Father—he will testify about me." (John 15:26)

The relationship and the interaction among the three Persons of the triune God are depicted in the Scriptures.

First of all, God put His Spirit in Christ (Isa. 42:1). God anointed Jesus of Nazareth with the Holy Spirit and power (Acts 10:38), and anointed and sent Him to proclaim the good news (Isa. 61:1). Christ received from the Father the promised Holy Spirit and poured out what His disciples saw and heard (Acts. 2:33). In addition, Christ promised to send to His disciples the Advocate, the Holy Spirit who goes out from the Father. And the Holy Spirit will testify Christ (John 15:26). Moreover, the Father sent the Holy Spirit, another Advocate in Christ's name to teach Christ's disciples all things and remind them of everything Christ has said to them (John 14:26); and the Holy Spirit will receive from Christ what He will make known to His disciples who also belong to the Father (John 16:15).

Finally, the Holy Spirit, who is from God acknowledges that Jesus Christ has come in the flesh (1 John 4:2). Paul keeps asking that the God of our Lord Jesus Christ, the glorious Father, may give Ephesian Christians the Spirit of wisdom and revelation, so that they may know Christ better (Eph. 1:17).

Reflection: There is not such a word, "Trinity" in the Scriptures. Does this mean that the doctrine of Trinity is wrong? Absolutely not. Christian faith is a revelation-based faith. Our knowledge of God comes from the revelation of God, who has freely revealed Himself. Although not explicit in the Scriptures, Trinity is a theological concept induced from God's self-revelation. Hebrew culture did not emphasize on analytical thinking as the Greek culture did. In fact, we cannot find a single theological concept that is defined in the Scriptures. Influenced by the reason-emphasized Greek philosophy, the early Christians and fathers of the Church formulated the doctrine of Trinity based on the biblical revelation with the methods of reasoning, when they attempted to understand the relationships among the three Persons of the Triune God. As a matter of fact, the relationship among the three Persons of the Godhead is the most important of all relationships. We always look at the relationships of our own: our relationships with nature, with men, with ourselves and with God. However, our own relationships are secondary in the universe. The relationship among the three Persons of the Godhead is the primary relationship in the universe. This relationship is pre-existent, and everything else is contingent. The Scriptures have fully revealed the relationship among the three Persons of the Godhead. The three Persons of the Godhead are one God, the same in substance, equal in power and glory. In other words, they have the same essential properties of God. Nevertheless, the three Persons of the Godhead are distinguished from each other in their personal properties. The Father begets the Son from all eternity; the Son is eternally begotten of the Father; and the Holy Spirit proceeds eternally from the Father and the Son.

March 21

The Trinity (III)

May the grace of the Lord Jesus Christ, and the love of God, and the fellowship of the Holy Spirit be with you all. (2 Corinthians 13:14)

We can see more of the relationships and the interactions among the three Persons of the triune God that are depicted in the Scriptures. God sent the Spirit of His Son into our hearts, and the Spirit calls out, "Abba, Father." (Gal. 4:6). Through the eternal Spirit, Christ offered Himself unblemished to God (Heb. 9:14). And through Christ we have access to the Father by the Holy Spirit (Eph. 2:18). God, who has raised Jesus from the dead, will give life to our mortal bodies through His Spirit who lives in us (Rom. 8:11).

Because of the grace God gave him, being a minister of Christ Jesus to the Gentiles, Paul was given the priestly duty of proclaiming the gospel of God, so that the Gentiles might become an offering acceptable to God, sanctified by the Holy Spirit (Rom. 15:15-16). And we, who boast in Christ, serve God by his Spirit (Phil. 3:3). In fact, all the believers have been chosen according to the foreknowledge of God the Father, through the sanctifying work of the Spirit, to be obedient to Jesus Christ and sprinkled with His blood (1 Pet. 1:2). Thus, the grace of the Lord Jesus Christ, and the love of God, and the fellowship of the Holy Spirit are with us all (2 Cor. 13:14).

Reflection: The three Persons of the Godhead are all actively involved in everything: creation, election, justification, and sanctification, etc. Without any one of the three Persons of the Godhead, nothing would happen. While recognizing the distinct roles that each Person has, we should never think of their roles as so separate that the other Persons are not involved. Rather, everything that one Person is involved in, the other two are also involved in, one way or another. Without cooperation and collaboration of the three Persons nothing would be accomplished. Although having distinct role, each Person of the Godhead is actively involved in creation, election, justification, and sanctification. In creation, the Creator God the Father ordained the creation by His command (Gen. 1, 2). Creation was made through the Son (Col. 1:15-17). And the Holy Spirit was actively involved in the process (Gen. 1:2). Election has been done according to the foreknowledge of God the Father, through the sanctifying work of the Spirit, and has been accomplished by the Son with His blood (1 Pet. 1:2). In justification, God the Father saved us through the washing of rebirth and renewal by the Holy Spirit, whom he poured out on us generously through Jesus Christ our Savior, so that, having been justified by his grace, we might become heirs having the hope of eternal life. (Titus 3:5-7). Sanctification has been ordained by God the Father, accomplished by the Son, and applied by the Holy Spirit (1 Pet. 1:2).

March 22

The Spirit of God (I)

For prophecy never had its origin in the human will, but prophets, though human, spoke from God as they were carried along by the Holy Spirit. (2 Peter 1:21)

The Spirit of God was involved in the Creation (Gen, 1:2). And He makes a person, and gives a person life (Job 33:4). In the Old Testament, the Spirit of God occasionally comes on a person (Num. 24:2; 2 Chron. 15:1; 2 Chron. 20:14; 2 Chron. 24:20; Judges 3:10, 6:34, 11:29). And He comes on a person in power (1 Samuel 11:6; Judges 14:6, 19, 15:14, 16:13). He tells a person what to say (Ezek. 11:5), or speaks through a person (2 Sam. 23:2), or empower a person to prophesy (1 Sam. 10:6, 10, 19:20, 23), for prophecy never had its origin in the human will, but prophets, though human, spoke from God as they were carried along by the Holy Spirit (2 Pet. 1:21).

The Spirit of God sometimes stirs a person (Judges 13:25). And sometimes He is in motion (Matt. 3:16; Ezek. 11:24; 1 Kings 18:12; 2 Kings 2:16; Ezek. 37:1; Acts. 8:39). He may rest on someone (Isa. 11:2). And we may be given rest by the Spirit of the Lord (Isa. 63:14). He may fill a person (Exod. 31:3, 35:31; Micah 3:8), or live in a person (Rom. 8:9). The Spirit of the Lord anointed Christ to proclaim the good news (Luke 4:18), and empower Him to drive out demons (Matt. 12:28). Through the Spirit of God, Paul led the Gentiles to obey God (Rom. 15:18-19).

Reflection: The Spirit of God was involved in the "old creation" that is recorded in the Book of Genesis. However, the "new creation" was completed in the Spirit. "New creation" means being born of the water and the Spirit (John 3:5); just as the "old creation" was done through Christ, whereas the "new creation" was done in Christ. Put it this way, the "old creation" was done by God, while the "new creation" was not only done by God, but also done in God. This is one of the differences between "the two creations". "If anyone is in Christ, the new creation has come: The old has gone, the new is here!" (2 Cor. 5:17). Regeneration is actually a new creation. Regeneration is a new birth, being born again of the Spirit, and in Christ. Whenever we are born again, the old creation has gone, the new creation is here. Whenever we receive Christ, we receive the Spirit of God. When we receive the Spirit of God, the Spirit of God will live in us. In the Old Testament, the Spirit of God occasionally comes on a person. And He comes on a person in power. He tells a person what to say, or speaks through a person, or empower a person to prophesy. The Spirit of God sometimes stirs a person. He may rest on someone. He may fill a person. However, the Spirit of God did not live in someone as He does in the Christians of the New Testament era. The Spirit of God we have received doesn't make us slave, but the children of God. Regeneration is an act of God which makes us not only a new creation in Christ, but God's children by adoption (Rom. 8:14-16).

MARCH 23

THE SPIRIT OF GOD (II)

Who can fathom the Spirit of the Lord, or instruct the Lord as his counselor? (Isaiah 40:13)

Who can fathom the Spirit of the Lord, or instruct the Lord as His counsellor (Isa. 40:13)? In fact, no one knows the thoughts of God except the Spirit of the Lord (1 Cor. 2:11). The person without the Spirit does not accept the things that comes from the Spirit of God but considers them foolishness, and cannot understand them because they are discerned only through the Spirit (1 Cor. 2:14). And, if you are filled with the Spirit of God, you are filled with wisdom, with understanding, with knowledge, with all kinds of skills (Exod. 31:3, 35:31), with power, and with justice and might (Mic. 3:8). Jews have ever rebelled against the Spirit of God (Ps. 106:33). But we cannot conspire to test the Spirit of the Lord (Acts 5:9).

The Spirit of God acknowledges that Jesus Christ has come in the flesh (1 John 4:2). And no one can say, "Jesus is Lord," except by the Spirit of the Lord (1 Cor. 12:3). Anyone who does not have the Spirit of Christ does not belong to Christ (Rom. 8:9). And those who are led by the Spirit of God are the children of God (Rom. 8:14). If the Spirit of God lives in you, you are not controlled by the sinful nature but are in the Spirit (Rom. 8:9). Where the Spirit of the Lord is, there is freedom (2 Cor. 3:17).

Reflection: Where the Spirit of the Lord is, there is true freedom. True freedom is to yield our freedom to the authority of God, and let the Spirit of God has total control of us: "If the Spirit of God lives in you, you are not controlled by the sinful nature but are in the Spirit" (Rom. 8:9). True freedom is freedom not to sin. True freedom is to submit to God. This is the paradox of authority and freedom. The Spirit of God is the Spirit of truth: "When he, the Spirit of truth, comes, he will guide you into all the truth." (John 16:13). And "the truth will set you free", free from bondage of sin. The Spirit of God is life-giving Spirit, because through Christ Jesus the law of the Spirit who gives life has set us free from the law of sin and death (Rom. 8:2). Who can fathom the Spirit of the Lord, or instruct the Lord as his counselor? As a matter of fact, as the heavens are higher than the earth, so are His ways higher than our ways and His thoughts than our thoughts (Isa. 55:9). Spiritual paradoxes are not only the secret of the kingdom, but the wisdom of God. Human wisdom cannot understand the spiritual paradoxes, and deem them foolishness. But God chose the foolish things of the world to shame the wise (1 Cor. 1:27), for the foolishness of God is wiser than human wisdom (1 Cor. 1:25). This is the wisdom of God. If we understand the wisdom of God, we will be willing to submit to God, and let ourselves be controlled by the Spirit of God. And we will have true freedom, true freedom in Christ, and true freedom not to sin. Moreover, if we are filled with the Spirit of God, we are filled with wisdom, with understanding, with knowledge, with all kinds of skills, with power, and with justice and might. No wonder the Apostle Paul exclaims, "Oh, the depth of the riches of the wisdom and knowledge of God! How unsearchable his judgments, and his paths beyond tracing out!" (Rom. 11:33).

March 24

The Son and the Spirit (I)

Regarding his Son, who as to his earthly life was a descendant of David, and who through the Spirit of holiness was appointed the Son of God in power by his resurrection from the dead: Jesus Christ our Lord. (Romans 1:3-4)

The Spirit was not only involved in the birth of the Son (Matt. 1:18; Luke 1:35), but also involved in the baptism of the Son (Matt. 3:16; Mark 1:10; Luke 3:22). When the Spirit had not yet come on some believers, they had simply been baptized into the name of the Son (Acts 8:16).

The Son has received from the Father the promised Holy Spirit (Acts 2:33). Jesus Christ was appointed through the Spirit of holiness the Son of God (Rom. 1:3-4); God anointed His Son with the Spirit and power (Acts 10:38); and the Spirit anointed the Son and sent the Son to preach the good news (Luke 4:18). The Son was led by the Spirit into the wilderness to be tempted by the devil (Matt. 4:1; Luke 4:1). The Son was full of the Spirit (Luke 4:1), full of joy through the Spirit (Luke 10:21), and in the power of the Spirit (Luke 4:14). And by the Spirit, the Son drove out demons (Matt. 12:28). Through the Spirit of holiness, Christ was appointed the Son of God (Rom. 1:4).

The Son promised the Holy Spirit by asking the Father to send another advocate (John 14:15). When the Son was not glorified, the Spirit was not given (John 7:39). Whoever repents and is baptized in the name of the Son will receive the gift of the Holy Spirit (Acts 2:38), who raised the Son from the dead (Rom. 8:11). The Son redeemed us, and by faith we received the promise of the Spirit (Gal. 3:14). Then we were included in the Son, and marked with a seal, the promised Holy Spirit (Eph. 1:13).

Reflection: Jesus Christ was appointed through the Spirit of holiness the Son of God (Rom. 1:3-4); And when we were born again in Christ, we were marked with a seal, the promised Holy Spirit. This seal indicates that we are children of God. This seal also signifies God's ownership of us. As the Son has received from the Father the promised Holy Spirit, we Christians have also received from God the promised Holy Spirit. However, when the Son was not glorified, the Spirit was not given. Jesus Christ went to the cross, and entered to the glory, and was glorified. Then we were be able to receive the promised Holy Spirit, who is the Advocate, sent by the Father. The Holy Spirit is our Advocate, our Comforter, and our Helper. The author of the Hebrews encourages us, "Let us then approach God's throne of grace with confidence, so that we may receive mercy and find grace to help us in our time of need." (Heb. 4:16). Because Jesus died on the cross, "we have confidence to enter the Most Holy Place by the blood of Jesus, by a new and living way opened for us through the curtain, that is, his body." (Heb. 10:19-20). Because Jesus died on the cross, we are able to approach God's throne of grace. Because Jesus died on the cross, we are able to receive from God the promised Holy Spirit, and the Holy Spirit will help us in our time of need. What a grace! This grace was what God's chosen people in the Old Testament era not even dreamt of. The seal of the Holy Spirit signifies God's ownership of us, and we are a letter from Christ, written not with ink but with the Spirit of the living God, not on tablets of stone but on tablets of human hearts (2 Cor. 3:3). And with the seal of the Holy Spirit, we are able to approach God's throne of grace, and call Him Abba, Father (Rom. 8:15), because the Spirit himself testifies with our spirit that we are God's children (Rom. 8:16).

March 25

The Son and the Spirit (II)

But Stephen, full of the Holy Spirit, looked up to heaven and saw the glory of God, and Jesus standing at the right hand of God. (Acts 7:55)

When Stephen was full of the Holy Spirit, he saw the glory of God, and the Son standing at the right hand of the Father (Acts 7:55). Meanwhile, after encountering with the Son, Paul was filled with the Holy Spirit (Acts 9:17). Thus, we can say, whenever you encounter the Son, you will be filled with the Spirit; and whenever you are full of the Spirit, you will see the Son.

The Spirit testifies the Son (John 15:26; 1 Cor. 12:3; 1 John 4:2, 5:6), for the testimony of Jesus is the Spirit of prophecy (Rev. 19:10). The Spirit also revealed the Son (1 Pet. 1:11) And with the Spirit of wisdom and revelation, we may be able to know the Son better (Eph. 1:17). Furthermore, the Spirit will teach us all things and remind us of the words of the Son (John 14:26). The truth of the Son may be confirmed through the Spirit (Rom. 9:1). And the letter from the Son is written with the Spirit (2 Cor. 3:3).

The Son was put to death in the body but made alive in the Spirit (1 Pet. 3:18). Likewise, the Spirit gives us life if the Son is in us (Rom. 8:10). And through the Son, the law of the Spirit who gives us life has set us free from the law of sin and death (Rom. 8:2). Whoever does not belong to the Spirit does not belong to the Son (Rom. 8:9). Whoever is sanctified and justified in the name of the Son is sanctified and justified by the Spirit (1 Cor. 6:11), through whom even the Son Himself offered Himself unblemished to God (Heb. 9:14).

Reflection: Whenever we encounter the Son, we will be filled with the Spirit; and whenever we are filled with the Spirit, we will see the Son. When Stephen was full of the Holy Spirit, he saw the Son (Acts 7:55), because the Spirit testified and revealed the Son. Meanwhile, after encountering with the Son, Paul was filled with the Holy Spirit (Acts 9:17), also because the Spirit testified and revealed the Son. These two incidents prove that the Spirit testifies the Son, and reveals the Son. Moreover, the Spirit will teach us all things and remind us of the words of the Son, as well as confirm the truth of the Son. In a word, the Spirit plays a key role in the revelation of the Son. Furthermore, the Spirit and the Son work together in justification and sanctification, because whoever is sanctified and justified in the name of the Son is sanctified and justified by the Spirit (1 Cor. 6:11), through whom even the Son Himself offered Himself unblemished to God

(Heb. 9:14). In fact, salvation won't be accomplished without the cooperation and collaboration of the three Persons of the Godhead. If we don't have the indwelling of the Holy Spirt in our heart, we won't be able to understand the Word of God, and won't be able to submit ourselves to Christ. Whereas, if we are filled with the Holy Spirt, we will be able to understand the Word of God, and will be able to accept Christ as our Lord and Savior. Do you want to be filled with the Holy Spirt, so that you may be able to understand the Word of God, so that you may be able to encounter the Resurrected Lord Jesus Christ? If you are filled with the Holy Spirit, you will know the secrets of the kingdom, you will understand the manifold wisdom of God, you will know the power of Christ's resurrection, and your life will be transformed for sure.

March 26

Children of God

See what great love the Father has lavished on us, that we should be called children of God! (1 John 3:1)

The creation waits in eager expectation for the children of God to be revealed (Rom. 8:19). The creation itself will be liberated from its bondage to decay and brought into the freedom and glory of the children of God (Rom. 8:21).

See what great love the Father has lavished on us, that we should be called children of God! And that is what we are! The reason the world does not know us is that it did not know him (1 John 3:1). So in Christ Jesus you are all children of God through faith (Gal. 3:26). To all who did receive him, to those who believed in his name, he gave the right to become children of God (John 1:12). Those who are led by the Spirit of God are the children of God (Rom. 8:14). Dear friends, now we are children of God, and what we will be has not yet been made known. But we know that when Christ appears, we shall be like him, for we shall see him as he is (1 John 3:2). No one who is born of God will continue to sin, because God's seed remains in them; they cannot go on sinning, because they have been born of God. This is how we know who the children of God are and who the children of the devil are: Anyone who does not do what is right is not God's child, nor is anyone who does not love their brother and sister (1 John 3:9-10). This is how we know that we love the children of God: by loving God and carrying out his commands (1 John 5:2). We know that we are children of God, and that the whole world is under the control of the evil one (1 John 5:19). Blessed are the peacemakers, for they will be called children of God (Matt. 5:9), so that you may become blameless and pure, children of God without fault in a warped and crooked generation. Then you will shine among them like stars in the sky (Phil. 2:15).

Reflection: As Christians, we have many different identities. Among them, "the children of God" is our most important and precious identity. Abraham is the father of faith, our spiritual father. In Christ, we are all children of God through faith. The lineage of God's family is defined by faith, not by blood. We were born again in Jesus Christ through faith. Therefore, we are children of God through faith. And we are children of God in Jesus Christ, God's only begotten Son. Therefore, we are children of God in Jesus Christ through faith. Because of God's only begotten Son, Jesus Christ, we have been adopted by God as His children. All the human-beings were made in the image and likeness of God, but not all of them are children of God. Only do those who receive the Son, and believe in His name become children of God. Only are those who are led by the Spirit of God children of God. In other words, when we are born again in Christ and by the Spirit of God, we are imparted with eternal life, the life of the Son of God. Christ is the first-born, and God's only begotten Son; whereas we become the children of God by adoption. As children of God, we will not continue to sin, because we are born of God. If we continue to sin, we will not be children of God. We know that we are children of God, and we know that we love children of God.

MARCH 27

CRUCIFIXION

For I resolved to know nothing while I was with you except Jesus Christ and him crucified. (1 Corinthians 2:2)

Crucifixion has multi-fold meaning in the Scriptures:

First and foremost, crucifixion means that Christ was crucified on the Cross. Christ crucified is a stumbling block to Jews who demand miraculous signs and foolishness to Gentiles who look for wisdom (1 Cor. 1:22-23). Actually, God was pleased through the foolishness of the massage of the cross to save those who believe (1 Cor. 1:21); whereas the message of cross is foolishness to those who are perishing (1 Cor. 1:18).

On the other hand, Christ crucified is God's power and God's wisdom. And this is God's secret wisdom which the rulers of this age did not understand; otherwise, they would not have crucified the Lord of glory (1 Cor. 2:7-8). Christ was crucified in weakness, but He lives by God's power (2 Cor. 13:4).

Besides, crucifixion means the believers' salvation. Paul resolved to know nothing except Jesus Christ and Him crucified (1 Cor. 2:2). Paul also claimed that he had been crucified with Christ and he no longer lived, but Christ lived in him (Gal. 2:20). And he had been crucified to the world (Gal. 6:14).

Last but not least, crucifixion means the removal of our sinful nature. We, who belong to Christ have crucified the sinful nature with its passions and desires (Gal. 5:24). Our old self was crucified with Christ on the cross, and we are no longer slaves to sin (Rom. 6:6). Like Paul, we boast in the cross of Christ through which the world has been crucified to us, and us to the world (Gal. 6:14).

Reflection: Christ crucified is God's power and wisdom. And it is God's secret wisdom, which the ruler of this age did not understand. However, Paul knew this secret wisdom of God. He knew that "fear of the Lord is the beginning of wisdom, and knowledge of the Holy One is understanding". He was so wise that he resolved to know nothing except Jesus Christ and Him crucified. In fact, the Holy One is Jesus Christ and Him crucified, who is God's power and wisdom, and God's secret wisdom. Christ crucified is God's wisdom, because on the cross, many paradoxes exist: the paradox of foolishness and wisdom (1 Cor. 1:18-25, 27), the paradox of weakness and strength (1 Cor. 1:25, 27), the paradox of lowliness and nobleness (1 Cor. 1:26, 28), the paradox of humiliation and exaltation (Phil. 2:6-11), the paradox of destruction and salvation (1 Cor. 1:18-21), the paradox of punishment and peace as well as the paradox of wounds and healing (Isa. 53:5), the paradox of division and reconciliation as well as the paradox of hostility and unity (Eph. 2:14-16), the paradox of disgrace and glory (1 Cor. 2:8), the paradox of death and life (Gal. 2:20), the paradox of curse and blessing (Gal. 3:13-14). Crucifixion is the most important act in God's salvation plan, and a crucial event in the history of salvation. It has achieved more than any previous achievement in the history of salvation has. On the cross, many significant paradoxical transformations have taken place. On the cross, foolishness has turned into wisdom, weakness into strength, lowliness into nobleness, humiliation into exaltation, destruction into salvation, punishment into peace, wounds into healing, division into reconciliation, hostility into unity, disgrace into glory, death into life, curse into blessing.

March 28

God and the Spirit (I)

For the one whom God has sent speaks the words of God, for God gives the Spirit without limit. (John 3:34)

God is Spirit (John 4:24; 2 Cor. 3:18). With His Holy Spirit, God anointed His Son (Isa. 61:1; Acts 10:38). The Lord put His Spirit on His servant (Isa. 42:1). He gives Him the Spirit without limit (John 3:34). Christ received the promised Holy Spirit from God (Acts 2:33). Likewise, God endowed His prophets with His Spirit (Num. 11:29; Isa. 48:16). And, God sent His Spirit to come down upon the apostles ten days after the Ascension of Christ (Act. 2:1-13).

In addition, God pours out His Spirit on the house of Israel (Ezek. 39:29), and on all people (Joel 2:28; Acts 2:17). He gives His Spirit to those who obey Him (Acts 5:32), to those He accepts (Acts 15:8), to those who ask Him (Luke 11:33), by their believing His word (Gal. 3:5). He gives us the Spirit of wisdom and revelation (Eph. 1:17), the Spirit as a deposit, guaranteeing what is to come (2 Cor. 5:5). The very God gives us His Holy Spirit (Rom. 5:5; 1 Thess. 4:8), the gift distributed according to His will (Heb. 2:4).

God sent the Spirit of His Son into our hearts (Gal. 4:6). We have received the Holy Spirit from God (1 Cor. 6:19). The Spirit gives us power, love, and self-discipline (2 Tim. 1:7). When God puts His Spirit in us, we will live (Ezek. 37:14). On the other hand, God lives in us by His Spirit (1 Cor. 3:16; Eph. 2:22).

God sent us His law and His word by His Spirit (Zech. 7:12). The sword of Spirit is the word of God (Eph. 6:17). Moreover, He sent us the Holy Spirit, the Advocate to teach us all things and remind us of the word of Christ (John 14:26). And His love has been poured out into our hearts through the Holy Spirit (Rom. 5:5).

Reflection: The history of salvation is the history that God sends His Spirit. The Spirit is involved in each and every aspect of God's salvation plan, and in each and every event in the history of salvation. Christ was sent to the world as the first visible missionary, and the Spirt was commissioned as the invisible missionary. God endowed His prophets in the Old Testament era with His Spirit; and God sent His Spirit to come upon the apostles in the New Testament era. The Lord promises to pour out His Spirit on the house of Israel; and He has sent His Spirit to the apostles and started the church, which was built on the foundation of the apostles and prophets, with Christ Jesus himself as the chief cornerstone (Eph. 2:20). Moreover, His Spirit is the Spirit of wisdom and revelation, which enables us to know Jesus Christ, the Son of God. And God sent His law and His word by His Spirit. Furthermore, the Spirit testifies the Son, who has been anointed by God with His Spirit. God gives His Spirit to us if we believe His word, and obey Him. God sent the Spirit of His Son into our hearts (Gal. 4:6). This verse summarizes how the three Persons of the Godhead work together in our salvation. This is the brief description of the New Creation. When God puts His Spirit in us, we will live. After we were born again, our lives are sustained by the Spirit. And God lives in us by His Spirit. We no longer live, but Christ lives in us. Oh, this is the secret of the eternal life. As a matter of fact, eternal life is the very life which the triune God lives in. When we have the triune God living in us, we will have everlasting life, because the Spirit is the life-giving Spirit, who sets us free from the law of sin and death (Rom. 8:2).

March 29

God and the Spirit (II)

In reading this, then, you will be able to understand my insight into the mystery of Christ, which was not made known to people in other generations as it has now been revealed by the Spirit to God's holy apostles and prophets. (Ephesians 3:4-5)

The Spirit leads prophets in the vision of God (Ezek. 8:3, 11:1, 24). And prophets spoke from God as they were carried along by the Holy Spirit (2 Pet. 1:21). In the Acts, the disciples were filled with the Holy Spirit and spoke the word of God (Acts 4:31). The mystery of Christ has been revealed by the Spirit to God's holy apostles and prophets (Eph. 3:5). God has revealed His secret wisdom to us by His Spirit (1 Cor. 2:10). Let's ask God to fill us with the knowledge of His will through all the wisdom and understanding that the Spirit gives (Col. 1:9).

The Spirit searches all things, even the deep things of God (1 Cor. 2:10). And the Spirit of God knows the thoughts of God (1 Cor. 2:11). Besides, the Spirit intercedes for God's people in accordance with the will of God (Rom. 8:27).

The person without the Spirit does not accept the things that come from the Spirit of God, and cannot understand them as they are discerned only through the Spirit (1 Cor. 2:14). Those who speak in a tongue speak to God as they utter mysteries by the Spirit (1 Cor. 14:2). He who has an ear, let him hear what the Spirit says to the churches. The one who is victorious will be given the right to eat from the tree of life, which is in the paradise of God (Rev. 2:7).

We praise God in the Spirit (1 Cor. 14:16; Col. 3:16), worship the Father in the Spirit and in truth (John 4:23-24), and serve God by His Spirit (Phil. 3:3). Just as Christ offered Himself unblemished to God through the eternal Spirit (Heb. 9:14), we may become an offering acceptable to God, sanctified by the Holy Spirit (Rom. 15:16). God chose us as first-fruits to be saved through the sanctifying work of the Spirit (2 Thess. 2:13).

Reflection: Two words in the Scriptures means "spirit" in English, one is Hebrew word *"ruach"* in the Old Testament, the other is Greek word *"pneuma"*. Appearing about 380 times in the Scriptures, Ruach means "wind" or "breath". Also appearing about 380 times, pneuma means wind, breath, human emotions and thought, the life-force of the person, or great power. In the Old Testament, the Spirit leads prophets in the vision of God, and carries along the prophets to speak from God. Especially, the Spirit plays a key role in the prophecy of the Messiah. Messiah is the Anointed One who ushers in the era of the New Covenant. And, at Pentecost, the age of messianic Spirit dawns, which leads to the fulfillment of the New Covenant. The Spirit is not only actively involved in the creation of the heaven and the earth, but plays an indispensable role in the revelation, especially in the revelation of mystery of Christ. The Spirt is actively involved in the ultimate revelation of God which is the incarnation of Christ. The Spirit testifies Christ, and converts the sinners to the New Creation in Christ (2 Cor. 5:17). In the New Creation (2 Cor. 5:17) and the New Covenant (Jer. 31:31), the Holy Spirit plays a pivotal role. The New Creation was completed in the Holy Spirit; and the New Covenant was made in the Holy Spirit. "By calling this covenant 'new', he has made the first one obsolete; and what is obsolete and outdated will soon disappear." (Heb. 8:13). Christ offered Himself unblemished to God through the eternal Spirit. Likewise, we may become an offering acceptable to God, sanctified by the Holy Spirit. This is why we don't have to observe the laws of sanitation and cleanliness prescribed in the Old Covenant: "But now, by dying to what once bound us, we have been released from the law so that we serve in the new way of the Spirit, and not in the old way of the written code." (Rom. 7:6). The Spirit guarantees the fulfillment of the New Covenant, because, through the Spirit, God will put His law in our minds and write it on our hearts (Jer. 31:33). Furthermore, the Spirit sanctifies us through and through, and keeps our whole spirit, soul and body blameless at the coming of our Lord Jesus Christ (1 Thess. 5;23).

March 30

The Law of the Spirit of Life

Therefore, there is now no condemnation for those who are in Christ Jesus, because through Christ Jesus the law of the Spirit who gives life has set you free from the law of sin and death. (Romans 8:1-2)

The law of the Spirit of life has set us free from the law of sin and death (Rom. 8:1-2). This law is not the one which is the written code: "But now, by dying to what once bound us, we have been released from the law so that we serve in the new way of the Spirit, not in the old way of the written code." (Rom. 7:6). Instead, this is the law of the Spirit of life.

In fact, we do not receive the Spirit by observing the law which is the written code (Gal. 3:2, 5). Although the righteous requirements of the Law may be fully met in us who live according to the Spirit (Rom. 8:4), if we are led by the Spirit, we are not under the law which is the written code (Gal. 5:18). Instead, the righteousness would certainly have come by the law that could impart life (Gal. 3:21). This is the law of the Spirit of life, for the Spirit gives life (John 6:63; Rom. 8:6, 11; 1 Cor. 15:45; 2 Cor. 3:6), and reaps eternal life (Gal. 6:8).

The law of the Spirit of life not only gives life and reaps eternal life, but also preserves life (Ps. 119: 149.156). So, the psalmist exclaims: "But his delight is in the law of the Lord, and on his law he meditates day and night. He is like a tree planted by the streams of water, which yields its fruit in season and whose leaf does not wither." (Ps.1:2-3). The law of the Spirit of life is indeed the Word of Life (John 5:24; 6:23, 28; Phil. 2:16; 1 John 1:1). And this law of the Spirit of life secures our shares in the tree of life (Rev. 22:19).

Reflection: In the Scriptures, the term "law" often means written code, such as Mosaic Law. However, the term "law" in the phrase "the law of the Spirit of life" does not refer to any written code; instead, it means the authority and power. The law of the Spirit of life is the authority and power of the Spirit. In contrast, the law of sin and death is the authority and power of sin and death. The Apostle Paul describes conflict between these two "laws" that he struggles between. The law of the Spirit of life gives life; while the law of sin and death gives death. The law of the Spirit of life sets us free from the law of sin and death (Rom. 8 :2), since Christ has destroyed death and has brought life and immortality to light through the gospel (2 Tim. 1 :10). The law of the Spirit of life has power of liberating us from the enslaving law of death-giving sin. In fact, the law of the Spirit of life is the life-giving power. The law mentioned in the new covenant (Jer. 31:33) is actually the law of the Spirit. God has put his law in our minds and written it on our hearts (Jer. 31:33). This law is not a written code, which was engraved in letters on stone. This law was written in our hearts by the finger of the Spirit. And this law is the law of the Spirit of life that has set us free from the law of sin and death, and has imparted life. Christ is the last Adam, a life-giving Spirit. Christ is the culmination of the law. Thus, He is the law of the Spirit of life (John 5:24; 6:23, 28; Phil. 2:16; 1 John 1:1). He has set us free from the law of sin and death.

March 31

Resurrection

Jesus said to her, "I am the resurrection and the life. The one who believes in me will live, even though they die; and whoever lives by believing me will never die". (John 11:25-26a)

Martha answered, "I know he will rise again in the resurrection at the last day." (John 11:24). Jesus said to her, "I am the resurrection and the life. The one who believes in me will live, even though they die; and whoever lives by believing me will never die." (John 11:25-26a). It is necessary to choose one of the men who have been with us the whole time the Lord Jesus was living among us, beginning from John's baptism to the time when Jesus was taken up from us. For one of these must become a witness with us of His resurrection (Acts 1:21-22). With great power the apostles continued to testify to the resurrection of the Lord Jesus. And God's grace was so powerfully at work in them all (Acts 4:33).

A group of Epicurean and Stoic philosophers began to debate with him (Paul). Some of them asked, "What is this babbler trying to say?" Others remarked, "He seems to be advocating foreign gods." They said this because Paul was preaching the good news about Jesus and the resurrection (Acts 17:18). When they heard about the resurrection of the dead, some of them sneered, but others said, "We want to hear you (Paul) again on this subject." (Acts 17:32).

The Sadducees say that there is no resurrection, and that there are neither angels nor spirits, but the Pharisees believe all these things (Acts 23:8). Paul, knowing that some of them were Sadducees and the others Pharisees, called out in the Sanhedrin, "My brothers, I am a Pharisee, descended from Pharisees. I stand on trial because of the hope of the resurrection of the dead." (Acts 23:6). (Paul said,) And I have the same hope in God as these men themselves have, that there will be a resurrection of both the righteous and the wicked (Acts 24:15)."

Reflection: The Apostle Paul's life of dedication to Jesus the Christ started on the road to Damascus (Acts 9:3-31). The Light of all lights shone around him and the resurrected Jesus appeared to him. He encountered the resurrected Lord. And his life had been dramatically changed after encountering the resurrected Lord. Although not one of the men who had been with the apostles the whole time the Lord Jesus was living among them, beginning from John's baptism to the time when Jesus was taken up from them

(Acts 1:21-22), although not one of the apostles commissioned during the life of Jesus, although not one of the original twelve, Paul was called by the resurrected Jesus Himself during his Road to Damascus vision and he started to use his Roman name "Paul" afterwards. His use of his Roman name "Paul" indicated the beginning of his career as the "Apostle to the Gentiles". He had seen and was anointed by Jesus while on the road to Damascus, and his life had been changed dramatically. Like Paul, without encountering the risen Lord, our lives won't be changed. Have you ever encountered the risen Lord in your spiritual journey? Have you ever had such a life-changing experience that transmitting to you the resurrection power from the Lord Jesus Christ? If you have never had such a life-changing experience, you should "put out into deep water" (Luke 5:4), and deepen your relationship with the Lord.

April 1

God Reveals

The secret things belong to the Lord our God, but the things revealed belong to us and to our children forever, that we may follow all the words of this law. (Deuteronomy 29:29)

No man can reveal difficult things (Dan. 2:11). But God reveals things (Isa. 43:12). And He reveals deep and hidden things (Dan. 2:22); He reveals the deep things of darkness and brings deep shadows into the light (Job 12:22). He usually reveals things to His servants (1 Sam. 9:15; 2 Sam. 7:27; 2 Kings 8:10; 1 Chron. 17:25; Jer. 11:18, 38:21; Amos 3:7), and to the descendants of the house of Jacob (1 Sam. 2:27; Ezek. 20:5). Interestingly, God is delighted in hiding things from the wise and learned, but revealing them to little children (Matt. 11:25; Luke 10:21). The secret things belong to the Lord our God, but the things revealed belong to us and to our children forever, that we may follow all the words of this law (Deut. 29:29).

God reveals to man His plan (Gen. 41:25, Num. 23:3), His thoughts (Amos 4:13), and His word (1 Sam. 3:7). God reveals Himself to somebody (Gen. 35:7). He even reveals Himself to those who did not ask for Him (Isa. 65:1; Rom. 10:20). He revealed Himself to the Israelites by bringing them out of Egypt (Ezek. 20:9). He reveals Himself in vision (Num. 12:6), or in dreams (Num. 12:6), or through His word (1 Sam. 3:7, 21). Sometimes, He reveals His word in hearing (Isa. 22:14). He reveals His word to Jacob, His laws and decrees to Israel (Ps. 147:19). And He is a revealer of mysteries (Dan. 2:29, 47). God in heaven reveals mysteries (Dan. 2:28, 30). Sometimes, the mystery is revealed in a vision (Dan. 2:19).

Moreover, in the Scriptures, righteousness from God is revealed (Ps. 98:2; Isa. 56:1; Rom. 1:17), the wrath of God is revealed from heaven (Rom. 1:18). And His righteous judgment will be revealed (Rom. 2:5). His righteous acts have been revealed (Rev. 15:4). His arm has been revealed (Isa. 53:1; John 12:38). And His glory will be revealed (Isa. 40:5; Rom. 8:18).

God has revealed to Simeon by the Holy Spirit that he would not die before he had seen the Lord's Christ (Luke 2:26). And He has revealed what He has prepared for those who love him by His Spirit (1 Cor. 2:9-10). And the salvation is ready to be revealed in the last time (1 Pet. 4:5).

Reflection: "The secret things belong to the Lord our God, but the things revealed belong to us and to our children forever, that we may follow all the words of this law." (Deut. 29:29) This verse tells us that God reveals things to us in order that we may follow all the words of His law. God, at His own disposal, chooses whatever He wants to reveal to us, or He doesn't want to reveal to us. He absolutely has the sovereignty. Whatever He has revealed to us we need to listen and obey. Ironically, we eager to know what He has kept hidden, and don't pay attention to what He has revealed. Our intellectual curiosity craves to figure out the secret things that belong to the Lord our God. By doing this, we violate God's sovereignty. Moreover, this shows our attitude of disobedience. If we are obedient to God, we will follow all the words of His law unconditionally, and not inquire about the secret things that belong to Him only. We diligently seek the will of God in our life on some specific aspects, for instance, our marriage, our job, our career; unfortunately, we always neglect His will that has been written in black and white in the Scriptures which is related to our spirituality. As a matter of fact, the will of God is the words of His law that are written in black and white in the Scriptures; and it has been fully and clearly revealed to us; and it is most important to our spiritual life. We ought to follow all the words of His law with absolute obedience.

April 2

The Revelation of Jesus Christ

The revelation from Jesus Christ, which God gave him to show his servants what must soon take place. He made it known by sending his angel to his servant John, who testifies to everything he saw—that is, the word of God and the testimony of Jesus Christ. (Revelation 1:1-2)

Christ was chosen before the creation of the world, but was revealed in these last times for our sake (1 Pet. 1:20). The mystery of Christ is revealed through the prophetic writings (Rom. 16:25-26), by the Sprit to God's holy apostles and prophets (Eph. 3:4-5). The revelation of Jesus Christ, which God gave him to show his servants what must soon take place. He made it known by sending his angel to his servant John, who testifies to everything he saw—that is, the word of God and the testimony of Jesus Christ (Rev. 1:1-2).

John the Baptist came baptizing with water so that Christ might be revealed to Israel (John 1:31). God reveals His Son in Paul (Gal. 1:15-16). Christ chose believers to reveal Himself (Matt. 11:25). Christ's life may be revealed in our body (2 Cor. 4:10), in our mortal body (2 Cor. 4:11).

Christ revealed His glory by His miraculous signs (John 2:11). The fact that Jesus is Christ is not revealed by man, but by our Father in heaven (Matt. 16:17). On the other hand, Jesus has revealed the Father to His disciples (John 17:6).

God's grace has been revealed through the appearing of our Savior, Christ Jesus (2 Tim. 1:9-10). We shall set our hope fully on the grace to be given us when Jesus Christ is revealed (1 Pet. 1:13). We eagerly wait for our Lord Jesus Christ to be revealed (1 Cor. 1:7). And our faith will be proved genuine when Jesus Christ is revealed (1 Pet. 1:7). On the day the Son of Man is revealed (Luke 17:30), He is revealed from heaven in blazing fire with His powerful angels (2 Thess. 1:7). We will be overjoyed when Christ's glory is revealed (1 Pet. 4:13).

Reflection: Our Christian faith is not based human reasoning, but on divine revelation. God has revealed Himself not only in creation, history, and human conscience, but in the Scriptures, the written Word, as well as the revelation of Jesus Christ, the Incarnate Word. God has spoken to Israel, His chosen people through the prophets at many times and in various ways, and finally, He has spoken to us by his Son, who is the radiance of God's glory and the exact representation of His being (Heb. 1:1-3). As a matter of fact, the salvation history is the history throughout which the revelation of Jesus Christ takes place. Christ was chosen before creation of the world, but was revealed in these last times for our sake. The creation was done in a particular moment, whereas the revelation takes place throughout the history of salvation. Just as they all are involved in creation, all of the three Persons of the triune God play key roles in the revelation of Jesus Christ. Christ is revealed by the Father, and by the Spirit to God's holy apostles and prophets. On one hand, God reveals His Son; on the other hand, the Son has revealed the Father. The mystery of Christ has been revealed through the prophetic writings, especially the Messianic prophecies. And finally, the mystery of Christ has been revealed through incarnation and church. Christ has been revealed as our Savior. And God's grace has been revealed through the appearing of the Son. And we will be overjoyed when Christ's glory is revealed.

April 3

The Mystery of God

Now to him who is able to establish you in accordance with my gospel, the message I proclaim about Jesus Christ, in keeping with the revelation of the mystery hidden for long ages past, but now revealed and made known through the prophetic writings by the command of the eternal God, so that all the Gentiles might come to the obedience that comes from faith— to the only wise God be glory forever through Jesus Christ! Amen. (Romans 16:25-27)

The mystery of God is the secret things of God (1 Cor. 4:1). The mystery was hidden for long ages past (Rom. 16:25; 1 Cor. 2:7; Eph. 3:4); it was kept hidden in God for ages and generations (Eph. 3:9; Col. 1:26). However, it was destined for our glory before time began (1 Cor. 2:7). And, as it was purposed in Christ, it will be put into effect when the times will have reached their fulfillment (Eph. 1:9-10).

It is God's good pleasure to disclose the mystery of His will (Luke 10:21; Eph. 1:9). He makes His mysteries known by revelation (Eph. 3:2). Instead of the wise and learned, He reveals them to little children (Matt. 11:25; Luke. 10:21). He reveals mysteries by the Spirit to God's holy apostles and prophets (Rom 16:26; Eph. 3:5; Eph. 6:19). We shall proclaim the mystery of Christ (Col. 4:3), so that the manifold wisdom of God may be made known to the rulers and authorities in the heavenly realm (Eph. 3:9). He disclosed mysteries to the saints (Col. 1:26), and made them known among the Gentiles (Col. 1:27). And they can only be fathomed with the gift of prophecy (1 Cor. 13:2).

At the end, what is the mystery of God? The mystery of God is, in fact, God's secret wisdom (1 Cor. 2:7). It is the manifold wisdom of God (Eph. 3:10). The mystery of God is Christ in whom are hidden all the treasures of wisdom and knowledge (Col. 2:2).

Reflection: Unlike its modern usage which means something that is difficult to understand or explain, in the Biblical time, "mystery" refers to something that will be revealed exclusively to the initiated. But in the New Testament, "mystery" refers to something formerly hidden or obscure but now revealed by God for all to know and understand (Rom 16:25-26; 1 Cor. 2:7; Eph. 1:9-10; 3:3-6, 9-11; Col. 1:25-27). In the New Testament, the mystery of God refers to : (1) Christ's Incarnation (1 Tim. 3:16); (2) The Atoning death of Christ (1 Cor. 2:7); (3) The Unity between Christ and the Church (Eph. 5:31-32); (4) God's purpose to sum up all things in Christ (Eph. 1:9) and especially to include both Jews and Gentiles, in the body of Christ (Eph. 3:3-6); (5) The change that will take place at the resurrection (1 Cor. 15:51-52); (6) The Eventual Inclusion of Jews and Gentiles in His kingdom (Rom. 11:25-26). The mystery of God is, in fact, God's secret wisdom. What is God's secret wisdom? It is Christ, Christ is the wisdom of God. The mystery of God is Christ in whom are hidden all the treasures of wisdom and knowledge. Paul knows this secret. He would rather to abandon everything in order to gain Christ.

April 4

Two Creations (I)

In the beginning, God created the heavens and the earth. (Genesis 1:1)

The Scriptures mention two creations. The first one is known as "the creation" recorded in the Book of Genesis: "In the beginning God created the heavens and the earth" (Gen. 1:1). He created all things through the Word (John 1:3). And He created man in His image and likeness (Gen. 1:26-27; 5:1; 9:6). He created them male and female (Gen. 1:27; 5:2).

God created man on the earth (Deut. 4:32). God formed the man from the dust of the ground and breathed into his nostrils the breath of life, and the man became a living being (Gen. 2:7; 1 Cor. 15:45). He created man for His glory (Isa. 43:7).

Although God made mankind upright, men have gone in search of many schemes (Eccl. 7:29). Although man is the image and glory of God (1 Cor. 11:2), he has sinned and falls short of the glory of God (Rom. 3:23). God decided to wipe mankind whom He created (Gen. 6:7).

In the first creation, the first man Adam became a living being (1 Cor. 15:45). He was of the dust of earth (1 Cor. 15:47). Death came through him (1 Cor. 15:21), and in him all die (1 Cor. 15:22).

Reflection: This is the first creation, the old creation, the physical creation. God created man in His image and likeness. He created them male and female. God created man on the earth. God formed the man from the dust of the ground and breathed into his nostrils the breath of life, and the man became a living being. He created man for His glory. The old creation was done through the Word, and not in the Word. In the first creation, man was created in the image and likeness of God, but he was not imparted with the eternal life until he was born again in Christ. In other words, man becomes a "new creation" when he is born again in Christ, and is imparted with the eternal life. Christ creates in Himself a new man (Eph. 2:15). This is the new self, which is created to be like God in true righteousness and holiness (Eph. 4:24), and renewed in the knowledge in the image of its Creator (Col. 3:10). This is the "new creation", which gives man the image and likeness of God of true righteousness and holiness, and imparts to man eternal life, as eternal life is life of righteousness and holiness.

Pearls of Wisdom VOLUME 1

April 5

Two Creations (II)

Therefore, if anyone is in Christ, the new creation has come: The old has gone, the new is here! (2 Corinthians 5:17)

The old creation took place through Christ, the Word of God (John 1:3; 1 Cor. 8:6). The new creation took place in Christ (2 Cor. 5:17). In the old creation of man, God formed man from dust of ground (Gen. 2:7). In the new creation, man is born of the Spirit (John 3:5, 8; Tit. 3:5), and born again of imperishable, through the living and enduring word of God (1 Pet. 1:23). In the old creation, God created man on earth (Deut. 4:32). Thus, we have borne the likeness of the earthly man (1 Cor. 15:49). In the new creation, we bear the likeness of the man from heaven (1 Cor. 15:49), who is the Son of Man (John 3:13). Just as the Scriptures say, "Flesh gives birth to flesh, but the Spirit gives birth to spirit." (John 3:6).

In the new creation, we are in Christ (2 Cor. 5:17), and Christ is in us, (Rom. 8:10). And He is formed in us (Gal. 4:19). The old has gone (1 Cor. 5:17). Our body is dead because of sin (Rom. 8:10). But we have been born again of imperishable through the living and enduring word of God (1 Pet. 1:23). And our spirit is alive because of righteousness (Rom. 8:10), because, if by the Spirit we put to death the misdeeds of the body, we will live (Rom. 8:13). In Christ all will be made alive (1 Cor. 15:22). And we are made alive in Christ (Eph. 2:4; Col. 2:13). We no longer live, but Christ lives in us (Gal. 2:20).

Christ creates in Himself a new man (Eph. 2:15). This is the new self, which is created to be like God in true righteousness and holiness (Eph. 4:24), and renewed in the knowledge in the image of its Creator (Col. 3:10).

Reflection: There are two creations that are recorded in the Scriptures. Everybody knows about the old creation, few the new creation. The old creation has created our natural body, and the new creation has created our spiritual body (1 Cor. 15:44). In the old creation the first man Adam, who is a living being, was created. In the new creation, the second Adam, who is a life-giving spirit, created. The old creation was done THROUGH the Word, whereas the new creation was done IN the Word (2 Cor. 5:17). In the old creation, man was created in the image and likeness of God; whereas in the new creation, man is created to be like God in true righteousness and holiness (Eph. 4:24), and renewed in the knowledge in the image of his Creator (Col. 3:10). In the old creation, which is the realm of the flesh, the sinful passions aroused by the law were at work in us, so that we bore fruit for death (Rom. 7:5). Our sinful mature hijacks us to do evil and not to do good (Rom. 7:17-18). In the realm of flesh, the law of sin and death controls us, thus, we cannot please God (Rom. 8:8). In the new creation, which is the realm of the Spirit, through Christ Jesus the law of the Spirit who gives life has set us free from the law of sin and death (Rom. 8:2). By dying to what once bound us, we have been released from the law so that we serve in the new way of the Spirit, and not in the old way of the written code (Rom. 7:6), and we live in accordance with the Spirit and our minds set on what the Spirit desires, and the mind governed by the Spirit is life and peace (Rom. 8:5-6). The old way of written code belongs to the Old Covenant; whereas the new way of the Spirit belongs to the New Covenant.

APRIL 6

TWO COVENANTS (I)

By calling this covenant "new," he has made the first one obsolete; and what is obsolete and outdated will soon disappear. (Hebrews 8:13)

The Lord gave Abraham the covenant of circumcision (Acts. 7:8), and required Abraham and his descendants to undergo circumcision that would be the sign of covenant between the Lord and them (Gen. 17:9-13). And that was His covenant in their flesh which was to be an everlasting covenant (Gen. 17:13). Any uncircumcised male broke His covenant (Gen. 17:14).

However, even those who were circumcised did not obey the law (Gal. 6:13). The Lord will punish all who are circumcised only in the flesh (Jer. 9:25). Circumcision is not merely outward and physical (Rom. 2:28); instead, circumcision is circumcision of the heart, by the Spirit, not by the written code (Rom. 2:29). Unfortunately, Israel is uncircumcised in heart (Jer. 9:26).

Then the Lord made a new covenant with the house of Israel and with the house of Judah (Jer. 31:31; Heb. 8:8). It was not like the covenant He made with their forefathers (Jer. 31:32; Heb. 8:9). With this new covenant, the Lord puts His law in their minds and writes it on their hearts (Jer. 31:33; Heb. 8:10, 10:16), not on tablets of stone but on tablets of human hearts (2 Cor. 3:3). By calling this covenant "new", He has made the first one obsolete (Heb. 8:13).

Reflection: The old covenant was the covenant of circumcision which was made in the flesh. That was to be an everlasting covenant. Through circumcision, a proselyte converted to a Jew, and entered the Covenant the Lord made with Israel, which circumcision served as the "sign" for (Gen. 17:11). Although the ritual of circumcision was also observed by the Egyptians, Arabs, or some other Semitic groups in the ancient time, in the history of Israel, this ritual started from Abraham as a sign of the covenant the Lord made with Israel through him, and all male Israelites must observe it in order to enter this covenant with the God of Israel. Even the Gentiles who lived among the Israelites must undergo circumcision as prerequisite for observance of the Passover. To the Israelites, circumcision was the sign of covenant the God of Israel had made with them, symbolizing and reminding them that they were God's chosen people, and they must keep the covenant by obeying the law. Unfortunately, even those who were circumcised did not obey the law, because they were circumcised only in flesh, not in heart; their circumcision was outward and physical (Rom. 2:28). Then the Lord has made the first covenant obsolete (Heb. 8:13) and made a new one with the house of Israel and with the house of Judah, in which the Lord would put His law in their minds and write it on their hearts (Jer. 31:31-33). This new covenant is the covenant of circumcision of heart, by the Spirit, not by the written code (Rom. 2:29). Those who serve God by his Spirit, who boast in Christ Jesus, and who put no confidence in the flesh are truly circumcised (Phil. 3:3).

April 7

Two Covenants (II)

For this reason Christ is the mediator of a new covenant, that those who are called may receive the promised eternal inheritance—now that he has died as a ransom to set them free from the sins committed under the first covenant. (Hebrew 9:15)

The first covenant had regulations for worship and also an earthly sanctuary (Heb. 9:1). And circumcision was the sign of Abrahamic covenant (Gen. 17:11). However, neither circumcisions nor uncircumcision means anything; what counts is a new creation (Gal. 6:15). We, who are letters from Christ written with the Spirit of living God (2 Cor. 3:3), worship God by His Spirit (John 4:24; Phil. 3:3), for we are ministers of a new covenant - not of the letter but of the Spirit (2 Cor. 3:6).

As the mediator of a new covenant (Heb. 9:15; 12:24), Christ has died as a ransom to set us free from the sins committed under the first covenant (Heb. 9:15). Since even the first covenant was not put into effect without blood (Heb. 9:18), Christ established the new covenant with His blood (Luke 22:20; 1 Cor. 11:25) instead of the blood of the covenant in the first covenant (Heb. 9:20). And this blood of covenant, the blood of eternal covenant (Heb. 13:20) sanctifies us (Heb. 10:29). As the High Priest of a New Testament,

Christ went through a tabernacle that is not a part of this creation (Heb. 9:11). He entered the Most Holy Place once for all with His own blood, having obtained, eternal redemption (Heb. 9:12).

Reflection: Undoubtedly, Moses is the mediator of the old covenant. And Christ is the mediator of the new covenant. In this aspect, Moses is a type of Christ. Nevertheless, Christ is not only the mediator of the new covenant, but also the messenger, the author as well as the guarantor of the new covenant. The reason is that Moses is a servant of God, whereas Christ is the Son of God. In the old covenant, God is the author, who established his covenant with Israel through the mediator, Moses. In the new covenant, Christ made the new covenant with His own blood with the church (Matt. 26:28; Mark 14:24; Luke 22:20; 1Cor. 11:25). Although the eternal blessings of the new covenant were guaranteed to God's people because the final sacrifice was foreordained (Acts 2:23; 3:18; 1 Peter 1:20), Christ had to come to world and die on cross in order to guarantee the eternal blessings of the new covenant. When Christ died on the cross and shed his blood for the redemption of the transgressions that were under the first testament, He was inaugurating and establishing the New Covenant. Moreover, Christ came to this earth as a Messenger from God the Father, as well as the Messenger of the New Covenant: "'Behold, I send My messenger, and he will prepare the way before Me. And the Lord, whom you seek, will suddenly come to His temple, even the Messenger of the covenant, in whom you delight. Behold, He is coming,' says the LORD of hosts" (Mal. 3:1). In this verse, John the Baptist is alluded as the first messenger from God the Father, who paved the way for the second Messenger, "the Messenger of the covenant," who is Jesus Christ. Furthermore, in the first covenant, an animal sacrifice for their sins could never fully and finally secure their forgiveness. In the New Covenant, Christ is not only the mediator, but the High Priest, whose high priesthood is superior to the high priesthood of Aaron and his descendants, because Christ offered His own body as sacrifice as atonement for the sins. He is not only the High Priest, but the Sacrifice. He is the guarantor of a better covenant with better promises.

APRIL 8

TWO CREATIONS AND TWO COVENANTS

But when Christ came as high priest of the good things that are now already here, he went through the greater and more perfect tabernacle that is not made with human hands, that is to say, is not a part of this creation. (Hebrews 9:11)

As we know, in the Scriptures, there are two creations, and two covenants that are mentioned. As the mediator of the new covenant, Christ went through a tabernacle which is greater and more perfect than the earthly one (Heb. 9:11) that the old covenant had regulations for (Heb. 9:1). This greater and more perfect tabernacle is not man-made and not a part of this creation (Heb. 9:11) which is accounted in the Book of Genesis. In other words, this tabernacle belongs to the other creation, which is the new creation (2 Cor. 5:17; Gal. 6:15).

The old covenant was related to the old creation. The signs of old covenant are physical (Gen. 9:12, 13, 17, 17:13, Rom. 2:28). The old covenant was inscribed in flesh (Gen. 17:13) in the form of circumcision (Gen. 17:13, 14; Jer. 9:25; Acts. 7:8). Likewise, the new covenant is related to the new creation. New creation takes place in Christ (2 Cor. 5:17). In the new creation, a man is born again of the Spirit (John 3:5, 8; Tit. 3:5). Neither circumcision nor uncircumcision of the flesh means anything, what counts is a new creation (Gal. 6:15), for circumcision is circumcision of heart by the Spirit (Rom. 2:29).

The Lord circumcises our hearts (Deut. 3:6) with His Spirit as the new covenant is of the Spirit (2 Cor. 3:6). By the new creation, we are marked in Christ with a seal, which is the promised Holy Spirit (Eph. 1:13). With the Spirit, we are sealed for the day of redemption (Eph. 1:14, 4:30). We will bear the seal of God on our foreheads (Rev. 9:4) which is the sign of the new covenant.

Reflection: Now the first covenant had regulations for worship and also an earthly sanctuary (Heb. 9:1). When the Lord gave Moses, the mediator of the old covenant, divine instruction on how to build the tabernacle, He also revealed to him what the heaven looked like, because the design of the tabernacle is based on "the greater and more perfect tabernacle" (Heb. 9:11) in heaven. And earthly worship of God was patterned after the heavenly worship of God. When Christ came as high priest of the good things that are already here, he went through the greater and more perfect tabernacle that is not man-made, that is to say, not a part of this creation (Heb. 9:11). For Christ did not enter a sanctuary made with human hands that was only a copy of the true one; he entered heaven itself, now to appear for us in God's presence (Heb. 9:24). These verses tell us that the tabernacle Christ went through was heaven itself, and it is not a part of this creation, namely the old creation. It is a part of the new creation. The first covenant, namely the old covenant had an earthly sanctuary. In contrast, the new covenant has a heavenly sanctuary, which Christ went through. The Scriptures reveal us glimpses of heavenly worship (see Isa. 6, Dan. 7, Rev. 4,5). In addition, the greater and more perfect tabernacle is in our heart, as it is the kingdom of heaven (Luke 17:21), which was not made with hands because God made it. And through it God has established with us a most personal and direct relationship: "Since we have a great high priest who has ascended into heaven, Jesus the Son of God, ...Let us then approach God's throne of grace with confidence, so that we may receive mercy and find grace to help us in our time of need." (Heb. 4:14,16).

April 9

New Creation

Neither circumcision nor uncircumcision means anything; what counts is a new creation. (Galatians 6:15)

If anyone is in Christ, he is a new creation; the old has gone, the new has come (2 Cor. 5:17), for in Adam he died (1 Cor. 15:22), and in Christ he is made alive (1 Cor. 15:22; Eph. 2:4; Col. 2:13), and he is made alive by the Spirit (1 Pet. 3:18), for Christ is a life-giving Spirit (1 Cor. 15:45).

New creation is regeneration. New creation is to be born again (John 3:3, 7; 1 Pet. 1:23) - born of the Spirit (John 3:5, 8). Through the washing of rebirth and renewal by the Holy Spirit (Tit. 3:5), and through the living and enduring word of God, we have been born again (1 Pet. 1:23). In the new creation, we have been put on the new self, which is being renewed in knowledge in the image of its Creator (Col. 3:10); in the new creation, we have been put on the new self, created to be like God in true righteousness and holiness (Eph. 4:24). In other words, new creation is creation of a new man (Eph. 2:15).

New creation is sanctification. In the new creation, a pure heart is created by God in us, and a steadfast spirit is renewed within us (Ps. 51:10). New creation is formation, when Christ is formed in us (Gal. 4:19), and we no longer live, but Christ lives in us (Gal. 2:20).

New creation is transformation. In the new creation, we are being transformed into His likeness with ever-increasing glory (1 Cor. 15:22), and our lowly bodies will be transformed to be like Christ's glorious body (Phil. 3:21). New creation is Christ's resurrected life in us: God raised us up with Christ (Eph. 2:6); Christ will be exalted in our bodies (Phil. 1:20); and we are saved by the resurrection of Christ (1 Pet. 3:21).

Reflection: Neither circumcision nor uncircumcision means anything; what counts is a new creation (Gal. 6:15). New creation starts with reconciliation. Cross was the place where reconciliation took place. On the cross, Christ reconciled Jews and Gentiles. And in the new creation, Christ created in Himself one new humanity out of the two, and made peace. So we can say that peace is reconciliation through Christ and in Christ. On the cross, Christ also reconciled both of them to God. He has made peace between God and this new humanity. Reconciliation has brought about creation of the new humanity (Eph. 2:14-17). And we can also say that when Christ died on the cross, and obtained us eternal redemption, the cross, tree of curse, turned into Tree of Life. Whoever accept Christ as his Lord and Savior will be definitely given eternal life, as partaking of the Tree of Life is the assurance of eternal life. Put it this way, cross is where Christ died, and where new creation takes place: "I have been crucified with Christ and I no longer live, but Christ lives in me. The life I now live in the body, I live by faith in the Son of God, who loved me and gave himself for me." (Gal. 2:20). New creation is regeneration in essence. Moreover, new creation is sanctification as well as transformation. Furthermore, new creation is Christ's resurrected life in us.

April 10

The Creator of Heaven and Earth

And he blessed Abram, saying, "Blessed be Abram by God Most High, Creator of heaven and earth. (Genesis 14:19)

In the beginning, God created the heavens and the earth (Gen. 1:1; Rev. 10:6). The Lord made the heavens and the earth (Gen. 2:4; Exod. 20:11, 31:17; 2 Kings 19:15; 2 Chron. 2:12; Neh. 9:6; Isa. 37:16, 45:18; Acts 4:24, 14:15; Rev. 14:7). He made the heavens and the earth by His great power and outstretched arm (Jer. 32:17). And the heavens and the earth were completed in all their vast array (Gen. 2:1).

In the beginning God laid the foundations of the earth (Ps. 102:25; Isa. 48:13, 51:13, 16; Zech 12:1; Heb. 1:10), set the heavens in place (Isa. 51:16); and the heavens are the work of His hands (Ps. 102:25; Heb. 1:10). By wisdom the Lord laid the earth's foundations, by understanding he set the heavens in place (Prov. 3:19). He made the earth by His power; he founded the world by His wisdom and stretched out the heavens by His understanding (Jer. 10:12, 51:15). He made all of His works in wisdom (Ps. 104:24). He has established all the ends of the earth (Prov. 30:4). He unleashes his lightning beneath the whole heaven and sends it to the ends of the earth (Job 37:3). He stretched out the heavens (Isa. 40:22, 42:5, 44:24, 45:12, 48:13, 51:13; Zech. 12:1), and spread out the earth and all that came out of it (Isa. 42:5, 44:24). He created man on the earth (Deut. 4:32; Isa. 45:12); in the heavens, He has pitched a tent for the sun (Ps. 19:4). The heavens declare the glory of God; the skies proclaim the work of hands (Ps. 19:4).

God Most High is the Creator of heaven and earth (Gen. 14:19, 22); the Lord is the Maker of heaven and earth (Ps. 115:15, 121:2, 124:8, 134:3, 146:6). By His Son, all things were created: things in heaven and on earth, visible and invisible (Col. 1:16). By God's word the heavens existed and the earth was formed (2 Pet. 3:5). Even if there are so-called gods, whether in heaven or on earth, these gods, who did not make the heavens and the earth will perish from the earth and from under the heaven (Jer. 10:11).

Reflection: We all know that God is the Creator of heaven and earth and He created the heavens and the earth, as the Scriptures tell us. However, have you ever been wondering how God created the heavens and the earth? In fact, the Scriptures have explicit answers: "By wisdom the Lord laid the earth's foundations, by understanding he set the heavens in place" (Prov. 3:19). "He made the earth by His power; he founded the world by His wisdom and stretched out the heavens by His understanding" (Jer. 10:12, 51:15). God created the heavens and the earth by His wisdom and understanding. God created the heavens and the earth with wisdom and understanding. In fact, wisdom comes from the Lord (Prov. 2:6), and is one of His divine traits, which He always possesses. Wisdom is as eternal as God Himself. Wisdom was present at each and every point of creation, from "the beginning" to the creation of man. At every stage of creation, from Day 1 to Day 6, wisdom played a key role in developing the universe from formless and empty state to a perfect inhabited world. God made creation to perfection with wisdom in which He Himself was delighted. Moreover, wisdom was also a major organizing principle for God's creation, which determined how things would proceed, as the creation account in Genesis 1 tells us. Because God created the heavens and earth with wisdom, the creation has been perfectly done.

APRIL 11

THE LORD OF THE HEAVENS AND THE EARTH

This is what the Lord says: "If I have not made my covenant with day and night and established the laws of heaven and earth, then I will reject the descendants of Jacob and David my servant and will not choose one of his sons to rule over the descendants of Abraham, Isaac and Jacob. For I will restore their fortunes and have compassion on them." (Jeremiah 33:25-26)

The God who made the world and everything in it is the Lord of heaven and earth and does not live in temples built by hands (Acts 17:24). The Lord fills heaven and earth (Jer. 23:24). The name of the Lord is majestic in all the earth; and He has set His glory above the heavens (Ps. 8:1). He is exalted above the heavens; and His glory is over all the earth

(Ps. 57:5, 11, 108:5). His splendor is above the earth and the heavens (Ps. 148:13). He performs signs and wonders in the heavens and on the earth (Dan. 6:27; Joel 2:30; Acts 2:19). The Lord measures the heavens above and searches out the foundation of the earth below (Jer. 31:37). He has marked off the heavens with the breadth of His hand, and held the dust of the earth in a basket (Isa. 40:12). Nobody knows the laws of the heavens; nobody can set up God's dominion over the earth (Job 38:33). The Lord established laws of heaven and earth (Jer. 33:25).

The Lord our God is God in heaven above and on the earth below (Josh. 2:11). To the Lord our God belong the heavens, even the highest heavens, the earth and everything in it (Deut. 10:14; 1 Chron. 29:11; Ps. 89:11). Everything in heaven and earth belongs to the Lord (1 Chron. 29:11), who made heaven and earth (2 Chron. 2:12). Our Lord is the God of heaven and the God of earth (Gen. 24:3; Deut. 4:39; Josh. 2:11; 2 Chron. 36:23; Ezra 1:2, 5:11).

The multitudes of heaven worship Him (Neh. 9:6). Every creature in heaven and on earth and under the earth and on the sea praises Him (Rev. 5:13), and worships Him who made the heavens, the earth, the sea and the springs of water (Rev. 14:7). The heavens rejoice, the earth is glad, saying among the nations, "The Lord reigns!" (1 Chron. 16:31).

Reflection: The God who made the world and everything in it is the Lord of heaven and earth. God created the world with wisdom which is His will for creation. Wisdom is essential in the act of creation in which she is woven into its very fabric. And creation is perfectly designed to follow the will of God; therefore, creation is in essence the wisdom design from God. As a matter of fact, God not only created the heaven and the earth, but also established laws of heaven and earth. And the entire universe and cosmos are governed by these laws. Because He created the heaven and the earth by His wisdom and understanding, by His great power and outstretched arm, the universe and cosmos are put in order by the laws He has established. Natural laws are hierarchical in nature; secondary laws of nature are derivatives from primary laws of nature, which have to be just right in order for our universe to be possible. The universe was created by the Creator in a logic, consistent, and orderly fashion, who is logical and has imposed order on His universe. Everything in the universe must obey these laws that describe the way God normally accomplishes His will in the universe. The Scriptures tell us: "The Son is the radiance of God's glory and the exact representation of his being, sustaining all things by his powerful word." (Heb. 1:3). In other words, the Creator God upholds and sustains the universe He has created by His powerful Word. The Lord of the heavens and the earth who has established the laws for all creation deserves of all honor, praise, and glory!

April 12

The King of the Heavens and the Earth

He sits enthroned above the circle of the earth, and its people are like grasshoppers. He stretches out the heavens like a canopy, and spreads them out like a tent to live in. (Isaiah 40:22)

The Lord does not dwell on earth (1 Kings 8:27; 2 Chron. 6:18). Heaven is His dwelling place (1 Kings 8:43; 2 Chron. 6:33), although even the highest heaven cannot contain Him (1 Kings 8:27; 2 Chron. 6:18). He builds His lofty palace in the heavens and sets its foundation on the earth (Amos 9:6). He alone is God over all the kingdoms of the earth (2 Kings 19:15).

Heaven is His throne, and the earth is His footstool (Isa. 66:1; Acts 7:49). The Lord, who sits enthroned above the circle of the earth (Isa. 40:22), is God over all the kingdoms of earth (2 Kings 19:15; Isa. 37:16). The Lord our God, the One who sits enthroned on high, stoops down to look on the heavens and the earth (Ps. 113:5-6). He looks down from His sanctuary on high, from heaven He views the earth (Ps. 102:19). He views the ends of the earth and sees everything under the heavens (Job 28:24).

Father, Lord of heaven and earth (Matt. 11:25; Luke 10:21) has given all authorities in heaven and on earth to His Son (Matt. 28:18). God brings unity to all things in heaven and on earth under Christ (Eph. 1:10). In heaven and on earth and under the earth, every knee should bow at the name of Jesus (Phil. 2:10), who is the firstborn over all creation (Col. 1:15).

Reflection: The Lord our God is the king of the heaven and the earth. Heaven is His throne, and the earth is His footstool. He is not only the creator of the heaven and the earth, but also the Lord of the heaven and the earth. He is not only the Lord of the heaven and the earth, but also the King of the heaven and the earth. The scope of our faith is how much we know God. The more we know God, the larger the scope of our faith is, and the stronger our commitment is. If you only know God is the Creator of the heaven and the earth, you don't have to be Christian, because a theist may have the same belief. When you know God is your Lord and your Savior and your King, you are a Christian. When you know God is the King of the kings, and Lord of the lords, you will have genuine Christian faith. Jesus Christ is the King who rules over heaven and earth, who reigns throughout all time and space. He establishes the eternal kingdom of heaven through his cross and resurrection. Like King David, Jesus Christ is a king who will shepherd His people with justice. He has all authority; and His throne will never fall. He is not only the king of the heavens and the earth, but the ruler of our hearts. As Christians, we must recognize His kingship over the heavens and the earth as well as over our lives, and be completely obedient to His will: "Our Father in heaven, hallowed be your name, your kingdom come, your will be done, on earth as it is in heaven." (Matt. 6:9-10). Amen!

APRIL 13

THE JUDGE OF THE HEAVENS AND THE EARTH

The Lord will judge the ends of the earth. (1 Samuel 2:10)

The Lord summons the heavens above, and the earth (Ps. 50:4; Isa. 48:13). He will judge the ends of the earth (1 Sam. 2:10). When He thunders, the waters in the heavens roar; He makes clouds rise from the ends of the earth (Jer. 51:16). The earth shook, the heavens poured down the rain (Ps. 68:8). In the flood, the Lord brought floodwaters on the earth to destroy all life under the heavens; and everything on earth perished (Gen. 6:17). The earth trembled and quaked, the foundations of the heavens shook; they trembled because he was angry (2 Sam. 22:8; Isa. 13:13; Hag. 2:6, 21; Heb. 12:26). The Lord will punish the powers in the heavens above and the kings on the earth below (Isa. 24:21).

The Lord is the sovereign God, who does whatever pleases Him (Ps. 135:6), who can destroy everything under the heavens and on the earth at His disposal (Gen. 6:17). Heaven and earth are His witness (Deut. 4:26, 30:19, 31:28).

And we shall not make for ourselves an idol in the form of anything in heaven above or on the earth beneath or in the water below (Exod. 20:4; Deut. 5:8), for there is no god in heaven or on earth who can do the deeds and mighty works He does (Deut. 3:24; 1 Kings 8:23; 2 Chron. 6:14), and who keeps His covenant of love with His servants (1 kings 8:27; 2 Chron. 6:14), even if there are so-called gods, whether in heaven or on earth (1 Cor. 8:5).

Reflection: The Lord our God is not only the creator of the heaven and the earth, but also the Lord of the heaven and the earth. He is not only the Lord of the heaven and the earth, but also the King of the heaven and the earth. He is not only the King of the heaven and the earth, but also the judge of the heaven and the earth. The Lord summons the heavens above, and the earth (Ps. 50:4; Isa. 48:13). He will judge the ends of the earth (1 Sam. 2:10). He has absolute sovereignty so that He may do everything that pleases Him, and destroy everything under the heavens and on the earth at His disposal. At the end time, when Jesus Christ returns, He will act as the Judge who judge the living and the dead. The judgements He will execute at the end time include: (1) the judgments of the tribulation period (Revelation 6—16); (2) The judgment executed on the judgment seat of Christ (2 Corinthians 5:10); (3) The judgment of the nations (Matthew 25:31–46); (4) The judgment of angels (1 Corinthians 6:2–3); (5) The Great White Throne Judgment (Revelation 20:11–15). Judgments will begin with God's household. As in creation, separation will play pivotal role in judgment. At the end of the age, Jesus Christ will judge the world, by separating the "sons of the kingdom" (the wheat) from the "sons of the evil one" (the tares or weeds) (Matt. 13:24-30), separating the good fish from the bad fish (Matt. 13:47-50), and separating the sheep from the goats (Matt. 25:31-46). All of these metaphors allude to the separation of the unsaved sinners from the saved believers during the Last Judgment. The saved believers will go into the eternal kingdom (Matt. 25:34); whereas the unsaved sinners will go into eternal punishment which is hell or the Lake of Fire (Matt. 25:46).

April 14

The Heavens vs. the Earth

For God was pleased to have all his fullness dwell in him, and through him to reconcile to himself all things, whether things on earth or things in heaven, by making peace through his blood, shed on the cross. (Colossians 1:19-20)

Heavens and earth are two completely different domains. The highest heavens belong to the Lord; whereas He has given the earth to mankind (Ps. 115:16). That is why God is in heaven, and we are on earth (Eccl. 5:2). No wonder the Lord, the God of heaven has given all the kingdoms of earth to Cyrus King of Persia (2 Chron. 36:23; Ezra 1:2).

As the children of God who have one Father in heaven (Matt. 18:19), we shall not store up for ourselves treasures on earth, but store up for ourselves treasures in heaven (Matt. 6:19-20); because we know that if the earthly tent we live in is destroyed, we have a building from God, an eternal house in heaven, not built by human hands (2 Cor. 5:1).

Nicodemus did not believe earthly things Jesus had spoken to him of, let alone he believed heavenly things Jesus had spoken to him of (John 3:12). Verily, if we do not understand earthly things, how can we understand heavenly things? Paul says, "There are also heavenly bodies and there are earthly bodies; but the splendor of the heavenly bodies is one kind, and the splendor of the earthly bodies is another." (1 Cor. 15:40). The splendor of heavenly bodies is truly beyond our imagination and our comprehension.

In the old creation, the prototype of man was Adam, the first man who was of dust of the earth; whereas, in new creation, the prototype of man is Christ, the second man who is from heaven (1 Cor. 15:47). As was the earthly man, so are those who are of earth, and who have borne the likeness of the earthly man; and as is the man from heaven, so also are those who are of heaven, and who bear the likeness of the man from heaven (1 Cor. 15:48, 49).

For God was pleased to have all his fullness dwell in him, and through him to reconcile to himself all things, whether things on earth or things in heaven, by making peace through his blood, shed on the cross." (Col. 1:19-20).

Reflection: In the old creation, our earthly bodies were created. And the prototype of man was Adam, the first man who was of dust of the earth. In the new creation, our heavenly bodies were created. And the prototype of man is Christ, the second man who is from heaven (1 Cor. 15:47). The splendor of the heavenly bodies is different than the splendor of the earthly bodies, because there are from two different creations. The old creation has been achieved by separation: (1) separation of light from darkness (Gen. 1:4); (2) separation of the water under the vault from the water above it (Gen. 1:7); (3) separation of land from the seas (Gen. 1:9). On the other hand, the new creation has been achieved through reconciliation. After we are reconciled with God by Christ's physical body through death (Col. 1:22), we are new creation in Christ (2 Cor. 5:17). Moreover, after Jews and Gentiles are reconciled with God and they are reconciled with each other, a new humanity is created (Eph. 2:14-16). The new humanity is also a new creation. Furthermore, as a matter of fact, the New Heavens and the New Earth are not simply the old ones that will be renewed, but a creation that will be achieved through reconciliation: "For God was pleased to have all his fullness dwell in him, and through him to reconcile to himself all things, whether things on earth or things in heaven, by making peace through his blood, shed on the cross." (Col. 1:19-20). In short, the old creation has been achieved through separation; whereas the new creation has been achieved through reconciliation.

APRIL 15

THE DOOM OF HEAVENS AND THE EARTH

But the day of the Lord will come like a thief. The heavens will disappear with a roar; the elements will be destroyed by fire, and the earth and everything in it will be laid bare. (2 Peter 3:10)

In Genesis, God promised to bring floodwaters on the earth to destroy all life under the heavens, every creature that has the breath of life in it (Gen. 6:17), because He saw that evil and wickedness had filled men's hearts, and men became enormously sinful (Gen. 6:4-5). The flood was the first judgment upon humankind decreed by God. By the flood the world of that time was deluged and destroyed (2 Pet. 3:6).

Moreover, the Lord is going to lay waste the earth, and devastate it (Isa. 24:1). The earth will be completely laid waste and totally plundered (Isa. 24:3). It will dry up and wither (Isa. 24:4), as it is defiled by its people who have disobeyed the laws, violated the statutes and broken the everlasting covenant (Isa. 24:5). This is the cursed earth (Isa. 24:6).

The earth will be formless and empty, and, at the heavens, their light will be gone (Jer. 4:23). The earth will mourn, and the heavens above will grow dark (Jer. 4:28). The floodgates of the heavens will be opened, and the foundations of the earth will shake (Isa. 24:18). In that day, the Lord will punish the powers in the heavens above and the kings on the earth below (Isa. 24:21). Those gods, who did not make the heavens and the earth, will perish from the earth and from under the heavens (Jer. 10:11). And the one, who has been fallen from heaven, and has been cast down to the earth (Isa. 14:12) will be punished as well (Rev. 20:2-3, 7-10).

When the day of the Lord comes, the heavens will vanish; and the earth and everything in it will be laid waste; and the elements will be consumed by fire (2 Pet. 3:10, 12). The world was destroyed by the waters at the first time, and finally, the heavens and the earth will be destroyed by fire (2 Pet. 3:6-7, 10). However, by God's promise, a new heaven and a new earth, the home of righteousness is imminent (2 Pet. 3:13).

Reflection: The doom of the heavens and the earth is part of God's judgment. It signifies the consummation of God's salvation plan (Isa. 51:5-6). The old creation will be terminated (2 Peter 3:10). Although the term "heavens and earth" is accepted to mean the world God created for mankind to dwell in (2 Peter 3), the Apostle Peter describes three distinct phases of creation with the phrase "the heavens and the earth": (1) the ancient heavens and the earth God created in the beginning and later destroyed by the Great Flood; (2 Pet. 3:4, Gen. 1); (2) the present heavens and earth that has existed since the Great Flood and will one day be destroyed by fire at the second coming of Christ (2 Pet. 3:7, 10); (3) the new heavens and the new earth that is the world we will inhabit after the second coming of Christ (2 Pet. 3:13). In the beginning, when God created the heavens and the earth, everything that was created was good. However, sin came to the universe because of Satan's rebellion and the fall of Adam and Eve. The ancient heavens and earth were under God's judgment when He purged of all wickedness with the Great Flood. Nevertheless, God's salvation plan was not consummated due to sins of mankind. As righteousness is a prerequisite for existence in the new order of things, God will purge away all that is evil with fire at the end of age, and will usher in a new era of the new heavens and the new earth. By God's promise, a new heaven and a new earth, the home of righteousness will come into existence. A new heaven and a new earth are not part of this creation, but part of the new creation. The new heavens and the new earth are in fact "the eternal kingdom of our Lord and Savior Jesus Christ" (2 Pet. 1:11), and the place which Jesus went to prepare for us (John 14:1-3)

APRIL 16

THE NEW HEAVENS AND THE NEW EARTH

See, I will create new heavens and a new earth. The former things will not be remembered, nor will they come to mind. (Isaiah 65:17)

God will create new heavens and a new earth. This will be part of the new creation, besides our rebirth (2 Cor. 5:17). A new creation will take place in the spiritual dimension in which a new life in Christ is created (2 Cor. 5:17) before it is completed in the physical dimension in which new heavens and a new earth will be created (Isa. 65:17). In the spiritual dimension, new creation means that God puts a new spirit in us (Ezek. 11:19). Also, the new covenant is of the Spirit (2 Cor. 3:6); and the mediator of the new covenant is Christ (Hew. 9:15, 12:24). In contrast, the old covenant was made in the physical dimension; and the mediator of the old covenant was Moses.

Just as the first covenant was made obsolete (Hew. 8:13), the first creation was terminated: "That day will bring about the destruction of the heavens by fire, and the elements will melt in the heat." (2 Pet. 3:12). Not only the first heaven, but also the first earth will pass away; and there will be no longer any sea (Rev. 21:1). The former things will not be remembered, nor will they come to mind (Isa. 65:17). We can say that the old time and space, the old universe and the old cosmos will disappear.

Reflection: The old heavens and the old earth are what we can see now. They are visible in this physical dimension, thus they are temporary (2 Cor. 4:18). The new heavens and the new earth are what we cannot see now. They are invisible in this physical dimension, thus they are eternal (2 Cor. 4:18), as the Lord declares that the new heavens and the new earth will endure before Him (Isa 66:22). Interestingly, the visible in the old creation will become invisible in the new creation. In contrast, the invisible in the old creation will become visible in the new creation. In the old heavens and the old earth, no one can see God. The one who sees God must die. In the new heavens and the new earth, we will see God face to face, and will live forever. We can see the old heavens and the old earth now, but we cannot see God. In the future, the old heavens and the old earth will vanish, and God will be seen by us. Interestingly, the visible in the old creation will become invisible in the new creation; in contrast, the invisible in the old creation will become visible in the new creation; because the Lord promises: "See, I will create new heavens and a new earth. The former things will not be remembered, nor will they come to mind." (Isa. 65:17).

April 17

All Things (I)

For God was pleased to have all his fullness dwell in him, and through him to reconcile to himself all things, whether things on earth or things in heaven, by making peace through his blood, shed on the cross. (Colossians 1:19-20)

From God, the Father all things came; and through the Lord, Jesus Christ all things came (1 Cor. 8:6). Through the Word, all things were made; without Him nothing was made that has been made (John 1:3). Through His Son, God made the universe (Heb. 1:2). Furthermore, by Him all things were created: things in heaven and on earth, visible and invisible, whether thrones or powers or rulers or authorities; all things were created by Him and for Him (Col. 1:16).

God has brought unity to all things in heaven and on earth under Christ (Eph. 1:10). The Father has placed all things under Christ's feet and appointed Him to be head over everything for the church (Eph. 1:22). The Father has put all things under the power of Christ (John 13:3), and has committed all things to His Son (Matt. 11:27; Luke 10:22). The Father has appointed His Son heir of all things (Heb. 1:2). In all things God may be praised through Christ (1 Pet. 4:11). If we lose all things for His sake (Phil. 3:8), we will in all things grow up into Him who is the head, that is, Christ (Eph. 4:15).

The Son is before all things, and in Him all things hold together (Col. 1:17). The Son sustains all things by His powerful word (Heb. 1:3). Through His Son, God has reconciled to Himself all things, whether things on earth or things in heaven, by making peace through His blood, shed on the cross (Col. 1:20). For from him and through him and to him are all things. To him be the glory forever! Amen (Rom. 11:36).

Reflection: What is peace? Peace is reconciliation through Christ and in Christ on the cross. On the cross, Christ reconciled Jews and Gentiles. On the cross, Christ also reconciled both of them to God. Through His Son, God has reconciled to Himself all things, whether things on earth or things in heaven, by making peace through His blood, shed on the cross (Col. 1:20). In a word, cross was the place where reconciliation took place (Eph. 2:14-17). Moreover, Jesus Christ, Prince of Peace (Isa. 9:6), is the peacemaker. He Himself has fulfilled the Beatitudes: "Blessed are the peacemakers, for they will be called children of God." (Matt. 5:9). Furthermore, because Jesus made peace on the cross, He reconciled Jews and Gentiles, Peter was able to minister to Cornelius. Peter said to people gathering in Cornelius' house: "You are well aware that it is against our law for a Jew to associate with or visit a Gentile. But God has shown me that I should not call anyone impure or unclean." (Acts 10:28). Because of the reconciliation Christ made on the cross, the dividing wall of hostility has been destroyed, by setting aside in his flesh the law with its commands and regulations, and Jews and Gentiles have been made one, as Paul says, "For he himself is our peace, who has made the two groups one and has destroyed the barrier, the dividing wall of hostility, by setting aside in his flesh the law with its commands and regulations." (Eph. 2:14-15). And the Mosaic dietary laws have been abolished, because all things have been made clean by the precious blood of Jesus. "Through His Son, God has reconciled to Himself all things, whether things on earth or things in heaven, by making peace through His blood, shed on the cross" (Col. 1:20). Because of the reconciliation, the unclean have been made clean. Because of the reconciliation, in His flesh, the commands and regulations have been set aside.

April 18

All Things (II)

He who did not spare his own Son, but gave him up for us all—how will he not also, along with him, graciously give us all things? (Romans 8:32)

God is the Maker of all things (Eccl. 11:5; Jer. 10:16, 51:19). He created all things (Eph. 3:9; Rev. 4:11), and made all things (Isa. 44:24). All things were created by His will and have their being (Rev. 4:11). God is the ruler of all things (1 Chron. 29:12). All things serve Him (Ps. 119:91). And God has exalted above all things His name and His word (Ps. 138:2). He knows all things (John 16:30, 21:17). God can do all things (Job 42:2), for all things are possible with God (Matt. 19:26; Mark 10:27).

God graciously gives us all things (Rom. 8:32). All things are ours (1 Cor. 3:21). God is able to make all grace abound to us, so that in all things, having all that we need, we will abound in every good work (2 Cor. 9:8). He who did not spare his own Son, but gave him up for us all—how will he not also, along with him, graciously give us all things (Rom. 8:32)? And in all things God works for the good of those who love Him, who have been called according to His purpose (Rom. 8:28).

The Spirit searches all things, even the deep things of God (1 Cor. 2:10). The Holy Spirit will teach us all things and remind us everything Jesus has said to us (John 14:26). As His anointing teaches us about all things (1 John 2:27), the spiritual man makes judgments about all things (1 Cor. 2:15).

Reflection: As we know, a merchandise's value is determined by the price it will attract; likewise, the value of a human soul is measured by what God is willing to pay to purchase it. As God did not spare His own Son, how would we imagine that He would not give us all things that are less valuable than His only-begotten Son? (Romans 8:32). However, although a human soul is precious in His eyes, God is willing to pay the price of His only-begotten Son not because of our merits, but because of His grace. Grace is that we get what we don't deserve, free of charge. Although grace is free, it is not cheap. It is too costly for us to afford; but God has paid it a great price. In other words, the redemption of Jesus Christ is too costly for us. Nevertheless, without our costly redemption we would have not been able to become the children of God. As long as we become His children, God also will freely go on providing everything that we need. He will graciously give us all things, out of His grace. He gives us immeasurably more than all we ask or imagine, because He is full of grace. As a matter of fact, we do not deserve anything, but He lavishes His great love on us which is so wide and long and high and deep, just because we are His children and because He loves us. However, we have to receive His only-begotten Son before we receive all things that He graciously gives us along with Him. We have to bear in mind that "all things" that God will graciously give to His children are not the riches of this world, but all spiritual blessings in the heavenly realms in Christ (Eph. 1:3) with the purpose of achieving our glorification. Our God who will meet all our needs according to the riches of His glory in Christ Jesus (Phil. 4:19), will work "all things" together for the good of those who love him, who have been called according to his purpose (Rom. 8:28); and the purpose is our glorification (Rom. 8:30).

April 19

The Word and the World

He (the Word) was in the world, and though the world was made through him, the world did not recognize him. (John 1:10)

The creation of the world was done through the Word. By God's word the heavens existed and the earth was formed out of water and by water (2 Pet. 3:5). Moreover, through the Word, all things were made; without the Word nothing was made that has been made (John 1:3). However, we should keep in mind that the world was created by the Word and for the Word (Col. 1:16). Furthermore, the Son is the radiance of God's glory and the exact representation of his being, sustaining all things by his powerful word (Heb. 1:3).

Unfortunately, the Word encounters the rejection from the world: "He (the Word) was in the world, and though the world was made through him, the world did not recognize him. He came to that which was his own, but his own did not receive him." (John 1:10-11).

Nevertheless, the Word plays a pivotal role in reconciliation between God and the world. Through the Word, God has reconciled to Himself all things, whether things on earth or things in heaven (Col. 1:20).

By the same Word the heavens and the earth came to existence, the present heavens and earth are reserved for fire, being kept for judgment and destruction of ungodly men (2 Pet. 3:7). When the times will have reached their fulfillment, the world (all things) will be brought under the Word (Christ) (Eph. 1:10). Heaven and earth will pass away, the Word will never pass away (Matt. 24:35; Mark 13:31; Luke 21:33).

Reflection: The Word plays a key role in creation. The creation of the world was done through the Word (John 1:3, 10), by the Word, and for the Word. And all things are sustained by His powerful Word. Moreover, the Word plays a key role not only in the creation, but also in reconciliation. Although encountering rejection from the world, the Word plays a pivotal role in reconciliation between God and the world. And the Word also plays an important role in the consummation of redemption: when the times will have reached their fulfillment, the world will be brought under the Word (Eph. 1:10). In other words, in God's plan, the Word is indispensable. God has done everything through the Word; and everything has been done by the Word, and for the Word; everything God has done, no matter creation or salvation, God has done through the Word. Put it this way, the Word acts as God's agent in doing everything. The Word is Jesus Christ, Son of God. Jesus Christ is the Wisdom of God (1 Cor. 1:18). God has created the heavens and the earth through the Word, by His Wisdom: "By wisdom the Lord laid the earth's foundations, by understanding he set the heavens in place" (Prov. 3:19). Compare the following verses, you will know the Word in the John 1 is identical with the Wisdom in Provers 8: "In the beginning was the Word, and the Word was with God, and the Word was God. He was with God in the beginning. Through him all things were made; without him nothing was made that has been made" (John 1:1-3); "The Lord brought me (wisdom) forth as the first of his works, before his deeds of old; I was formed long ages ago, at the very beginning, when the world came to be." (Prov. 8:22-23).

April 20

A Copy and Shadow

They serve at a sanctuary that is a copy and shadow of what is in heaven. This is why Moses was warned when he was about to build the tabernacle: "See to it that you make everything according to the pattern shown you on the mountain." (Hebrews 8:5)

Men who offer the gifts prescribed by the law serve at a sanctuary that is a copy and shadow of what is in heaven (Heb. 8:5). And it was made according to the pattern shown on the mountain (Heb. 8:5). Moses was entrusted to make this sanctuary on earth, through whom the old covenant was established. We can see that this earthly sanctuary is associated with the old covenant, as the Scriptures read, "Now the first covenant had regulations for worship and also an earthly sanctuary (Heb. 9:1).

The law is only shadow of good things that are coming (Heb. 10:1), so are the rituals prescribed by the law (Col. 2:16-17). Neither of them is reality; the reality, however, is found in Christ (Col. 2:17; Heb. 10:1). The true tabernacle, of which man-made sanctuary is a copy and shadow, is what is in the heaven (Heb. 8:5, 9:24).

Just as the man-made sanctuary belongs to the old covenant and the old creation, the true tabernacle which is set by the Lord (Heb. 8:2) belongs to the new covenant and the new creation, as the Scriptures read, "When Christ came as high priest of the good things that are already here, he went through the greater and more perfect tabernacle that is not man-made, that is to say, not a part of this creation" (Heb. 9:11). This verse implies that the true tabernacle belongs to the new creation. Christ, our High Priest, who sat down at the right hand of the throne of the Majesty (Heb. 8:1), which is also the throne of grace (Heb. 4:16) in heaven, serves in this true sanctuary (Heb. 8:2). He entered heaven itself, now to appear for us in God's presence (Heb. 9:24).

Reflection: This earthly sanctuary is associated with the old covenant, and is part of the old creation. Christ "went through the greater and more perfect tabernacle that is not man-made, ... not a part of this creation" (Heb. 9:11). This greater and more perfect tabernacle belongs to the new creation and the new covenant. The earthly sanctuary is a copy and shadow of what is in heaven (Heb. 8:5). The heaven is the new creation which Christ went through: "For Christ did not enter a sanctuary made with human hands that was only a copy of the true one; he entered heaven itself, now to appear for us in God's presence." (Heb. 9:24). God's revelation is progressive. He always uses events and objects to symbolize His salvation plan. These events and objects serve as "shadow" to symbolize the "realities". In theological terms, "shadow" is called "type"; whereas "realities" "antitype". All the realities are found in Christ (Col. 2:17). For instance, all the temples, rituals, and objects based on the Mosaic Law in the Old Covenant are meant to be the "shadow" of God's real plan, which is fulfilled in Christ. The temple worship based on the Mosaic Law is the "shadow" of heavenly worship taken place in the heavenly tabernacle. This sanctuary of shadows is intended to point the worshipers of God to greater future realities about God and His plan of salvation. Moreover, the Levitical priesthood foreshadows to Jesus and His priesthood. Furthermore, the sacrificial system based on the Mosaic Law symbolizes Jesus' sacrificial death on the cross. As the author of Hebrews points out, Jesus, the mediator of the New Covenant is greater than Moses, the mediator of the Old Covenant (Heb. 3); His priesthood is greater than Levitical priesthood (Heb. 7); He is mediator of the New Covenant which is established on better promises (Heb. 8:6); the true tabernacle in heaven is better than the earthly tabernacle (Heb. 9); and Jesus' sacrifice on the cross is superior to the sacrifices of the Old Covenant; because realities are always better than shadow.

April 21

The New Order (I)

This is an illustration for the present time, indicating that the gifts and sacrifices being offered were not able to clear the conscience of the worshiper. They are only a matter of food and drink and various ceremonial washings—external regulations applying until the time of the new order. (Hebrews 9:9-10)

Christ introduces a new order, which is the new covenant, with its new priesthood, new sanctuary, and new sacrifices, because in the old order, the gifts and sacrifices being offered were not able to clear the conscience of the worshiper. They were only a matter of food and drink and various ceremonial washings—external regulations applying until the time of the new order (Heb. 9:9-10). The first covenant was no longer effective. If there had been nothing wrong with that first covenant, no place would have been sought for another (Heb. 8:7). By calling this covenant "new," The Lord has made the first one obsolete; and what is obsolete and outdated will soon disappear (Heb. 8:13). The Lord has made a new covenant with the house of Israel and with the house of Judah (Jer. 31:31; Heb. 8:8, 10:16). Christ is the mediator of this new covenant (Heb. 9:15, 12:24). Even the first covenant was not put into effect without blood, Christ established the new covenant with His own blood (Luke 22:20; 1 Cor. 11:25). And He did not enter the Most

Holy Place by means of blood of goats and calves, but He entered the Most Holy Place once for all by His own blood, having obtained eternal redemption (Heb. 9:12). Therefore, we have confidence to enter the Most Holy Place once for all by His blood, by the new and living way opened for us through His body (Heb. 10:19-20). And His sprinkled blood speaks a better word than the blood of Abel (Heb. 12:24).

Reflection: The Old Covenant is a covenant initiated by the Lord between Israel and Himself, with Moses as the mediator. It comes with the Mosaic Law, Levitical priesthood, Levitical sacrificial system, and tabernacle/temple worship. It is entailed with promises that the Lord is the God of Israel, Israel is His chosen people, and that He pledges prosperity and protection in the Promised Land. Christ introduces a New Order, which is the New Covenant. The New Order is the New Covenant established through and by Christ, with its new priesthood, new sanctuary, and new sacrifices. Because of the reconciliation Jesus has done on the cross, the New Order has been introduced. Jesus Christ has established the New Covenant between the Church and Himself with His own blood (1 Cor. 11:25). The contrast between these two covenants is works vs. grace. As the author of Hebrews expounds, the New Covenant is superior to the Old Covenant because: (1) As a mediator, Jesus who is the Son of God is superior to Moses who is a servant of God; (2) The priesthood Jesus represents, which was of the order of Melchizedek, is superior to the Levitical priesthood; (3) Unlike the sacrifices in the Old Covenant, Jesus' sacrifice was once for all, perfecting believers for eternal life; (4) Unlike the High Priest in the Old Covenant, Christ did not enter the Most Holy Place by means of blood of goats and calves, but He entered the Most Holy Place once for all by His own blood (Heb. 9:12), the greater and more perfect tabernacle that is not man-made, but a true tabernacle set by the Lord (Heb. 8:1). And He serves in this new sanctuary (Heb. 8:2). Christ sets aside the first covenant to establish the second covenant. And we have been made holy through the sacrifice of the body of Christ once for all (Heb. 10:9-10). As a matter of fact, in God's salvation plan, the Old Covenant was temporary and provisional. It was to be made null and void by the institution of the New Covenant (Jer. 31:32; Heb. 8:13; 10:9). Nevertheless, Christ has come to fulfill the laws, not to abolish them (Matt. 5:17). Because of Jesus' perfect fulfillment of the Law, we are saved through Him, saved by faith in Jesus Christ, the mediator of the New Covenant (Gal. 2:16).

April 22

The New Order (II)

This is an illustration for the present time, indicating that the gifts and sacrifices being offered were not able to clear the conscience of the worshiper. They are only a matter of food and drink and various ceremonial washings—external regulations applying until the time of the new order. (Hebrews 9:9-10)

If the Levitical priesthood is so great for bringing man and God together, then why did God start planning for a new order way back in the time of Abraham, in the order of Melchizedek, not in the order of Aaron? (Heb. 7:11). Therefore, Christ introduces a new order, which is the new covenant, with its new priesthood, new sanctuary, and new sacrifices that has abolished external regulations that were outward observances of the old covenant law (Heb. 9:9-10).

Christ is the High Priest of the new covenant, who sat down at the right hand of the throne of the Majesty in heaven (Heb. 8:1). He is the mediator of the new covenant (Heb. 12:24). The old covenant had an earthly sanctuary (Heb. 9:1). A tabernacle was set up (Heb. 9:2). But Christ went through the greater and more perfect tabernacle that is not man-made, but a true tabernacle set by the Lord (Heb. 8:1). And He serves in this new sanctuary (Heb. 8:2).

In the old covenant, the gifts and sacrifices being offered were not able to clear the conscience of the worshiper (Heb. 9:9). And the same sacrifices repeated endlessly year after year can never make perfect those who draw near to worship (Heb. 10:1). Christ sets aside the first covenant to establish the second covenant. And we have been made holy through the sacrifice of the body of Christ once for all (Heb. 10:9-10). By one sacrifice Christ has made perfect forever those who are being made holy (Heb. 10:14). And our hearts have been sprinkled to cleanse us from a guilty conscience and having our bodies washed with pure water.

Reflection: Because man could not get a perfect conscience under the Levitical priesthood after the order of Aaron, a new priesthood was required. In the Old Testament, according to Mosaic Law, the office of High Priest was based on genealogy and heredity. In contrast, Jesus represented a different priesthood than Levitical priesthood, a priesthood which was of the order of Melchizedek, a permanent order on the basis of an endless life. The Father promised the Messiah that He would be a priest according to the higher order of Melchizedek, and put Him in the office by an oath (Heb. 7:18-21). And

Jesus introduced a New Order based upon an atonement that was efficacious. Since the priesthood changed, the law and the sacrifices associated with it also changed. This New Order provides a better hope by which His New Covenant people can draw near to God (Heb. 7:11-18). As the High Priest of the new covenant, Christ sat down at the right hand of the throne of the Majesty in heaven (Heb. 8:1). He went through a greater and more perfect sanctuary that was not made with human hands, and He did not enter by means of the blood of goats and calves; but He entered the Most Holy Place once for all by his own blood, thus obtaining eternal redemption. All of these show that Christ introduces a New Order, which is the New Covenant, with its new priesthood, new sanctuary, and new sacrifices. Heavenly things themselves have been purified with better sacrifices that are the blood of Christ, because the blood of Christ, who through the eternal Spirit offered Himself unblemished to God, will cleanse our consciences from acts that lead to death, so that we may serve the living God! (Heb. 9:14).

April 23

Faith is Knowing Who Jesus Is (I)

When the wine was gone, Jesus' mother said to him, "They have no more wine." (John 2:3)

Maria reported to Jesus, "They have no more wine." She said to the Vine, "They have no more wine." (John 2:3). How could she say to the Vine, "They have no more wine", as Jesus Himself is the true vine (John 15:1)?

Jesus' disciples said to Jesus, "We have only five loaves of bread and two fish – unless we go and buy food for all this crowd." (Luke 9:13; Matt. 14:7; John 6:9). How could they say to the Bread of Life (John 6:35, 48, 51), "We have only five loaves of bread"? Later on, the disciples even forgot that Jesus fed five thousand with five loaves of bread and two fish, and four thousand with seven loaves of bread and a few small fish (Matt. 16:9-10).

In the storm, the disciples woke Jesus up, saying, "Lord, save us! We are going to drown." (Matt. 8:25). While walking on water, Peter cried out, "Lord, save me!" (Matt. 14:30). At those moments, they recognized Jesus as their Lord, but they seemed not knowing that Jesus Himself was their Savior, and His name means "the Lord Saves" (Matt. 1:21). If knowing that Jesus is their Savior, they would not have been panic.

The Samaritan woman wondered how Jesus could get the living water from the deep well without having anything to draw with. She did not know that Jesus Himself was the living water (John 4:11-12).

Reflection: Do we sometimes, like Maria, say to "the Vine", we have no more wine? Do we sometimes, like Jesus' disciples, say to "the Bread of Life", we have only five loaves of bread? Do we sometimes, like Peter and other disciples of Jesus, call to the Savior: "Save me"? Do we sometimes, like the Samaritan woman, wonder how "the living water" can get the living water from the deep well without having anything to draw with? Actually, we are not better than any of them. Our faith is not stronger than theirs. Faith is knowing who Jesus is. The more we know Jesus, the stronger our faith is. A Christian's spiritual journey starts with knowing that Jesus is his/her Lord and Savior. Knowing Jesus is more than knowing about Him; it is knowing Him personally and having a personal relationship with Him. In fact, a personal relationship with Jesus is the basis of truly knowing Him. Knowing Jesus is not only recognizing who He is, but acknowledging your need for Him, your need for your Savior who can save you from sin. Knowing Jesus in salvation is not based on what we do; knowing Jesus starts with faith in Him, and our continuing relationship with Him is always rooted in faith. And true faith is not only cognitively recognizing that He is Son of God, but also emotionally trusting in Him who is your Lord and Savior; it is not only emotionally trusting in Him who is your Lord and Savior, but also volitionally obeying Him who is the Lord your God.

APRIL 24

FAITH IS KNOWING WHO JESUS IS (II)

Then some Pharisees and teachers of the law came to Jesus from Jerusalem and asked, "Why do your disciples break the tradition of the elders? They don't wash their hands before they eat!" (Matthew 15:1-2)

Some Pharisees and teachers of the law blame Jesus' disciples for not washing their hands before eating, without knowing that Jesus Himself is the sanctifier (Matt. 15:1-2). In contrast, the man with leprosy knew that Jesus was the sanctifier, and entreated Jesus to make him clean. Jesus granted his request by healing him immediately (Matt. 8:1-3).

The Pharisees blamed Jesus and His disciples for doing what was unlawful on the Sabbath, without knowing that Jesus Himself is the Lord of Sabbath (Matt. 12:1-14).

When Jesus healed a demon-possessed man who was blind and mute, all the people were astonished and said, "Could this be the Son of David?" (Matt. 12:22-23) Pharisees believed, by Beelzebub, Jesus drove out demons (Matt. 12:24). Actually, even demons recognized that Jesus was the Son of God (Matt. 8:28-31).

Some of the Pharisees and teachers of the law wanted to see a miraculous sign from Jesus, without knowing that He was the greatest miracle worker (Matt. 12:38). The Pharisees and Sadducees asked Jesus to show them a sign from heaven, without knowing that He Himself was from heaven (Matt. 16:1).

The collector of two-drachma tax wondered whether or not Jesus had paid tax, without knowing that Him is the Son of God (Matt. 17:24-27).

Reflection: The Pharisees knew the law very well, but they didn't know Jesus. They were well-versed in the Mosaic Law, and added human traditions to the Law of God. They showed very high degree of piety with commitment to obeying to the Mosaic Law. In fact, one sect among the Pharisees believed that if they could keep every item of the Mosaic Law for just twenty-four hours, then that would prompt God to send the Messiah to Israel. Ironically, when the Messiah stood in front of them, they denied Him, hated Him, and assaulted Him. They were jealous of Him because of His popularity among the people. They hated Him because their hypocrisy was exposed by His true and genuine holiness, and they feared losing their power and authority. They denied that He was the Messiah and the Son of God. They knew the Written Word of God, but they didn't know the Incarnated Word of God. As a matter of fact, we cannot truly know the Written Word of God, without knowing the Incarnated Word of God. The Written Word of God witnesses the Incarnated Word of God. And both of them are the ultimate revelation of the triune God. In fact, faith is knowing who Jesus is. Pharisees knew the law very well, but didn't know who Jesus was. Therefore, they didn't have true faith at all. Likewise, no matter how well we know the Scriptures, no matter how many Bible verses we memorize, no matter how knowledgeable we are in theology, if we don't recognize that sin separates us from God and others, we must repent and ask God for forgiveness, if we don't accept Jesus Christ as our Lord and Savior, and establish a personal relationship with Him, we won't have true faith at all.

April 25

Faith Is Knowing Who Jesus Is (III)

As Jesus went on from there, two blind men followed him, calling out, "Have mercy on us, Son of David!" When he had gone indoors, the blind men came to him, and he asked them, "Do you believe that I am able to do this?" "Yes, Lord," they replied. Then he touched their eyes and said, "According to your faith let it be done to you"; and their sight was restored. (Matthew 9:27-30)

As Jesus went on from there, two blind men followed him, calling out, "Have mercy on us, Son of David!" (Matthew 9:27). These two blind men recognized Jesus as Son of David, Jesus healed them according to their faith. (Matt. 9:27-30).

The centurion recognized Jesus' healing power and His authority, Jesus commended him, "It will be done just as you believe it would." (Matt. 8:13).

The bleeding woman believed if she only touched Jesus' cloak, she would be saved. Jesus commended her, "Your faith has healed you.", because she knew that Jesus was the Healer (Matt. 9:20-22).

To reward the Canaanite woman's great faith, who recognized Jesus as Lord and Son of David, Jesus healed her demon-possessed daughter (Matt. 15:21-28).

The ruler beseeched Jesus to raise his daughter from dead. Jesus granted his request as he recognized Jesus as Resurrection (Matt. 9:18-19, 23-26).

The men at Gennesaret recognized Jesus, so the sick from all the surrounding country were healed by just touching the edge of Jesus' cloak (Matt. 14:34-36).

As soon as Peter recognized Jesus as Christ, the Son of living God, Jesus entrusted him the keys to the kingdom of heaven (Matt. 16:13-20), although Peter still did not understand Jesus' mission on the earth (Matt. 16:21-23).

Jesus said, "Whoever acknowledges me before men, I will also acknowledge him before my Father in heaven. But whoever disowns me before men, I will disown him before my Father in heaven (Matt. 10:32-33).

Reflection: What is faith? Faith is knowing who Jesus is. Look at these two blind men, when they recognized who Jesus was, Jesus healed them according to their faith (Matt. 9:27-30). How much faith you have is virtually how much you know Jesus. And He will reveal to you who He is if you recognize Him. If you know the seven redemptive names of the Lord, you will truly know God. If you know that Jesus is the Lord my Shepherd (Jehovah Rohi), you shall not want (Psalm 23:1). If you know that Jesus is the Lord-Will-Provide (Jehovah Jireh), God will meet all your needs according to the riches of his glory in Christ Jesus (Eph. 4:19). If you know that Jesus is the Lord Who Heals (Jehovah Rapha), you will be healed by His wound (Isa. 53:5). If you know that Jesus is the Lord my Peace (Jehovah Shalom), the peace of God, which transcends all understanding, will guard your hearts and your minds in Christ Jesus (Eph. 4:7). If you know that Jesus is the Lord my Banner (Jehovah Nissi), you will fight the good fight of the faith (1 Tim. 6:12). If you know that Jesus is the Lord my Righteousness, God will make Him who knows no sin to be sin on your behalf, so that you will become the righteousness of God in Him (2 Cor. 5:21). If you know that Jesus is "the Lord is there for me" (Jehovah Shammah), the Lord your God is with you wherever you go (Josh. 1:9). If you know that Jesus is the Savior, He will save you, because His name is the Lord Saves (Matt. 1:21).

April 26

Cleansing

The blood of goats and bulls and the ashes of a heifer sprinkled on those who are ceremonially unclean sanctify them so that they are outwardly clean. How much more, then, will the blood of Christ, who through the eternal Spirit offered himself unblemished to God, cleanse our consciences from acts that lead to death, so that we may serve the living God! (Hebrews 9:13-14)

In the Old Testament, bull's blood or goat's blood is used for the purpose of cleansing. The Lord told Moses that Aaron should sprinkle some of the blood on the altar with his finger seven times to cleanse it and to consecrate it from the uncleanness of the Israelites (Lev. 16:19). And the plant of hyssop is also used for the purification rites (Lev. 14:4-7, 14:49-52, 19:6, 18). King David entreated to the Lord, "Wash away all my iniquity and cleanse me from my sin. ......Cleanse me with hyssop, and I will be clean" (Ps. 51:2,7). On the tenth day of the seventh month, atonement will be made for Israelites to cleanse their sins. However, the blood of goats and bulls and the ashes of a heifer sprinkled on those who are ceremonially unclean sanctify them so that they are outwardly clean. How much more, then, will the blood of Christ, who through the eternal Spirit offered himself unblemished to God, cleanse our consciences from acts that lead to death, so that we may serve the living God! (Heb. 9:13-14). In fact, the Lord Himself is the one who cleanses: "The Lord will wash away the filth of the women of Zion; he will cleanse the bloodstains from Jerusalem by a spirit of judgment and a spirit of fire." (Isa. 4:4).

The Lord cleanses us from all the sin we have committed against Him (Ps. 51:2; Jer. 33:8; Ezek. 36:33). He cleanses us from all our impurities (Ezek. 24:13, 36:25) and from all our idols (Ezek. 36:25). A fountain will be opened to the house of David and the inhabitants of Jerusalem, to cleanse them from sin and impurity (Zech. 13:1). The Lord will cleanse them; and they will be His people, and He will be their God (Ezek. 37:23).

Not only people, but land will be cleansed (Ezek. 39:12, 14, 16). The altar will be cleansed as well (Ezek. 43:26).

Not only Christ cleanses those who have leprosy (Matt. 10:8), but the blood of Christ cleanses our consciences from acts that lead to death (Heb. 9:14). We shall have our hearts sprinkled to cleanse us from a guilty conscience (Heb. 10:22). Sometimes, evil will be cleansed away by blows and wounds (Prov. 20:30).

Reflection: As the author of the Hebrews asserts, the New Covenant with Jesus Christ as the mediator is superior to the Old Covenant with Moses as the mediator, His priesthood is greater than the Levitical priesthood, and His blood is more efficacious than the blood of goats and bulls in the Levitical sacrificial system. In the Old Covenant, priests of the Levitical priesthood offered repeated sacrifices for sins, including their own. In contrast, Christ, the High Priest in the New Covenant offered Himself as the perfect sacrifice, cleansed people's sins once for all, with His all-efficacious blood, and without Himself having any sin to be forgiven of (Heb. 7:26-28; 9:12). Although used by the Lord in the Old Covenant to atone for Israel's sin, to cleanse the Tabernacle, the Priests, the Israelites, and the land from the defilement by Israel's sin, the temple sacrifices served as symbols to symbolize Jesus' sacrifice on the cross. In the Old Covenant, bull's blood or goat's blood is used for the purpose of cleansing, to provide ritual purity to the physical flesh. It is the means of cleansing in the earthly tabernacle in the Old Covenant. It does type the blood of Christ in the New Covenant, the blood shed on the cross that has immeasurable power to resolve man's inner sin. In the New Covenant, only does the precious blood of Jesus Christ have the function of cleansing: "Heavenly things themselves have been purified with better sacrifices" (Heb. 9:23) that are the blood of Christ, because "the blood of Christ, who through the eternal Spirit offered himself unblemished to God, will cleanse our consciences from acts that lead to death, so that we may serve the living God!" (Heb. 9:14).

April 27

Purification (I)

The Lord said to Moses: "Take the Levites from among the other Israelites and make them ceremonially clean. To purify them, do this: Sprinkle the water of cleansing on them; then have them shave their whole bodies and wash their clothes, and so purify themselves." (Numbers 8:5-7)

Purification appears even in the first book of the Bible. Jacob instructed his household to abandon the foreign gods and purify themselves and change their clothes (Gen. 35:2). According to Mosaic Law, whoever touches the dead body of anyone must purify himself with the water on the third day and on the seventh day in order to be clean; otherwise, they will not be clean (Num. 19:12), and will defile the Lord's tabernacle (Num. 19:13). Whoever has killed anyone or touched anyone who was killed must purify himself and his captives on the third and seventh days (Num. 31:19). The man who is clean is to purify the man who is unclean (Num. 19:19). The man who is not unclean and fails to purify himself must be cut off from the community (Num. 19:20). Those who consecrate and purify themselves to go into the gardens, following the one in the midst of those who eat the flesh of pigs and rats and other abominable things will perish (Isa. 66:17).

To achieve ceremonial cleanness, Levites were purified by being sprinkled the water of cleansing, being shaved and washing their clothes (Num. 8:6-7). Levites were presented as a waving offering before the Lord and were made atonement for them to be purified (Num. 8:21). Levites were commanded to purify themselves and go and guard the gates of Jerusalem in order to keep the Sabbath day holy (Neh. 13:22). They will be purified and refined like gold and silver, then they will bring offerings in righteousness (Mala. 3:3).

Reflection: In biblical usage the term "purification" refers to a certain rite in the external worship of God. Purification, in its legal and technical sense, is applied to the ritual observances for the purpose of absolution from the ceremonial uncleanness. The rites of purification are indicated in the Law of Purity as part of the Priestly Code (Lev. 11–16). The purpose of purification is to remove ceremonial uncleanness of a person deemed by the Mosaic Law, and help him/her meet the requirements of holiness according to the Mosaic Law (Num. 8:5-7). The rites of purification are part of the Mosaic Law with emphasis on both the separation of the Israelites from pagans and the holiness of Yahweh. The origin of the rites may be traced back to the Patriarchs of Israel and be inherited from the common Semitic culture. Although other nations in the ancient Near East had the concept of uncleanness, Israel was the only nation that viewed uncleanness from the spiritual perspective, and their rites of purification involved not only ablution, but expiatory sacrifices and offerings. In other words, the distinctiveness of the Mosaic rites of purification is their expiatory character. The Mosaic rites of purification that deal with outward uncleanness are closely linked to forgiveness of sin which deals with the inward impurity. Moreover, the Mosaic rites of purification, as part of the Mosaic Law, have been observed by Israel as part of their obligation to the Old Covenant with Moses as the Mediator. And they are observed by the Levites as means to preserve the priestly purity. Jesus' mother, Mary performed the rite of purification in the temple of Jerusalem 40 days after giving birth to Christ in order to meet the requirements of the Mosaic Law regarding the purification of a woman from the ceremonial uncleanness incurred at childbirth. In other words, this ritual observance has received much deeper significance in the light of Mosaic Covenant. Furthermore, anyone who is not unclean and fails to purify himself must be cut off from the community (Num. 19:20). And exposure to contamination was presented by the prophets as a punishment of Yahweh for the people who broke the covenant (Amos 7.17; Hos. 9.3–4; Ez. 4.13–14).

April 28

Purification (II)

Sacrifice a bull each day as a sin offering to make atonement. Purify the altar by making atonement for it, and anoint it to consecrate it. (Exodus 29:36)

In the Old Testament, not only people need to be purified, but also anything which is used to serve the Lord. According to Mosaic Law, altar needs to be purified by making atonement for it, and to be anointed in order to be consecrated (Exod. 29:36). Blood of bull or of ram was used to purify the altar (Lev. 8:15; Ezek. 43:20) and made atonement for the altar (Ezek. 43:20-24).

According to Mosaic Law, a house with spreading mildew is supposed to be purified as well (Lev. 14:49, 52). Those who killed anyone or touched anyone who was killed must purify their garments as well (Num. 31:20). Whoever touches the dead body of anyone and fails to purify himself defiles the Lord's tabernacle, and must be cut off from Israel (Num. 19:13).

As King Hezekiah ordered, Levites purified the temple of the Lord, following the word of the Lord (2 Chron. 29:15). And priests purified the sanctuary of the Lord (2 Chron. 29:16). A young bull without defect was used to purify the sanctuary (Ezek. 45:18). To purify the land and the temple, King Josiah had the temple of the Lord repaired (2 Chron. 34:8).

As the Temple of the Lord, we, as God's people who are His own need to be purified for Himself (Tit. 2:14). Our lips must be purified ((Zeph. 3:9). Our hearts must be purified (James 4:8). We must purify ourselves from everything that contaminates body and spirit (2 Cor. 7:1), and from all unrighteousness (1 John 1:9).

Reflection: In the Old Covenant, purification means the outward cleanness, or ceremonial cleanness. As a sign of the covenant (Gen. 17:11), circumcision as Israel's obligation to the covenant, is an act of purification. According to Jewish thought, the foreskin was understood as a source of defilement; and the circumcision of the foreskin symbolizes the circumcision of hearts (Deut. 30:6; Jer. 4:4). And it secures the cleanliness of the whole body in a way that is suited to the people consecrated to God.

Nevertheless, in the New Covenant, circumcision is an unnecessary burden, because God purifies the hearts of both Jewish and Gentile believers through faith (Acts 15:9). In the Old Testament, not only people need to be purified, but also anything which is used to serve the Lord needs to be purified (Exod. 29:36). In the Old Covenant, Levites serve at a sanctuary that is a copy and shadow of what is in heaven. And the ceremonial cleanness is a copy of shadow of the spiritual cleanness in the New Creation. Nevertheless, purification of the sacred vessels in the tabernacle symbolizes purification of our lives in the spiritual sense. Even today, this principle is still valid. After we were born again, we are part of the New Creation; thus, purification to us means inward cleanness or spiritual cleanness. Not only do we need to be purified, but also anything which is used to serve the Lord need to be purified. We can say a consecration prayer and ask the Lord to purify everything which we use to serve Him. As the Temple of the Lord, we, as God's people who are His own need to be purified for Himself (Tit. 2:14). Our lips must be purified (Zeph. 3:9). Our hearts must be purified (James 4:8). We must purify ourselves from everything that contaminates body and spirit (2 Cor. 7:1), and from all unrighteousness (1 John 1:9).

April 29

Sanctification

May God himself, the God of peace, sanctify you through and through. May your whole spirit, soul and body be kept blameless at the coming of our Lord Jesus Christ. (1 Thessalonians 5:23)

Sanctification is the work of the triune God. God Himself is the one who sanctifies us (1 Thess. 5:23). We are sanctified by truth; and the word of God is truth (John 17:17). Christ sanctifies Himself so that His disciples may be truly sanctified (John 17:19). Sanctification is also the work of the Holy Spirit (2 Thess. 2:13; 1 Pet. 1:2). In a word, all Three Persons in the Godhead are involved in the sanctification of a believer.

Even election has been done through sanctifying work of the Spirit, as we are chosen to be saved through sanctifying work of the Spirit (2 Thess. 2:13; 1 Pet. 1:2). We are to be wholly sanctified – our whole spirit, soul, and body may be kept blameless at the coming of Our Lord Jesus Christ (1 Thess. 5:23). And we may become an offering acceptable to God, sanctified by the Holy Spirit (Rom. 15:16).

Sanctification is progressive, because God sanctifies us through and though (1 Thess. 5:23). Sanctification may make us go deeper and deeper in our spiritual life, as God sanctifies us through and through. Ultimately, we will be entirely sanctified, thus our whole spirit, soul, and body are kept blameless at the coming of our Lord Jesus Christ (1 Thess. 5:23).

Reflection: Today's theme scripture is a key Bible verse to substantiate Wesleyan doctrine of "Entire Sanctification", one of Wesleyan theological distinctives. Sanctification starts upon justification, and ends with glorification. It is a lifelong process, while transformation from human to divine nature takes place. Sanctification is progressive: "May God himself, the God of peace, sanctify you through and through." (1 Thess. 5:23a). Sanctification is also comprehensive, "May your whole spirit, soul and body be kept blameless at the coming of our Lord Jesus Christ." (1 Thess. 5:23b). In other words, sanctification is both progressive and comprehensive. And the end result of the progressive and comprehensive sanctification will be entire sanctification, in which our whole spirit, soul and body will be sanctified (1 Thess. 5:23b). God sanctifies us progressively and comprehensively until we are wholly sanctified. Also called the second work of grace, entire sanctification is a sanctification in which our sinful nature is cleansed away. It is an entire cleansing in the sense that no carnality, nor original sin remains to deprave our faculties, to incline us to acts of sin. According to the Wesleyan theology, entire sanctification may be received in this life, not as many assume that it can only be received at the time of death. Entire sanctification is not so early as justification, nor so late as death; a Christian can reach such a state of holiness that he or she ceases to sin in this life, as John Wesley maintains. Entire sanctification is provided for every Christian by the precious blood of our Lord Jesus Christ. It is by grace through faith and follows our willing, complete surrender to the Lordship of Jesus Christ. Entire sanctification is to offer our bodies as a living sacrifice, holy and pleasing to God (Rom. 12:1), to give our utmost for His highest.

April 30

Eternal life is the life of holiness

But now that you have been set free from sin and have become slaves to God, the benefit you reap leads to holiness, and the result is eternal life. For the wages of sin is death, but the gift of God is eternal life in Christ Jesus our Lord. (Romans 6:22-23)

As a matter of fact, eternal life is not physical immortality as many people understand, not an enjoyable life after death as Muslims understand, not a life that leaves a good name for generations as Confucianists understand, nor a life of nothingness as Buddhists understand. Indeed, eternal life is a life of eternity that God sets in the hearts of men

(Eccles. 3:11). And it is in the Son of God (Rom. 6:23) and is given to a Christian at the price of God's only begotten Son (John 3:16). We know also that the Son of God has come and has given us understanding, so that we may know him who is true. And we are in him who is true—even in his Son Jesus Christ. He is the true God and eternal life (1 John 5:20). Eternal life is to know Jesus Christ, Son of God (John 17:3). God has given us eternal life, and this life is in his Son. He who has the Son has life; he who does not have the Son of God does not have life (1 John 5:12). In other words, eternal life is the life of the Son of God.

Eternal life is not only the life of eternity that transcends time and space, but also the life of holiness (Rom. 6:22). It is not only an everlasting life, but also an abundant life, a life of fullness (John 10:10). It is not only of quantity, but of quality. To those who by persistence in doing good seek glory, honor and immortality, God will give eternal life (Rom. 2:7). And the result of holiness is eternal life (Rom. 6:22).

Reflection: Although sometimes translated as "holiness", sanctification is different than holiness. Sanctification is a process of transformation that our lives are transformed more and more like Christ. Holiness is the end result of this transformation process when we have attained Christlikeness. Sanctification is the sovereign act of God to set the elected apart from the world, and to Himself, and for His divine purpose. With the means of sanctification, God posits the elected into a proper relationship with Himself. As a matter of fact, holiness is our proper relationship with Jesus Christ in which we partake His divine nature, share in His life, and are imparted with His righteousness. Ultimately, Christlikeness, which manifests in the fruit of the Spirit, will be attained as the end result. And the result of holiness is eternal life (Rom. 6:22). "And this is the testimony: God has given us eternal life, and this life is in his Son. Whoever has the Son has life; whoever does not have the Son of God does not have life." (1 John 5:11-12). Eternal life is the life of the Son of God; and the life of the Son of God is the life of holiness (1 Cor. 1:30). Therefore, eternal life is life of holiness per se. Holiness is the quality of the eternal life, while everlastingness is the quantity of the eternal life. Quality determines quantity. Holiness is an attribute of God. When we are imparted holiness from God, our life is everlasting as Him. And we will participate in the glories of God forever (Rom. 5:2).

May 1

The Splendor of His Holiness

Ascribe to the LORD the glory due his name; worship the LORD in the splendor of his holiness. (Psalms 29:2)

Holiness is from God (2 Cor. 1:12). God shows the holiness of His great name (Ezek. 36:23); He shows His greatness and His holiness (Ezek. 38:23). He has sworn by His holiness (Ps. 89:35; Amos 4:2). He is majestic in holiness (Exod. 15:11), and holiness adorns His house (Ps. 93:5). The holiness of the Holy One of Jacob will be acknowledged (Isa. 29:23). The Holy One, Jesus Christ, is our righteousness, holiness and redemption (1 Cor. 1:30). Through the Spirit of holiness, He was declared with power to be the Son of God by His resurrection from the dead (Rom. 1:4). We praise God for the splendor of His holiness (2 Chron. 20:21), and we worship Him in the splendor of His holiness (1 Chron. 16:29; Ps. 29:2, 96:9).

Without holiness, no one will see the Lord (Heb. 12:14). We, believers of the Son of God, are created to be like God in true righteousness and holiness (Eph. 4:24). If we continue in faith, love and holiness with propriety (1 Tim. 2:15), we will live in all godliness and holiness (1 Tim. 2:2); and will be able to serve Him without fear in holiness and righteousness before Him all our days (Luke 1:74-75). If we do not uphold His holiness, we will break faith with the Lord (Deut. 32:50-51).

God disciplines us for our good so that we may share in His holiness (Heb. 12:10). We shall perfect holiness out of reverence of God by purifying ourselves from everything that contaminates body and spirit (2 Cor. 7:1). When we are set free from sin and have become slaves to God, the benefit we reap leads to holiness (Rom. 6:22), of which result is eternal life. Thus, we shall offer our body in slavery to righteousness leading to holiness (Rom. 6:19). If we seek glory, honor and immortality by persistence in doing good, God will give us eternal life (Rom. 2:7). And this is the Way of Holiness (Isa. 35:8).

Reflection: Holiness is one of God's most important attributes. Holiness is God's essence of who He is. Creation ascribes to God glory, honor, and majesty. And God sets Himself apart from all of the creation, because He is the Creator, and He is holy. He is holy because He is distinct from all the creation, sinless, and morally pure in every aspect of His nature and character. Redemption also ascribes to God glory, honor, and majesty, because "only redemption leads to holiness."; and "only holiness brings the assurance and enjoyment of redemption." (Andrew Murray, "Holy in Christ"). Our Redeemer,

Jesus Christ, Son of God is the splendor of God's holiness: "The Son is the radiance of God's glory and the exact representation of his being." (Heb. 1:3); "The Son is the image of the invisible God, the firstborn over all creation." (Col. 1:15). When we see the Son, we behold the splendor of God's holiness, because the infinite degree of God's holiness imparts to Him a beauty and magnificence beyond description. The Son of God, who is the beauty of all holiness and the splendor of His holiness deserves our due worship. We worship the Lord in the splendor of His holiness, because the Son cleansed our sins with His precious blood on the cross, and made us holy. Thus, we are imparted holiness from the Son of God. To us, God's adopted sons, holiness is a life free from sin, when we offer our body in slavery to righteousness. We shall perfect holiness out of reverence of God by purifying ourselves from everything that contaminates body and spirit (2 Cor. 7:1). When we are set free from sin and have become slaves to God, the benefit we reap leads to holiness (Rom. 6:22), of which result is eternal life.

May 2

Holiness

Ascribe to the LORD the glory due his name; bring an offering and come before him. Worship the LORD in the splendor of his holiness. (1 Chronicles 16:29)

The Lord is majestic in holiness, awesome in glory, working wonders (Exod. 15:11). Holiness adorns His house (Ps. 93:5). He has sworn by His holiness (Ps. 89:35; Amos 4:2). He will show the holiness of His great name (Ezek. 36:23); and He will show His greatness and His holiness (Ezek. 38:23). He enables us to serve Him without fear in holiness and righteousness before Him all our days (Luke 1:74-75). Jesus Christ our Lord was appointed the Son of God through the Spirit of holiness in power by His resurrection from the dead (Rom. 1:4). And He has become for us wisdom from God – that is, our righteousness, holiness and redemption (1 Cor. 1:30).

Although the holiness of the Lord was not upheld among the Israelites (Deut. 32:51), and the holiness of His great name had been profaned among the nations (Ezek. 36:23), the House of Jacob will acknowledge His holiness (Isa. 29:23). We will worship the Lord in the splendor of His holiness (1 Chron. 16:29; Ps. 29:2, 96:9).

Without holiness no one will see the Lord (Heb. 12:14), as we are created to be like God in true righteousness and holiness (Eph. 4:24). There will be a highway called the Way of Holiness, and it will be those who walk on that Way (Isa. 35:8). God disciplines us for our good, in order that we may share in His holiness (Heb. 12:10). We shall perfect holiness out of reverence for God (2 Cor. 7:1), live peaceful and quiet lives in all godliness and holiness (1 Tim. 2:2), continue in faith, love and holiness (1 Tim. 2:15). We must offer ourselves as slaves to righteousness leading to holiness (Rom. 6:19), and the result of holiness is eternal life (Rom. 6:22).

Reflection: God's righteousness is the natural expression of His holiness. His righteousness is in perfect agreement with His holy nature. We shall perfect holiness out of reverence for God, and offer ourselves as slaves to righteousness leading to holiness. Eternal life is virtually the life of holiness: "the result of holiness is eternal life" (Rom. 6:22). Righteousness is a gift from God through Jesus Christ who has made atonement for our sins on the cross, and it is imputed to us by His redemptive work; whereas holiness is what we ought to strive for and progressively imparted to us by the sanctification of the Holy Spirit. However, righteousness and holiness always go hand in hand. The glory of God is the brilliance of His holiness. His holiness sets Himself apart from the creation. As His chosen people, we won't be set apart until we behold the brilliance of His holiness. Moses, Isaiah, Ezekiel, and Paul were called to serve Him after they see the vision, encounter the presence of God, and behold His glory, the brilliance of His holiness. Moses encountered the presence of God in the burning bush (Exod. 3), and beheld the glory of God, the brilliance of His holiness; Isaiah encountered the presence of God by a burning coal – a physical embodiment of the holiness of God – which purified him, and beheld the glory of God, the brilliance of His holiness (Isa. 6); Ezekiel encountered the presence of God by the Kebar River, and beheld the glory of God, the brilliance of His holiness (Ezek. 1); Paul encountered the risen Lord on the road to Damascus, and beheld the glory of God, the brilliance of His holiness (Acts 9). All of them have been called to serve the Lord after they encountered the presence of God, and beheld the glory of God, the brilliance of His holiness. Have you ever had any experience to encounter the presence of God, and behold His glory? We have to be set apart for Him before we serve Him. However, without holiness no one will see the Lord. We must be set apart for holiness before encountering the presence of God.

May 3

The Bread of Life

Jesus said to them, "I tell you the truth, it is not Moses who has given you the bread from heaven, but it is my Father who gives you the true bread from heaven. For the bread of God is he who comes down from heaven and gives life to the world." (John 6:32-33)

What is the bread of life? The bread of life is the life-giving bread (John 6:33, 51), and this bread is actually the Son of God who comes down from heaven and gives life to the world (John 6:32-33). Jesus claims that He is the bread of life (John 6:35, 48).

The crowds were looking for Jesus as they ate the loaves and had themselves full (John 6:26). Actually, they looked bread from the earth, not the bread from heaven (John 6:32, 50). As their forefathers who ate the manna in the desert, yet died (John 6:49), they did not know what the true bread was and who gave them the true bread (John 6:32). The true bread has been given by the Father from heaven (John 6:32). Just like them, many of us work for the food that spoils, not the food that endures to eternal life (John 6:27).

This kind of food is only given by the Son of Man (John 6:27). He comes down from heaven and gives life to the world (John 6:33). He is the bread from heaven, which a man may eat and not die (John 6:50). He is the living bread that came down from heaven, which a man may eat and will live forever (John 6:51). And anyone who eats it will never go hungry nor thirsty (John 6:35). Because He Himself is the true God and eternal life (1 John 5:20), He is able to supply life to man (John 6:33). Anybody who believes in the bread of life will have everlasting life (John 6:47-48), because this Bread of Life Himself is eternal life (1 John 5:20). The bread of life is a life-giving bread (John 6:33).

Reflection: "I am the Bread of Life" is one of the seven "I am" statements Jesus made in the Gospel of John. And "the Bread of Life" is a name used by Christians to denote Jesus Christ figuratively. Just as bread is a staple food that we need for physical sustenance, the Bread of Life is the essential spiritual food that sustains our spiritual life, the spiritual food that brings eternal life. In the Scriptures, there are quite a few types that point to Christ. The manna which the Lord fed the Israelites when they were wandering in the desert types the Bread of Life, the Son of God. Jews in ancient time believed that the Messiah would miraculously bring manna when He came. Nevertheless, the physical manna was not of capable of satisfying the true hunger of soul. Only is the Bread of Life capable of nourishing of our spiritual life, because Christ is the Word of God who satisfies our spiritual hunger (Amos 8:11). In the Old Testament the bread of Presence placed on the table in the tabernacle provides a wonderful picture of Christ, the Bread of Life, who is holy before God, who provides true sustenance, and who is always present. The "unleavened bread" which plays an integral part of the Jewish Passover meal represents Christ who is sinless, morally pure, holy, and righteous. In other words, Christ is the "unleavened bread" in "the Feast of Unleavened Bread". The birthplace of Jesus, Bethlehem, which means "house of bread" implies that Jesus is the Bread of Life. The bread of life is the life-giving bread (John 6:33, 51), and this bread is actually the Son of God who comes down from heaven and gives life to the world (John 6:32-33). Jesus claims that He is the bread of life (John 6:35, 48). When we partake the Lord's Supper, we are partaking the Bread of Life ceremonially. At the Last Supper, Jesus Christ told His disciples to eat bread and drink wine as symbols of His body and blood. This New Testament Passover bread also reminds us of the close relationship Christians have with Jesus Christ, resulting in eternal life, life of holiness.

May 4

Wheat and Bread

And from the finest wheat flour make round loaves without yeast, thick loaves without yeast and with olive oil mixed in, and thin loaves without yeast and brushed with olive oil. (Exodus 29:2)

Jews were instructed by the Lord to make bread from the wheat (Exod. 29:2). And wheat is the principal ingredient of bread (Ezek. 4:9). In fact, wheat is one of the most important ingredients from which human's main food is made. Wheat is reproductive. However, it won't reproduce unless a kernel of wheat falls to the ground and dies; but if it dies, it produces many seeds (John 12:24). In other words, wheat is life-giving. Since bread is made from wheat, bread is also life-giving.

Just like a kernel of wheat, Jesus, God's only begotten Son (John 3:16) died; but many of God's sons have been born. Jesus is no longer God's only begotten Son, but the firstborn (Col. 1:15) among all of God's sons. As the Bread of Life (John 6:35, 48), Jesus gives life to the world (John 6:33); and He is the true bread the Father gives us from heaven (John 6:32). And He is the living bread that comes from heaven (John 6:51). This true and living bread is the food which endures to eternal life (John 6:27). The secret is that, Jesus, the Bread of Life, imparts His eternal life by dying for us (John 3:16, 12:23-24), just as a kernel of wheat does (John 12:24).

Whoever believes in Him, the Bread of Life, will not perish but has eternal life (John 3:16, 6:47). The bread is His flesh that whoever eats will live forever (John 6:51, 54). Without partaking of the life of the Son of Man, we will have no life in us (John 6:54).

Today, when we partake in the Lord's Supper, we shall remember that we are partaking of the life of the Bread of Life. The Bread of Life is broken for us so that He may supply life to us (1 Cor. 11:24). When Jesus died for us, He not only was glorified (John 12:23), but also was releasing His life (John 6:33, 51) so that whoever believes in Him may have eternal life (John 3:16, 6:47).

Reflection: As everybody knows, wheat is the principal ingredient of bread (Exod. 29:2). Bread is life-giving, because wheat is life-giving. And we all know that Jesus is the Bread of Life (John 6:35, 41, 48, 51). However, what are the main ingredients of the Bread of Life? The main ingredients of the Bread of Life are "the Way", "the Truth", "the Life", and "the Resurrection", as Jesus claims, "I am the way and the truth and the life. No one comes to the Father except through me." (John 14:6); and "I am the resurrection and the life. The one who believes in me will live, even though they die." (John 11:25). The ingredient of "the Way" in the Bread of Life leads us to come to the Father, enter the Holy of the Holies and approach His throne of grace; the ingredient of "the Truth" in the Bread of Life enables us to know God, and have knowledge of eternal life; the ingredient of "the Life", i.e. "the Eternal Life" in the Bread of Life helps us establish a vital relationship with God, and participate in the life of the Son of God; and the ingredient of "the Resurrection" in the Bread of Life triumphs over death, and imparts us with eternal life. These ingredients are life-giving, so the Bread of Life is life-giving. Jesus Christ, the Bread of Life, is life-giving bread. Just like a kernel of wheat, the main ingredient of the bread, produces many seeds when it falls to the ground and dies, the Son of God gives us life when He died on the cross. This exemplifies the great paradox of life and death. Death comes first, then does life. Death leads to life.

May 5

The Spirit and Life

The Spirit of God has made me; the breath of the Almighty gives me life. (Job 33:4)

The LORD God formed the man from the dust of the ground and breathed into his nostrils the breath of life, and the man became a living being (Gen. 2:7). The breath of life is the Spirit. The breath of the Almighty gives us life, and this is the way the Spirit of God has made us (Job 33:4). The Spirit gives life (John 6:63; 2 Cor. 3:6).

When man was made by God, God gave him His Spirit (Gen. 2:7). We were given life by God's Spirit (Job 33:4). When we were born again, the Spirit gave us life. "And if the Spirit of Him who raised Jesus from the dead is living in you, He who raised Christ from the dead will also give life to your mortal bodies through his Spirit, who lives in you." (Rom. 8:11). Jesus Christ, the last Adam, is a life-giving Spirit (1 Cor. 15:45). In other words, all of the three Persons of the triune God are involved in our new birth.

The words the Son has spoken to us are Spirit and they are life (John 6:63, KJV). Not only the Son and the Father are one (John 10:30), but the Son and the Spirit are one (John 6:63). And the Spirit gives Life (John 6:63), just as the Son give Life (John 10:28).

Through Christ Jesus the law of the Spirit of life has set us free from the law of sin and death (Rom. 8:2). And the mind controlled by the Spirit is life and peace (Rom. 8:6). He who sows to please the Spirit, from the Spirit will reap eternal life (Gal. 6:8). Since we live by the Spirit, let us keep in step with the Spirit (Gal. 5:25).

Reflection: There are many divine titles for the Holy Spirit in the Scriptures. Each of them has its own significance and reveals a certain aspect of the Holy Spirit. Among them, the divine title, "life-giving Spirit" reveals the aspect of the Holy Spirit for imparting life (Job 33:4). However, we may be wondering how the Spirit gives life. This divine mystery can be revealed in light of death and resurrection of Jesus Christ. Through death and resurrection, Jesus Christ passed through a process that transfigured Him from the flesh into the life-giving Spirit (1 Cor. 15:45), then He gave His disciples the Holy Spirit (John 20:22). A kernel of wheat gives life when it dies, just as Jesus Christ teaches His disciples, "I tell you the truth, unless a kernel of wheat falls to the ground and dies, it remains only a single seed. But if it dies, it produces many seeds." (John 12:24). In the same way, through His death and resurrection, Jesus Christ has imparted Himself as life into us so that we may be able to participate in His divine life. As a matter of fact, there is no life without Spirit. In the Spirit and through the Spirit, we have been born again. There is no doubt that the day of Pentecost was when Jesus' followers were born again, and when the church, the body of Christ itself was born. Without the Spirit, we would not have eternal life. Eternal life is the life of holiness, which is imparted by Jesus Christ, the life-giving Spirit.

May 6

The Most Holy Place (I)

And he measured the length of the inner sanctuary; it was twenty cubits, and its width was twenty cubits across the end of the outer main hall. He said to me, "This is the Most Holy Place." (Ezekiel 41:4)

In a tabernacle, the first room was called the Holy Place. Behind the curtain was a room called the Most Holy Place (Heb. 9:2-3). Both the outer sanctuary and the Most Holy Place had double doors (Ezek. 41:23), and had a rectangular doorframe (Ezek. 41:21). The inner doors to the Most Holy Place and the socket for the doors of the Most Holy

Place were gold (1 Kings 7:50; 2 Chron. 4:22). There was a curtain to separate the Holy Place and the Most Holy Place (Exod. 26:33; Lev. 16:2; Heb. 9:3).

The Most Holy Place was the inner sanctuary of the temple (1 Kings 6:16, 8:6; 2 Chron. 5:7). It was the innermost room (1 Kings 7:50). It was the sanctuary in the sacred district the Spirit of God showed Ezekiel (Ezek. 45:3). The Most Holy Place had a length corresponding to the width of the temple (2 Chron. 3:8). And interestingly, the three-dimensional structure of the Most Holy Place perfectly represented the heaven itself, God's eternal dwelling place (Ezek. 41:4). In the Most Holy Place, a pair of sculptured cherubim were made that were overlaid with gold (2 Chron. 3:10). The ark of the Lord's covenant as well as the atonement cover on it was placed in the Most Holy Place (Exod. 26:34; 2 Chron. 5:7), so were the golden altar of incense and the gold-covered ark of the covenant (Heb. 9:3-4).

Reflection: The tabernacle was an earthly dwelling place of the God of Israel. The Holy Place was part of the tabernacle tent, a room where priests conducted rituals to honor the God of Israel. Within the Holy Place of the tabernacle, there was an innermost chamber called the Most Holy Place, which was the Lord's special dwelling place in the midst of His people, with each dimension of a perfect cube in 15 feet. A veil, which was a thick curtain separated the Most Holy Place from the Holy Place, shielded the God of Israel from the sinful men. The veil served as a barrier between the sinful men and the holy God. It denied men's access to the awesome presence of the Lord due to their sinfulness. Only on the Day of Atonement, only could the high priest enter the Most Holy Place with some meticulous preparations: "But only the high priest entered the inner room, and that only once a year, and never without blood, which he offered for himself and for the sins the people had committed in ignorance." (Heb. 9:7). Nonetheless, upon Jesus' sacrificial death on the cross, the atonement for sin, the veil in the Jerusalem temple was torn in half, from the top to the bottom. From then on, God's awesome presence was accessible to those who have been redeemed by the precious blood of Jesus Christ: "We have confidence to enter the Most Holy Place by the blood of Jesus, by a new and living way opened for us through the curtain, that is, his body." (Heb. 10:19-20). That's why Jesus says He is the Way, the Truth, and the Life. He is the Way to the Most Holy Place. So, "Let us then approach the throne of grace with confidence, so that we may receive mercy and find grace to help us in our time of need." (Heb. 4:16). And interestingly, the three-dimensional structure of the Most Holy Place perfectly represented the heaven itself (Ezek. 41:4), God's eternal dwelling place; and the New Jerusalem was a perfect cube, just as the Most Holy Place was (Rev. 21:16).

May 7

The Most Holy Place (II)

He did not enter by means of the blood of goats and calves; but he entered the Most Holy Place once for all by his own blood, having obtained eternal redemption. (Hebrews 9:12)

Atonement was made for the Most Holy Place because of the uncleanness and rebellion of the Israelites (Lev. 16:16, 17, 20, 27, 33). The high priest carried the blood of animals into the Most Holy Place as a sin offering (Lev. 16:27; Heb. 13:11). No one was to be in the Tent of Meeting from the time the high priest went in to make atonement in the Most Holy Place until he came out (Lev. 16:17). "Only the high priest entered the inner room, and that only once a year, and never without blood, which he offered for himself and for the sins the people had committed in ignorance. The Holy Spirit was showing by this that the way into the Most Holy Place had not yet been disclosed as long as the first tabernacle was still standing." (Heb. 9:7-8).

When Jesus died on the cross, the curtain of the temple was torn in two from top to bottom (Matt. 27:51; Mark 15:38; Luke 23:45). Unlike those high priests in the Old Testament time who entered the Most Holy Place every year with blood that was not his own (Heb. 9:25), Jesus entered the Most Holy Place by His own blood, not by the blood of goats and calves (Heb. 9:12). Thus, we have confidence to enter the Most Holy Place by the blood of Jesus, by a new and living way opened for us through the curtain which was His body (Heb. 10:19-20). In fact, Jesus did not enter a man-made sanctuary that was only a copy of the true one; he entered heaven itself, now to appear for us in God's presence. He did not enter heaven to offer himself again and again, the way the high priest entered the Most Holy Place every year with blood that was not his own (Heb. 9:24-25). Because of what Jesus has done for us, we are able to cry for mercy, call to God for help, and lift up our hands toward His Most Holy Place (Ps. 28:2).

Reflection: The first covenant had regulations for worship and also an earthly sanctuary (Heb. 9:1). "But when Christ came as high priest of the good things that are now already here, he went through the greater and more perfect tabernacle that is not made with human hands, that is to say, is not a part of this creation." (Heb. 9:11). "For this reason Christ is the mediator of a new covenant." (Heb. 9:15). These verses imply that the first covenant, i.e. the old covenant is related to an earthy sanctuary which is a part of this creation, the old creation. Christ, who is the mediator of the new covenant, went through the greater and more perfect tabernacle that is not a part of this creation, but a part of the new creation. "He did not enter by means of the blood of goats and calves; but he entered the Most Holy Place once for all by his own blood, thus obtaining eternal redemption." (Heb. 9:12). "For Christ did not enter a sanctuary made with human hands that was only a copy of the true one; he entered heaven itself, now to appear for us in God's presence. (Heb. 9:24). These verses imply that Christ entered the Most Holy Place which is heaven itself. This Most Holy Place is a part of heavenly sanctuary, and a part of heaven itself.

MAY 8

THE THRONE OF GRACE

Let us then approach the throne of grace with confidence, so that we may receive mercy and find grace to help us in our time of need. (Hebrews 4:16)

Throne of grace, also called mercy seat or atonement cover is an important piece in the tabernacle. It was made of pure gold, with two and half cubits in length and a cubit and a half in width (Exod. 25:17, 37:6). It was made by craftsmen whom God had given skills (Exod. 31:6-8). It was placed on the ark of the Testimony in the Most Holy Place (Exod. 26:34, 35:12, 39:35, 40:20). Above the ark were the cherubim of the Glory, overshadowing the atonement cover (Heb. 9:5).

It was the place where the Lord was to meet Moses (Exod. 30:6). Moses heard the voice speaking to him from between the two cherubim above the atonement cover on the ark of the Testimony when he entered the Tent of Meeting to speak with the Lord (Num. 7:89). It was the place over where the Lord appeared in the cloud (Lev. 16:2). The smoke of incense would conceal the atonement cover above the Testimony so that the high priest would not die (Lev. 16:13). The blood of sacrifice was sprinkled on the front of the atonement cover seven times to make atonement for the Most Holy Place because of the uncleanness and rebellion of the Israelites, whatever their sins have been (Lev. 16:14-16).

God presented Christ as a sacrifice of atonement (Rom. 3:25). In other words, Christ is the mercy seat. Thus we can approach the throne of grace with confidence, so that we may receive mercy and find grace to help us in our time of need (Heb. 4:16).

Reflection: Throne of grace, also called mercy seat or atonement cover is an important piece in the tabernacle. As the utmost attributes of love, grace and mercy are two sides of a coin – and the coin is love. "Grace is the act of endowing unmerited favor, while mercy is the act of withholding deserved punishment. In His grace, God gives us the gift we do not deserve, namely heaven, while in His mercy, God does not give us punishment we deserve, namely hell" (Wilmington's Guide to the Bible). And we can discover the connection between the names, "throne of grace", "mercy seat" and "atonement cover", although there seems no connection between them in the literal sense. In fact, the Most Holy Place is not only the storeroom for God's presence, but the vehicle for atonement of sins on the Day of Atonement, when the High Priest enters it and sprinkles the blood of sacrificial animals on the "atonement cover". In other words, the "throne of grace", or the "mercy seat" shows its purpose of serving as the base of God's heavenly throne, whereas, the "atonement cover", as original Hebrew word suggests shows its purpose of serving as the vehicle for atonement. Only through the vehicle for atonement can we approach God's heavenly throne. God's love is manifested through Christ's atonement for sins. In the atonement of Christ, we can find grace and mercy from God. And the cross is where grace and mercy meet. God presented Christ as a sacrifice of atonement. Just because of Christ, a sacrifice of atonement, we can approach the throne of grace with confidence, so that we may receive mercy and find grace to help us in our time of need.

May 9

God is Love

God is love. (1 John 4:8,16)

Dear friends, let us love one another, for love comes from God. Everyone who loves has been born of God and knows God. Whoever does not love does not know God, because God is love. This is how God showed his love among us: He sent his one and only Son into the world that we might live through him. This is love: not that we loved God, but that he loved us and sent his Son as an atoning sacrifice for our sins. Dear friends, since God so loved us, we also ought to love one another. No one has ever seen God; but if we love one another, God lives in us and his love is made complete in us (1 John 4:7-12).

And so we know and rely on the love God has for us. God is love. Whoever lives in love lives in God, and God in them. This is how love is made complete among us so that we will have confidence on the day of judgment: In this world we are like Jesus. There is no fear in love. But perfect love drives out fear, because fear has to do with punishment. The one who fears is not made perfect in love. We love because he first loved us. Whoever claims to love God yet hates a brother or sister is a liar. For whoever does not love their brother and sister, whom they have seen, cannot love God, whom they have not seen. And he has given us this command: Anyone who loves God must also love their brother and sister (1 John 4:16-21).

Reflection: A hallmark is a guarantee of quality and purity. Moreover, a hallmark tells you where the product comes from, when it was made, and in some cases, what individual made it. As the disciples of Christ, our hallmark is a life that resembles His, a life of love. The hallmark that bears witness to the world that we are "in Christ" is our love for each other. Like the hallmark on a precious metal shows its genuineness and its origins, this hallmark indicates our genuineness and origins – we belong to Christ and we show that we love one another. This is Jesus' new command: "A new command I give you: Love one another. As I have loved you, so you must love one another. By this everyone will know that you are my disciples, if you love one another." (John 13:34-35). As we know, "love your neighbor as yourself" is one of the Old Testament commands, how come Jesus says "love one another" is a new command? In fact, the command is new, because Jesus commands His disciples to love one another in the way God loves us, in the way of "agape" love. Jesus says, "As I have loved you, so you must love one another.". To love one another with the "agape" love, the divine love that only belongs to God, is a new command. Moses promulgated the Ten Commandments. The Jews derived them to 613 commandments. Jesus sums up the Mosaic Law to two great commands, to love God and to love one another. The Apostle John combined the two great commands to one, which is to love God by loving our brothers and sisters. Therefore, if we don't love one another, we don't bear the hallmark of the "agape" love in our spiritual life. Whoever does not love does not know God, because God is love (1 John 4:8). If we love one another with the "agape" love, everyone will know that we are Christ's disciples.

MAY 10

GOD'S LOVE (I)

Give thanks to the LORD, for he is good. His love endures forever. (Psalm 136:1)

God is love (1 John 4:8, 16). He is the God of love (2 Cor. 13:11). Love comes from God (1 John 4:7). Our God is the compassionate and gracious God, slow to anger, abounding in love and faithfulness (Exod. 34:6; Neh. 9:17; Ps. 86:15; Joel 2:13; Jonah 4:2). God sends forth His love and His faithfulness (Ps. 57:3). He has not withheld His love (Ps. 66:20). He keeps his covenant of love (Neh. 9:32). He keeps his covenant of love to a thousand generations of those who love him and keep his commandments (Deut. 7:9, 12; Neh. 1:5; Dan. 9:4). He keeps his covenant of love with his servants who continue wholeheartedly in his way (1 Kings 8:23; 2 Chron. 6:14).

Although Israel doubts God's love (Mal. 1:2), God loves Israel (Deut. 23:5; Hos. 11:1). Because of His love, His eternal love for Israel, He made Solomon king to maintain justice and righteousness (1 Kings 10:9; 2 Chron. 9:8). He has remembered His love and His faithfulness to Israel (Ps. 98:3). God shows love to Judah (Hos. 1:7). He shows love to the one He called "Not my loved one" (Hos. 2:23). In His love, God will no longer rebuke us (Zeph. 3:17). God shows His love to thousands (Jer. 32:18). God demonstrates His own love for us in this: while we were still sinners, Christ died for us (Rom. 5:8). Because of His great love for us, God made us alive with Christ even when we were dead in transgression (Eph. 2:4-5). What great love the Father has lavished on us (1 John 3:1). This is how God showed His love among us: He sent His one and only Son into this world that we might live through Him (1 John 4:9). God's love endures forever (Ps. 136:1, 2, 3, 26).

Reflection: There are four types of love in Greek language: "storge" which is empathy bond; "philia" which is friend bond; "eros" which is romantic love; and "agape" which is God's unconditional love. All the human loves are conditional. No human love is unconditional. Only is God's love unconditional. God's unconditional love is one of His attributes. Grace and mercy are based on His love. God is love, and God is the God of covenant. God has entered the covenant of love with His children. "He is the faithful God, keeping his covenant of love to a thousand generations of those who love him and keep his commandments" (Deut. 7:9). God has not only taken the initiative to enter this covenant, but also has Himself bound by this covenant. And this is an everlasting covenant (Jer. 32:38, 40). He is the God of everlasting covenant, thus His love endures forever (Psalm 136:1, 2, 3, 26). His love is sacrificial love, everlasting love, unconditional love. It is a covenant love, "Agape". His covenant love is not based on our merits, but based on His grace. His covenant love is the love of grace. Although Israel has been unfaithful to God's covenant again and again, God has never changed. He has loved them with an everlasting love, and has drawn them with unfailing kindness (Jer. 31:3). God initiates His covenant with us for the purpose of bestowing us grace and blessings, because God is love.

May 11

God's love (II)

Woe to you Pharisees, because you give God a tenth of your mint, rue and all other kinds of garden herbs, but you neglect justice and the love of God. You should have practiced the latter without leaving the former undone. (Luke 11:42)

God loves those who love His Son (John 16:27). God so loved the world that He gave His one and only Son, that whoever believes in Him shall not parish but have eternal life (John 3:16). God demonstrates His own love for us in this: while we were still sinners,

Christ died for us (Rom. 5:8). Son of God loved me, and gave Himself for me (Gal. 2:20). When the kindness and love of God our Savior appeared, He saved us (Titus 3:4-5). This is love, not that we love God, but that He loved us and sent His son as an atoning sacrifice for our sins (1 John 4:10).

We shall rely on the love God has for us (1 John 4:16). Nothing can separate us from the love of God that is in Christ Jesus our Lord (Rom. 8:39). Those who cling to worthless idols turn away from God's love for them (Jon. 2:8). Pharisees neglected justice and the love of God (Luke 11:42). However, the righteous trust God's love forever and ever (Ps. 52:8). Solomon asked the Lord to remember the great love promised to David His servant (2 Chron. 6:42). David entreated God to have mercy on him according to His unfailing love (Ps. 51:1). Nehemiah asked the Lord to show mercy to him according to His great love (Neh. 13:22). How priceless is God's unfailing love (Ps. 36:7). Within His temple, we meditate on His unfailing love (Ps. 48:9). God's love has been poured into our hearts through the Holy Spirit (Rom. 5:5).

Reflection: God is love, and God loves. He loves sacrificially, unconditionally, and everlastingly. Nevertheless, He loves in justice, because He is the God of justice. Sometimes, God applies justice to us, but He applies justice out of love, because God is love. Love and justice go hand in hand in God. Love and justice constitute the message of cross. Pharisees did not know God, let alone the message of cross, so they neglected justice and the love of God, of course (Luke 11:42). In God, love and justice cannot be separated. In whatever He does, neither love nor justice is dispensable. Without either love or justice, the message of cross is incomplete. God loves, this statement sounds incredible to many non-believers, especially to some heathens. In many religions, their gods are the gods of punishment, and gods of tyranny. The gospel message that God so loved the world that He gave His one and only Son, that whoever believes in Him shall not perish but have eternal life (John 3:16) will melt people's hearts. To Christians, this gospel message has striking effect in our spiritual life. For Christians, knowing God is knowing His attributes, including experiencing His sacrificial, unconditional, and everlasting love. The more we experience His "agape" love, the closer we come to Him, as the Lord promises, "I have loved you with an everlasting love; I have drawn you with unfailing kindness." (Jer. 31:3)

May 12

Love and faithfulness (I)

The LORD, the LORD, the compassionate and gracious God, slow to anger, abounding in love and faithfulness. (Exodus 34:6)

The Lord proclaims, "The Lord, the Lord, the compassionate God, slow to anger, abounding in love and faithfulness (Exod. 34:6; Ps. 86:15). God sends forth His love and His faithfulness (Ps. 57:3), and appoints His love and His faithfulness to protect King David (Ps. 61:7). The Lord promises He will not take His love from him, nor will He ever betray His faithfulness (Ps. 89:33). He has remembered His love and His faithfulness to Israel (Ps. 98:3). The Lord is good and His love endures forever, His faithfulness continues through all generations (Ps. 100:5).

Love and faithfulness meet together (Ps. 85:10). Love and faithfulness go before the Lord (Ps. 89:14). Love and faithfulness keep a king safe (Prov. 20:28). In love a throne will be established; in faithfulness a man will sit on it (Isa. 16:5). Through love and faithfulness sin is atoned for (Prov. 16:6). Let love and faithfulness never leave us (Prov. 3:3), for great is His love toward us, and the faithfulness of the Lord endures forever (Ps. 117:2). Those who plan what is good find love and faithfulness (Prov. 14:22).

Reflection: Love and faithfulness are attributes of God, the God of covenant. God's love is the covenant love, the "faithful love" ("*hesed*" is the word in Hebrew). God has initiated a bond of covenant love with His covenant people, and He stays faithful to His covenant unconditionally. His love is the covenant love. His love is a steadfast love based on His covenant promise which He will never break. His faithfulness keeps Himself faithful to His covenant. This is why even Israel has broken His covenant many times, God has never violated His covenant. He has always kept His promises encompassed in His covenant. God's steadfast love and faithfulness form the basis for hope and confidence. As His covenant people, we can count on Him to fulfill His promises as He has done to Israel, who have failed to keep their promises many times. God is so good; and He is so kind, because of His love and faithfulness, Furthermore, God is so good that He shows His faithful love for his obedient covenant people by the blessings he confers upon them. We won't know God if we have not experienced His love and faithfulness. No wonder the Prophet Jeremiah sings, "Because of the Lord's great love we are not consumed, for his compassions never fail. They are new every morning; great is your faithfulness. I say to myself, 'The Lord is my portion; therefore, I will wait for him.'" (Lam. 3:22-24).

May 13

Love and faithfulness (II)

It is good to praise the Lord and make music to your name, O Most High, proclaiming your love in the morning and your faithfulness at night. (Psalms 92:1-2)

The psalmist asks the Lord, "Lord, where is your former great love, which in your faithfulness you swore to David?" (Ps. 89:49). The psalmist says to the Lord, "I have always been mindful of your unfailing love and have lived in reliance on your faithfulness." (Ps.26:3). The psalmist praises to the Lord, "Your love, Lord, reaches to the heavens, your faithfulness to the skies." (Ps. 36:5, 57:10, 108:4). The psalmist promises to the Lord, "I do not conceal your love and your faithfulness from the great assembly." (Ps. 40:10). "I will sing of the Lord's great love forever; with my mouth I will make your faithfulness known through all generations." (Ps. 89:1). "I will declare that your love stands firm forever, that you have established your faithfulness in heaven itself." (Ps. 89:2). "I will bow down toward your holy temple and will praise your name for your unfailing love and your faithfulness" (Ps. 138:2).

We shall proclaim His love in the morning and His faithfulness at night (Ps. 92:2), for great is His love toward us, and the faithfulness of the Lord endures forever (Ps. 117:2). Not to us, Lord, not to us but to your name be the glory, because of your love and faithfulness (Ps. 115:1).

Reflection: The psalmist says to the Lord, "I have always been mindful of your unfailing love and have lived in reliance on your faithfulness." (Ps.26:3). The psalmist has expressed what all of God's children have learned from their life experience. God's faithfulness is the only thing that we can live in reliance on. In this world, people think insurance policies give us peace of mind. However, your insurance provider may go bankrupt. In this world everything changes, except God's love and faithfulness. The psalmist knows God so well that he has written many psalms to praise His love and faithfulness. He has tasted and seen that the Lord is good (Ps. 34:8). Whenever we have experienced God's love and faithfulness, we will grow spiritually. We will eager to take refuge in Him, because we know that He will keep His promises written in the Scriptures. His steadfast love brings His promises to fruition, and His faithfulness is a result of His steadfast love. His love and faithfulness inspire our worship and praise, just as the psalmist sings, "It is good to praise the Lord and make music to your name, O Most High, proclaiming your love in the morning and your faithfulness at night." (Ps. 92:1-2). In fact, worship and praise we render to Him is merely the reaction to His love and faithfulness. Solomon has experienced God's love and faithfulness, and tasted and seen that God is so good. He teaches wisdom to his son, "Let love and faithfulness never leave you; bind them around your neck, write them on the tablet of your heart. Then you will win favor and a good name in the sight of God and man (Prov. 3:3-4).

MAY 14

RIGHTEOUSNESS AND FAITHFULNESS

Faithfulness springs forth from the earth, and righteousness looks down from heaven. (Psalms 85:11)

The Lord rewards everyone for their righteousness and faithfulness (1 Sam. 26:23). He will judge the world in righteousness and the people in His faithfulness (Ps. 96:13). Righteousness will be His belt and faithfulness the sash around His waist (Isa. 11:5). Oh, Lord, I do not hide your righteousness in my heart; I speak of your faithfulness and your saving help. I do not conceal your love and your faithfulness from the great assembly (Ps. 40:10), as love and faithfulness meet together; righteousness and peace kiss each other (Ps. 85:10). Righteousness and justice are the foundation of your throne; love and faithfulness go before you (Ps. 89:14). Lord, hear my prayer, listen to my cry for mercy; in your faithfulness and righteousness come to my relief (Ps. 143:1). In faithfulness a man will sit on a throne, and speed the cause of righteousness (Isa. 16:5). Faithfulness springs forth from the earth, and righteousness looks down from heaven (Ps. 85:11).

Reflection: Faithfulness springs forth from the earth, and righteousness looks down from heaven (Ps. 85:11). One meaning of "righteousness" in the Bible is moral uprightness. Perhaps a more basic meaning would be faithfulness. In Romans 3:1-8, the Apostle Paul discovers that God's righteousness is closely related to His faithfulness. As a matter of fact, God's righteousness is manifested in His covenantal faithfulness to His chosen people Israel. He is righteous because He is faithful to His covenant which He has enacted with His people Israel. He is righteous when He fulfills His promises encompassed in His covenant. His covenant with Israel is indeed a covenant of redemption. God has been faithful to His covenant with Abraham as well as with Moses. God has redeemed his chosen people Israel from Egypt with the covenant blood which was shed in the Passover. The Passover symbolizes redemption Jesus Christ has done to the church, the true descendants of Abraham to rescue them from sin and death that Egypt symbolizes. "The 'righteousness of God' is the divine covenant faithfulness, which is both a quality upon which God's people may rely and something visible in action in the great covenant-fulfilling actions of the death and resurrection of Jesus and the gift of the Spirit." (N. T. Wright). God's righteousness is not only the covenantal faithfulness, but the judging righteousness. Because God is the judge of all the earth, righteousness is very important for our relationship with Him. "God will bring into judgment both the righteous and the wicked, for there will be a time for every activity, a time to judge every deed." (Eccl. 3:17). In other words, the righteousness of God is displayed in the justice of His salvation.

May 15

Righteousness and faith

Abraham's faith was credited to him as righteousness. (Romans 4:9)

He received circumcision as a sign, a seal of the righteousness that he had by faith while he was still uncircumcised (Rom. 4:11). It was not through the law that Abraham and his offspring received the promise that he would be heir of the world, but through the righteousness that comes by faith (Rom. 4:13). Even gentiles, who did not pursue righteousness, have obtained a righteousness that is by faith (Rom. 9:30), as to the one who does not work but trust God who justifies the ungodly, their faith is credited as righteousness (Rom. 4:5). The person who does righteousness that is by the law will live by them (Rom. 10:5); but the righteous will live by faith, for in the gospel the righteousness of God is revealed – a righteousness that is by faith from first to last (Rom. 1:17). Apart from the law the righteousness of God has been made known, and this righteousness is given through faith in Jesus Christ to all who believe (Rom. 3:21-22). Through the Spirit we eagerly await by faith the righteousness for which we hope (Gal. 5:5), not a righteousness of my own that comes from the law, but that which is through faith in Christ – the righteousness that comes from God on the basis of faith (Phil. 3:9).

Reflection: Righteousness by faith is the most important and distinct doctrine of Christian faith. Unlike many other religions that advocate merit-based righteousness, Christianity's "righteousness by faith" doctrine is not only unique but revolutionary. The righteousness of God is a righteousness that comes from God. It is His covenantal faithfulness. The Scriptures prove that covenant is closely related to grace and faith. Grace and faith play key roles in obtaining righteousness. The righteousness of God is received as a gift, by faith: "For it is by grace you have been saved, through faith—and this is not from yourselves, it is the gift of God— not by works, so that no one can boast." (Eph. 2:8-9). Precisely speaking, this righteous is imputed righteousness: "Abraham's faith was credited to him as righteousness." (Rom. 4:9); "as to the one who does not work but trust God who justifies the ungodly, their faith is credited as righteousness."

(Rom. 4:5). Nevertheless, "faith is credited as righteousness" does not mean that faith is our righteousness. Instead, faith brings us in union with Christ, who is our righteousness. Because of the righteousness of Christ, and because of our union with Christ through faith, God counts the righteousness of Christ as ours. God has imputed His own righteousness to us on the basis of our faith that unites us with Christ. He puts His righteousness to our account, and reckons it as ours. God credits righteousness to us through our faith in Jesus Christ, and apart from our deeds and merits (Rom. 4:4-6). Through faith in Jesus Christ, we have received the righteousness of God, not a righteousness of my own that comes from the law, but that which is through faith in Christ – the righteousness that comes from God on the basis of faith (Phil. 3:9). Based on our faith in Jesus Christ, we are declared righteous and imputed with the righteousness of Christ, while our sins are imputed to Him. Imputed righteousness means that we are not becoming righteous, but being counted as righteous while we are still sinners.

MAY 16

RIGHTEOUSNESS AND JUSTICE (I)

Your righteousness is like the highest mountains, your justice like the great deep. (Psalm 36:6)

The Lord's justice will dwell in the desert, His righteousness live in the fertile field (Isa. 32:16). Righteousness and justice are the foundation of your throne (Ps. 89:14, 97:2). In His justice and great righteousness, He does not oppress (Job 37:23). Instead, the Lord works righteousness and justice for all the oppressed (Ps. 103:6). And the heavens proclaim His righteousness, for He is a God of justice (Ps. 50:6).

The Lord loves righteousness and justice (Ps. 33:5). The Lord will make justice the measuring line and righteousness the plumb line (Isa. 28:17). He exercises kindness, justice and righteousness on earth (Jer. 9:24). He puts on righteousness as His clothing; justice was His robe and His turban (Job 29:14). He will betroth the Israelites in righteousness and justice, in love and compassion (Hos. 2:19). Let justice roll on like a river, righteousness like a never-failing stream (Amos 5:24). Wisdom walks in the way of righteousness, along the paths of justice (Prov. 8:20).

Solomon prayed to the Lord, "Endow the king with your justice, O God, the royal son with your righteousness. May he judge your people in righteousness, your afflicted ones with justice" (Ps. 72:1-2). He has made him king to maintain justice and righteousness (1 Kings 10:9; 2 Chron. 9:8). The Lord says, "Maintain justice and do what is right, for my salvation is close at hand and my righteousness will soon be revealed (Isa. 56:1). My righteousness draws near speedily, my salvation is on the way, and my arm will bring justice to the nations (Isa. 51:5)."

Reflection: God's righteousness is virtually synonymous with His justice. The word just and the word righteous are identical in both the Old Testament and the New Testament. The most common Old Testament word for just means "straight," and the New Testament word means "equal," in a moral sense they both mean "right." "The Lord will make justice the measuring line and righteousness the plumb line" (Isa. 28:17). This verse implies that God sets the standard of righteousness. God's righteousness is closely connected to His holiness; and His justice is included in His righteousness. Not only does He set the standard of righteousness, but He Himself is righteousness. Yes, God is righteous, and He Himself is righteousness. He is the epitome of righteousness. The righteousness of God means that He is not only righteous in "doing", but righteous in "being". His nature and character are always righteous. Righteousness is one of His most important attributes. In His interaction with the creation, including humanity, His righteousness is manifested in His justice. Because of His righteousness, He rewards the upright; because of His righteousness, He cannot accept sin, and punishes those who sin. And because He is love, He applies justice out of love. He loves the world so much that He sacrifices His only begotten Son as the atonement of sin. The cross is epitome of His love and His justice. Love and justice, a pair of antitheses, have been reconciled on the cross by the precious blood of His Son. Both of His love and His justice have been satisfied on the cross.

May 17

Righteousness and Justice (II)

For to us a child is born, to us a son is given, and the government will be on his shoulders. And he will be called Wonderful Counselor, Mighty God, Everlasting Father, Prince of Peace. Of the greatness of his government and peace there will be no end. He will reign on David's throne and over his kingdom, establishing and upholding it with justice and righteousness from that time on and forever. The zeal of the LORD Almighty will accomplish this. (Isaiah 9:6-7)

Jerusalem once was full of justice; righteousness used to dwell in her – but now murderers (Isa. 1:21). And He looked for justice, but saw bloodshed; for righteousness, but heard cries of distress (Isa. 5:7). So justice is far from us, and righteousness does not reach us (Isa. 59:9). So justice is driven back, and righteousness stands at a distance (Isa.

59:14). There are those who turn justice into bitterness and cast righteousness to the ground (Amos 5:7). They have turned justice into poison and the fruit of righteousness into bitterness (Amos 6:12). Zion will be delivered with justice, her penitent ones with righteousness (Isa. 1:27). He will fill Zion with His justice and righteousness (Isa. 33:5).

Messiah will reign on David's throne and over his kingdom, establishing and upholding it with justice and righteousness (Isa. 9:7). In love a throne will be established; in faithfulness a man will sit on it – one from the house of David – one who in judging seeks justice and speeds the cause of righteousness (Isa. 16:5). With righteousness He will judge the needy, with justice He will give decisions for the poor of the earth (Isa. 11:4). See, a king will reign in righteousness and rulers will rule with justice (Isa. 32:1).

Reflection: Messiah will reign on David's throne and over his kingdom, establishing and upholding it with justice and righteousness (Isa. 9:7). He will fill Zion with His justice and righteousness (Isa. 33:5). Justice views conduct from the standpoint of man, whereas righteousness from the standpoint of God. No wonder the Scriptures say, "And Jesus grew in wisdom and stature, and in favor with God and man." (Luke 2:52). Jesus' growth process shows He is Messiah, as He establishes and upholds His kingdom with justice and righteousness. He is in favor of God for righteousness, and in favor of man for justice. When Christ returns to usher His millennial reign, He will land in Jerusalem: "On that day his feet will stand on the Mount of Olives, east of Jerusalem." (Zech. 14:4). He will establish His Kingdom in Jerusalem, the holy city, first. He will restore the nation of Israel. He will exercise His righteousness and justice on the throne of David: "The days are coming," declares the Lord, "when I will raise up for David a righteous Branch, a King who will reign wisely and do what is just and right in the land. In his days Judah will be saved and Israel will live in safety. This is the name by which he will be called: The Lord Our Righteous Savior." (Jer. 23:5-6). Starting with Jerusalem as where His throne is, He will expand His reign to the world. He will summon all the nations to come to Jerusalem, the learning center of the Law, to learn about His Law. And He will reward the saints on His judgment seat, and judge the world on the Great White Throne.

May 18

Faith and Promise

It was not through the law that Abraham and his offspring received the promise that he would be heir of the world, but through the righteousness that comes by faith. (Romans 4:13)

For if those who depend on the law are heirs, faith means nothing and the promise is worthless (Rom. 4:14). By faith Abraham, when God tested him, offered Isaac as a sacrifice. He who embraced the promises was about to sacrifice his one and only son (Heb. 11:17). By faith he made his home in the promised land like a stranger in a foreign country; he lived in tents, as did Isaac and Jacob, who were heirs with him of the same promise (Heb. 11:9). The promise comes by faith, so that it may be by grace and may be guaranteed to all Abraham's offspring – not only to those who are of the law but also to those who have the faith of Abraham (Rom. 4:16). He did not waver through unbelief regarding the promise of God, but was strengthened in his faith and gave glory to God (Rom. 4:20). God redeemed us in order that the blessing given to Abraham might come to the Gentiles through Christ Jesus, so that by faith we might receive the promise of the Spirit (Gal. 3:14).

Reflection: It was not through the law that Abraham and his offspring received the promise that he would be heir of the world, but through the righteousness that comes by faith (Rom. 4:13). This is grace: "The promise comes by faith.so that it may be by grace" (Rom. 4:16). The promise is the blessing that is entailed with the covenant that God has made with His people. As long as His people show obedience to the covenant, the blessing will be bestowed to them. In fact, their obedience is their faith that is able to withdraw the promise, for true faith is demonstrated in obedience. God's promise is the foundation of our faith. It is where our faith is anchored. The word of God is His promise, it is what we hope for. Faith is confidence in the word of God, in His promise. The word of God is His promise, it is what we do not see but faith is assurance about (Heb. 11:1). Our faith is not out of nothing, it is from God. Along with grace, faith is a gift from God (Eph. 2:8). Merits have no place in the promise of God. The promise of God comes by faith. On the other hand, the promise of God strengthens our faith. Therefore, the Scriptures say, "It was not through the law that Abraham and his offspring received the promise that he would be heir of the world, but through the righteousness that comes by faith." (Rom. 4:13). The heroes of faith in Hebrews 11, such as Abel, Enoch, Noah, Abraham, Moses, and many others, their faith was empowered and strengthened by the promises of God. "They were longing for a better country—a heavenly one. Therefore, God is not ashamed to be called their God, for he has prepared a city for them." (Heb. 11:16). Likewise, as we know God never lies, and will fulfill all of His promises in Jesus Christ, our faith anchored on the promises of God will be empowered and strengthened by His promises, so that we may be able to put faith in action by obedience. Furthermore, the call of God in our lives are always accompanied by many promises of God. We need strong faith to respond to the call of God. And that strong faith is solely anchored on the promise of God.

Pearls of Wisdom VOLUME 1

May 19

The Promise and the Covenant

Remember that at that time you were separate from Christ, excluded from citizenship in Israel and foreigners to the covenants of the promise, without hope and without God in the world. (Ephesians 2:12)

The sovereign Lord's covenant is trustworthy, and He has promised good things to His servants (2 Sam. 7:28). He found Abraham's heart faithful to Him, and He made a covenant with him to give his descendants the land of the Canaanites, Hittites, Amorites, Perizzites, Jebusites and Girgashites. He has kept His promise because He is righteous (Neh. 9:8). The covenants and the promises are of the people of Israel (Rom. 9:4). He made an everlasting covenant with them, His faithful love promised to David (Isa. 55:3). Because of the covenant He made with David, the Lord was not willing to destroy the house of David. He had promised to maintain a lamp for him and his descendants forever (2 Kings 8:19; 2 Chron. 21:7). He remembers His covenant forever, the promise He made, for a thousand generations (1 Chron. 16:15; Ps. 105:8).

Just as no one can set aside or add to a human covenant that has been duly established (Gal. 3:15), the law introduced 430 years later does not set aside the covenant previously established by God and thus do away with the promise (Gal. 3:17). The promises were spoken to Abraham and his seed, namely Christ (Gal. 3:16). In fact, the ministry Jesus received is as superior to the High Priests as the covenant He is mediator is superior to the old one, since the new covenant is established on better promises (Heb. 8:6). Christ is the mediator of the new covenant, that those who are called may receive the promised eternal inheritance (Heb. 9:15). He has died as a ransom to set them free from the sins committed under the first covenant (Heb. 9:15), who were separate from Christ, excluded from citizenship in Israel and foreigners to the covenant of the promise without hope and without God in the world (Eph. 2:12).

Reflection: The relationship between God and us is a covenant relationship. God's covenant consists of promises that God will fulfill on His side, and the law, the covenant stipulations that we must obey on our side. The divine covenants entail promises, stipulations, sanctions, and symbols, signs and seals. However, the central part of a divine covenant is a promise. All covenants in the Bible between God and man are originated by God and are an act of his grace. "God in his grace gave it (the inheritance) to Abraham through a promise" (Gal. 3:18). The covenant God made with Abraham is in nature a covenant of promise. In the Abrahamic covenant, God gives three promises to Abraham: (1) a promise to give him and his descendants the Promised Land; (2) a promise to bless him, and bless all the nations through him; (3) a promise to give him countless descendants. According to the order, the promises are for individual first, then for the nation, and finally for the world. Nevertheless, covenant of circumcision is set forth in the Abrahamic covenant as the stipulation. As long as Abraham and his descendants set themselves apart from all the other peoples by observing the covenant of circumcision, God will fulfill His promises entailed in the Abrahamic covenant. In fact, circumcision serves as the permanent sign of the Abrahamic covenant. In the Mosaic covenant, God promises to make Israel His treasured possession among all the nations, and a kingdom of priests and a holy nation. Ten commandments are set forth as the stipulation of the covenant. As long as Israel sets herself apart from all the other nations by observing the Mosaic Law, God will fulfill His promises encompassed in the Mosaic covenant. And Sabbath serves as the sign of the covenant. In His covenant with David, a covenant of kingdom, God promises that are entailed in both the Abrahamic and the Mosaic covenants are to be further fulfilled, and the promise of the Messiah comes on the scene. The throne serves as the sign of the covenant, which Jesus Christ, the Son of God, the Messiah whom the Jews have expected for centuries will ultimately sit on. God has initiatively made His covenants with Abraham, Moses and Israel, and David that encompass promises, in His grace. And He has made these covenants for the purpose of bestowing blessings to them.

May 20

The Promise and the Law

What I mean is this: The law, introduced 430 years later, does not set aside the covenant previously established by God and thus do away with the promise. (Galatians 3:17)

Although in the Old Testament, the Lord requires the Israelites to observe His law so that He will fulfill through them the promise He gave to David their father (1 Kings 6:12; 2 Chron. 6:16), it was not through the law that Abraham and his offspring received the promise that he would be heir of the world, but through the righteousness that comes by faith (Rom. 4:13). For if those who depend on the law are heirs, faith means nothing and the promise is worthless (Rom. 4:14). For if the inheritance depends on the law, then it no longer depends on the promise; but God in his grace gave it to Abraham through a promise (Gal. 3:18). Therefore, the promise comes by faith, so that it may be by grace and may be guaranteed to all Abraham's offspring—not only to those who are of the law but also to those who have the faith of Abraham. He is the father of us all (Rom. 4:16).

And the law does not set aside the covenant previously established by God and thus do away with the promise (Gal. 3:17). Why, then, was the law given at all? It was added because of transgressions until the Seed to whom the promise referred had come. The law was given through angels and entrusted to a mediator (Gal. 3:19). Is the law, therefore, opposed to the promises of God? Absolutely not! For if a law had been given that could impart life, then righteousness would certainly have come by the law (Gal. 3:21).

Reflection: The law does not set aside the covenant previously established by God and thus do away with the promise (Gal. 3:17). And the law is not opposed to the promise of God (Gal. 3:21). In fact, we receive the promise through the righteousness that comes by faith. The law was not designed to supplant grace but to show the need for grace. The Mosaic Law didn't change God's promises entailed in His covenant with Abraham. Israel's obligation to observe the Mosaic Law did not set aside the covenant God has made with Abraham 430 years ago, and did not do annul God's obligation to fulfill His promises entailed in His covenant with Abraham. On the other hand, if the inheritance depends on the law, then it no longer depends on the promise; but God in his grace gave it to Abraham through a promise (Gal. 3:18). The New Testament makes a clear distinction between the covenants of the Mosaic Law and the covenant of Promise. They are referred by the Apostle Paul as "two covenants", the former one as the covenant "from Mount Sinai", whereas the latter one as the covenant "from the Jerusalem above" (Gal. 4:24-26). The salve woman, Hagar gave birth to Ishmael in the ordinary way; in contrast, Isaac was born from Sarah, the free woman as the result of promise. The covenant of law defines a relationship between a master and the servant; whereas the covenant of promise defines the relationship between the father and the son. Like Isaac, we are no longer a slave, but God's child; and since we are His child, God has made us also an heir (Gal. 4:7). We are an heir to inherit the kingdom of God. We are born from above, from the Spirit, as the Scriptures say, "you are his sons, God sent the Spirit of his Son into our hearts, the Spirit who calls out, "Abba, Father." (Gal. 4:6); "For those who are led by the Spirit of God are the children of God. The Spirit you received does not make you slaves, so that you live in fear again; rather, the Spirit you received brought about your adoption to sonship. And by him we cry, 'Abba, Father.' The Spirit himself testifies with our spirit that we are God's children. Now if we are children, then we are heirs—heirs of God and co-heirs with Christ, if indeed we share in his sufferings in order that we may also share in his glory." (Rom. 8:14-17).

May 21

Law and Covenant

If you pay attention to these laws and are careful to follow them, then the Lord your God will keep his covenant of love with you, as he swore to your ancestors. (Deuteronomy 7:12)

(The Lord says to the Israelites) if you pay attention to these laws and are careful to follow them, then the Lord your God will keep his covenant of love with you, as he swore to your ancestors (Deut. 7:12). But if you will not listen to me and carry out all these commands, and if you reject my decrees and abhor my laws and fail to carry out all my commands and so violate my covenant, then I will do this to you; I will bring on you sudden terror, wasting diseases and fever that will destroy your sight and sap your strength. You will plant seed in vain, because your enemies will eat it (Lev. 26:14-16). The earth is defiled by its people; they have disobeyed the laws, violated the statues and broken the everlasting covenant (Isa. 24:5). They did not keep God's covenant and refused to live by His law (Ps. 78:10). The Lord will single them out from all the tribes of Israel for disaster, according to all the curses of the covenant written in this Book of Law (Deut. 29:21).

Moses gave command to the Levites who carried the ark of the covenant of the Lord, "Take the Book of the Law and place it beside the ark of the covenant of the Lord your God. There it will remain as a witness against you." (Deut. 31:26). Joshua made a covenant for the people, and there at Shechem he reaffirmed for them the decrees and laws (Josh. 24:25). The law does not set aside the covenant previously established by God and thus do away the promise (Gal. 3:17). Instead, God established a new covenant with His people, and put His law in their minds and write it on their hearts (Jer. 31:31-33; Heb. 8:10; 10:16).

Reflection: In the Biblical sense, a covenant implies much more than a contract or a simple agreement between two parties. However, there are some parallel points between a divine covenant and a human contract. Just as a contract entails terms and conditions, a conditional divine covenant entails the law for men to obey, in order to receive God's blessings. One of the major differences between a human contract and a divine covenant is: the terms and conditions are to protect both parties of the contract, whereas the law that is entailed by a divine covenant is to protect men from sinning and falling short of God's grace. As a matter of fact, contract is an interested-based agreement; whereas covenant is a grace-based agreement. In the contract, both parties try to set forth terms and conditions to protect themselves. Negotiation is often needed to reach an agreement. In contrast, in the covenant, God sets forth stipulation which is the law for the purpose to protect and to bless His chosen people. He invites them into a grace-based relationship with Himself. He enjoys this relationship, and lavish His amazing grace and abundant blessings upon them. There are two types of relationships in the world, interest-based one and grace-based one. Almost all the relationships in the world are interest-based, such as those between employers and employees, merchants and customers, landlords and tenants, etc. Only does parents-children relationship give us a glimpse of the grace-based relationship. The Lord makes covenant with His people, keeps His promises encompassed in the covenant, and bestows them His grace and blessings.

May 22

Law and Christ

For the law was given through Moses; grace and truth came through Jesus Christ. (John 1:17)

Thanks be to God, who delivers us through Jesus Christ our Lord! So then, we ourselves in our mind are a slave to God's law, but in our sinful nature a slave to the law of sin (Rom. 7:25). We who are trying to be justified by the law have been alienated from Christ; we have fallen away from grace (Gal. 5:4). However, we died to the law through the body of Christ (Rom. 7:4). Christ redeemed us from the curse of the law by becoming a curse for us (Gal. 3:13). And through Jesus Christ the law of the Spirit who gives life has set us free from the law of sin and death (Rom. 8:2).

The law is only a shadow of the good things that are coming (Heb. 10:1). Christ is the culmination of the law (Rom. 10:4). The law was our guardian until Christ came that we might be justified by faith (Gal. 3:24). We are not justified by the works of the law, but by faith in Christ (Gal. 2:15-17). If righteousness could be gained through the law, Christ died for nothing (Gal. 2:21). We do not have righteousness of our own that comes from the law, but that which is through faith in Christ – the righteousness that comes from God on the basis of faith (Phil. 3:9). We are not free from God's law but under Christ's law (1 Cor. 9:21). If we carry each other's burdens, we will fulfill the law of Christ (Gal. 6:2).

Reflection: In the Biblical era, there are two types of covenants, one is the promissory type (also called unconditional type), the other is obligatory type (also called conditional type). Promissory covenants were usually made between the suzerain and the vassal. Obligatory covenants were usually made between two parties with equal standing. In the Scriptures, the Noahic, the Abrahamic and Davidic Covenants are examples of the promissory covenants. In these covenants, the Lord has obligation to fulfill His promises encompassed in these covenants, and is willing to take upon the curse if He does not uphold His obligation. The Lord walked through the pieces of flesh when He made the covenant with Abraham. This incident signifies that the Abrahamic covenant is a promissory covenant. In the Scripture, the Mosaic Covenant is a major example of the obligatory (conditional) covenant. Although it is an administration of the unconditional Abrahamic covenant of grace, the Mosaic Covenant is a conditional covenant. It attaches the Mosaic Law as the stipulation of the covenant. The Mosaic Law sets boundaries for Israel to receive God's blessings promised in the covenant, including the Promised Land. The Mosaic Covenant is a conditional covenant made between God and the nation of Israel, which is centered around God's giving His divine law to Moses on Mount Sinai. Christ is the mediator of the new covenant which is superior to the old one (the Mosaic Covenant) of which Moses is the mediator. The new covenant is a better covenant because it is established on better promises. In fact, the new covenant is the covenant of promise under which we are justified by God's grace and mercy. The new covenant is the covenant of grace in essence.

May 23

Law and Sin (I)

They will pay for their sins because they rejected my laws and abhorred my decree. (Leviticus 26:43)

Jehu was not careful to keep the law of the Lord, the God of Israel, with all his heart. He did not turn away from the sins of Jeroboam, which he had caused Israel to commit (2 Kings 10:31). In fact, all Israel has transgressed His law and turned away, refusing to obey Him. The Lord warned them in order to turn them back to His law, but they became arrogant and disobeyed His commands. They sinned against His ordinances (Neh. 9:29). Therefore the curses and sworn judgments written in the Law of Moses, the servant of God, have poured out on them, because they have sinned against Him (Dan. 9:11). Just as it is written in the Law of Moses, disaster has come on them, yet they have not sought the favor of the Lord their God by turning away from their sins and giving attention to His truth (Dan. 9:13).

The Israelites will pay for their sins because they rejected the Lord's law and abhorred His decree (Lev. 26:43). Because they have burned incense and have sinned against the Lord and have not obeyed Him or followed His law or His decrees or His stipulations, disaster has come upon them (Jer. 44:23). They sinned against the Lord, and did not follow His ways nor obey His law (Isa. 42:24). They have sinned and done wrong. They have been wicked and have rebelled; they have turned away from His commands and laws (Dan. 9:5). For sins of Judah, the Lord will not relent, because they have rejected the law of the Lord and have not kept His decrees, because they have been led astray by false gods, the gods their ancestors followed (Amos 2:4). However, he who keeps His laws and follows His decrees will not die for his father's sin; he will surely live (Ezek. 18:17).

Reflection: Judaism regards the violation of any of the 613 commandments as a sin. Judaism uses the term "sin" to include violations of Jewish law that are not necessarily a lapse in morality. The doctrine of original sin is totally unacceptable to Jews. Jews believe that man enters the world free of sin, with a soul that is pure and innocent and untainted. A man sins because he is not a perfect being, and not, as Christianity teaches, because he is inherently sinful. The Old Testament substantiates that Jews sinned because they did not obey God's law (Neh. 9:29; Lev. 26:43; Jer. 44:23: Isa. 42:24: Dan. 9:5; Amos 2:4; Ezek. 18:17). The Mosaic sacrificial system deals with the sinful acts. Once every year, on the Day of Atonement, the high priest enters the Holy of Holies, prays for his Jewish brethren, and makes atonement for sins he and his Jewish brethren have committed with the blood of sacrifices. As the atonement made with the blood of sacrifices only deals with the sinful acts, not the sinful nature, it has to be made every year on the Day of Atonement, and therefore does not have eternal effectiveness. In contrast, the atonement made by Christ on the cross not only deals with our sinful acts, but cleanses our sinful nature. The atonement made with precious blood of the Son of the eternal God has eternal effectiveness for sin.

MAY 24

LAW AND SIN (II)

All who sin apart from the law will also perish apart from the law, and all who sin under the law will be judged by the law. (Romans 2:12)

All who sin apart from the law will also perish apart from the law, and all who sin under the law will be judged by the law (Rom. 2:12). No one will be declared righteous in God's sight by the works of the law; rather, through the law we become conscious of our sin (Rom. 3:20). To be sure, sin was in the world before the law was given, but sin is not charged against anyone's account where there is no law (Rom. 5:13). For when we were in the realm of the flesh, the sinful passions aroused by the law were at work in us, so that we bore fruit for death (Rom. 7:5). What shall we say, then? Is the law sinful? Certainly not! Nevertheless, I would not have known what sin was had it not been for the law. For I would not have known what coveting really was if the law had not said, "You shall not covet." (Rom. 7:7). But sin, seizing the opportunity afforded by the commandment, produced in me every kind of coveting. For apart from the law, sin was dead (Rom. 7:8). Once I was alive apart from the law; but when the commandment came, sin sprang to life and I died (Rom. 7:9).

Reflection: The Mosaic Law was enacted in order to put Israel within the boundary to receive the blessings from God promised in the covenants. As a matter of fact, law is not opposed to the promises of God. Before Jesus came when man was judged by faith, law had provided man supervision. Man was held prisoner by the law, locked up until faith should be revealed (Gal. 3:21-24). In other words, law had been given to prevent man from sinning before Jesus came. Unfortunately, sin abuses the law. It uses the law to put us to death. "Sin, seizing the opportunity afforded by the commandment, produced in me every kind of coveting. For apart from the law, sin was dead" (Rom. 7:8). "For sin, seizing the opportunity afforded by the commandment, deceived me, and through the commandment put me to death" (Rom. 7:11). This must be the "law of sin" (Rom. 7:23, 25) and "the law of sin and death" (Rom. 8:2). The law was powerless to overcome the sin because it was weakened by the flesh (Rom. 8:3). The law is not able to overpower sin. Conversely, sin avails itself of the loopholes of the law, and enslaves us in the sinful nature to the law of sin. The Pharisees diligently and meticulously observe the Mosaic Law as well as the commandments they added to the Law with the purpose of becoming holy. Unfortunately, they sin in doing so. For instance, they love to pray standing in the synagogue and on the street corners to be seen by others. By doing this, they commit the sin of hypocrisy (Matt. 6:5). When a Pharisee boasts how pious he is, he commits the sin of self-righteousness (Like 18:11-12).

May 25

Law and Sin (III)

Through Him everyone who believes is set free from every sin, a justification you were not able to obtain under the law of Moses. (Acts 13:39)

We know that the law is spiritual; but I am unspiritual, sold as a slave to sin (Rom. 7:14). I see another law at work in me, waging war against the law of my mind and making me a prisoner of the law of sin at work within me (Rom. 7:23). So then, I myself in my mind am a slave to God's law, but in my sinful nature a slave to the law of sin (Rom. 7:25).

Sin shall no longer be your master, because you are not under the law, but under grace (Rom. 6:14). The law was brought in so that the trespass might increase. But where sin increased, grace increased all the more (Rom. 5:20). However, shall we sin because we are not under the law but under grace? By no means! (Rom. 6:15).

The sting of death is sin, and the power of sin is the law (1 Cor. 15:56). For what the law was powerless to do because it was weakened by the flesh, God did by sending His own Son in the likeness of sinful flesh to be a sin offering. And He condemned sin in the flesh (Rom. 8:3). Through Him everyone who believes is set free from every sin, a justification you were not able to obtain under the law of Moses (Acts 13:39), because through Christ Jesus the law of the Spirit who gives life has set you free from the law of sin and death (Rom. 8:2). Everyone who sins breaks the law; in fact, sin is lawlessness (1 John 3:4).

Reflection: Through Christ Jesus the law of the Spirit sets us free. The law of the Spirit is the truth, because truth sets us free (John 8:32). Sin will no longer be our master, because we are not under the law, but under grace (Rom. 6:14). Christ has destroyed the power of sin with grace and truth, because He came from the Father, full of grace and truth (John 1:14). With grace, Christ imputes us righteousness; whereas with the truth (the law of Spirit that gives life) He imparts us righteousness. The law of the Spirit of life is indeed the Word of Life (John 5:24; 6:23, 28; Phil. 2:16; 1 John 1:1). The righteousness would certainly have come by the law that could impart life (Gal. 3:21). This law is the law of the Spirit, i.e. the Word of Life, which is the Truth. The law of the Spirit is the life-giving law. It sets us free from the law of sin. Our journey of salvation consists of three phases: justification, sanctification, and glorification. In the phase of justification, when we confess our sin, and accept Jesus Christ as our Lord and Savior, we are justified by faith in Christ. We are free from the penalty of sin. However, we are torn between the law of the Spirit and the law of sin as Paul does (Rom. 7:21-23). Sanctification is a process during which our condition is becoming like Christ. In this phase we are sanctified by the Spirit, and are free from the power of sin. In the final phase, glorification, our expectation is to be like Christ, and we are free from the presence of sin.

May 26

Wisdom and Understanding (I)

By wisdom the Lord laid the earth's foundations, by understanding He set the heavens in place. (Proverbs. 3:19)

God gave Solomon wisdom and very great insight, and a breadth of understanding as measureless as the sand on the seashore (1 Kings 4:29). His wisdom and understanding were shown to the nations (Deut. 4:6). But where can wisdom be found? Where does understanding dwell? (Job 28:12, 20) Is not wisdom found among the aged? Does not long life bring understanding? (Job 12:12) To God belong wisdom and power; counsel and understanding are His (Job 12:13), who gives the ibis wisdom or gives the rooster understanding (Job 38:36). The Lord gives wisdom; from his mouth come knowledge and understanding (Prov. 2:6). A shoot will come up from the stump of Jesse; from his root a branch will bear fruit. The Spirit of the Lord will rest on Him – the Spirit of wisdom and of understanding, the Spirit of counsel and of might, the Spirit of the knowledge and of the Lord (Isa. 11:1-2). Men are filled with the Spirit of God, with wisdom, with understanding (Exod. 31:3; 35:31; 1 Kings 7:14).

By wisdom the Lord laid the earth's foundations, by understanding He set the heavens in place (Prov. 3:19). God made the earth by His power; He found the world by His wisdom and stretched out the heavens by His understanding (Jer. 10:12; 51:15). By wisdom a house is built, and through understanding it is established (Prov. 24:3). By the strength of His hand He has done this, and by His wisdom, because He has understanding (Isa. 10:13). With all wisdom and understanding, He made known to us the mystery of His will according to His good pleasure, which He purposed in Christ (Eph. 1:8-9).

Reflection: We all know that God created the heavens and the earth. However, have you ever wondered about how God created the heavens and the earth? Actually, the Scriptures give us explicit answer: By wisdom the Lord laid the earth's foundations, by understanding He set the heavens in place (Prov. 3:19). God made the earth by His power; He found the world by His wisdom and stretched out the heavens by His understanding (Jer. 10:12; 51:15). These scriptures are the Biblical grounds for the theory of "Intelligent Design", which argues that the design of the living system as well as the nonliving elements of the universe suggests a Designer. It is a form of creationism which claims God as the sole creator of the universe, who created all things out of nothing, by an act of free will. In the Scriptures, the Wisdom of God plays a key role in creation. Wisdom is essential in the act of creation into which very fabric wisdom is woven. God created the world by His decree, and creation is designed to follow His will. Wisdom is the embodiment of the will of God that ensures creation is perfectly aligned with the will of God. Proverbs 8:22-26 hints that wisdom is the Word of God, who was appointed from eternity, from the beginning, before the world began (Prov. 8:22-26). This passage reminds us of John 1:1-3. As a matter of fact, Christ is the power of God and the wisdom of God (1 Cor. 1:24).

May 27

Wisdom and Understanding (II)

The fear of the Lord is the beginning of wisdom, and knowledge of the Holy One is understanding. (Proverbs 9:10)

The fear of the Lord is the beginning of wisdom; all who follow His precepts have good understanding. To Him belongs eternal praise (Ps. 111:10). And He said to the human race, "The fear of the Lord – that is wisdom, and to shun evil is understanding" (Job 28:28).

Does not wisdom call out? Does not understanding raise her voice? (Prov. 8:1). My mouth will speak words of wisdom; the meditation of my heart will give you understanding (Ps. 49:3). Get wisdom, get understanding; do not forget my words or turn away from them (Prov. 4:5). The beginning of wisdom is this: Get wisdom. Though it cost all you have, get understanding (Prov. 4:7). Do not let wisdom and understanding out of your sight (Prov. 3:21). If you accept my words and store up my commands within you, turning your ear to wisdom and applying your heart to understanding— indeed, if you call out for insight and cry aloud for understanding, and if you look for it as for silver and search for it as for hidden treasure, then you will understand the fear of the Lord and find the knowledge of God. For the Lord gives wisdom; from his mouth come knowledge and understanding (Prov. 2:1-6). We continually ask God to fill you with the knowledge of His will through all the wisdom and understanding the Spirit gives (Col. 1:9). A fool finds pleasure in wicked schemes, but a person of understanding delights in wisdom (Prov. 10:23). The one who gets wisdom loves life; the one who cherishes understanding will soon prosper (Prov. 19:8). Blessed are those who find wisdom, those who gain understanding (Prov. 3:13).

Reflection: Given the difference in their understanding of wisdom and knowledge, Greeks and Hebrews pursue wisdom and knowledge in completely different ways. For Greeks, knowledge is the avenue to virtue, and the "chief good". For Hebrews, wisdom and knowledge go hand in hand. They all come from God. In contrast to the Greek concept of wisdom which focuses mainly on the intellect and the acquisition of knowledge, the Hebrew concept of wisdom goes beyond intellectual pursuit to the practical, hands-on ability to live one's daily life successfully, applying knowledge in concrete ways. In other words, unlike Greek people, Hebrew people understand wisdom as an action, rather than abstract concepts. True wisdom starts from the fear of God, and the highest wisdom is to obey God in all things. "The fear of the Lord is the beginning of wisdom; all who follow His precepts have good understanding." (Ps. 111:10). True wisdom starts with action: fear the Lord and follow His precepts. And true wisdom is godly wisdom, which comes from heaven, and it is about morality rather than intellectuality (James 3:17). The fear of the Lord is the beginning of the true wisdom, the wisdom from the above. There are two kinds of wisdom that are distinguished in the Scriptures (1 Cor. 1-2; Jam. 3): the worldly wisdom or the wisdom from the below, and the divine wisdom or the wisdom from the above. The worldly wisdom is earthly, unspiritual, demonic (Jam. 3:15), characterized by envy and selfish ambition (Jam. 3:16); in contrast, the divine wisdom is first of all pure; then peace-loving, considerate, submissive, full of mercy and good fruit, impartial and sincere (Jam. 3:17). These two kinds of wisdom constitute spiritual paradox. With divine wisdom, God has paradoxically chosen those who were not wise by human standards, and put the wisdom of the wise to shame. The cross destroys the wisdom of the wise, and frustrates the intelligence of the intelligent (1 Cor. 1:19). Christ Crucified is God's power and wisdom. Christ is the personification of God's wisdom, a mystery that has been hidden and that God destined for our glory before time began (1 Cor. 2:7).

May 28

For the Lord's Name's sake

You will know that I am the LORD, when I deal with you for my name's sake and not according to your evil ways and your corrupt practices, you people of Israel, declares the Sovereign LORD. (Ezekiel 20:44)

For my own name's sake I delay my wrath; for the sake of my praise I hold it back from you, so as not to destroy you completely. See, I have refined you, though not as silver; I have tested you in the furnace of affliction. For my own sake, for my own sake, I do this. How can I let myself be defamed? I will not yield my glory to another (Isa. 48:9-11).

(David prays to the Lord:) The LORD is my shepherd, I lack nothing. He makes me lie down in green pastures, he leads me beside quiet waters, he refreshes my soul. He guides me along the right paths for his name's sake (Ps. 23:1-3). When our ancestors were in Egypt, they gave no thought to your miracles; they did not remember your many kindnesses, and they rebelled by the sea, the Red Sea. Yet he saved them for his name's sake, to make his mighty power known (Ps. 106:7-8). Sovereign LORD, help me for your name's sake; out of the goodness of your love, deliver me (Ps. 109:21). For your name's sake, LORD, preserve my life; in your righteousness, bring me out of trouble (Ps. 143:11). Help us, God our Savior, for the glory of your name; deliver us and forgive our sins for your name's sake (Ps. 79:9).

Reflection: The Lord does what He does for His name's sake, not ours. He guides us for His name's sake, forgives our sins for His name's sake, leads us for His name's sake, delivers us from sin for His name's sake, deals with us out of His goodness for His name's sake, and lets us live for His name's sake. More than a dozen times the phrase "for my name's sake" appears in the Bible. The Lord's name extols His character. His holy name is closely linked to His integrity, His reputation, His holiness, and even His glory, honor, and power. Yes, the Lord's great name is linked to His glory, honor, and power. The Lord deserves all glory, honor and power. And He does everything for His own glory, and for His name's sake. Some may think that the Lord is too proud and self-centered. As a matter of fact, no glory is too much for the Lord; no honor is too much for Him; and no power is too much for Him. He just deserves all glory, honor and power. And often the Lord acts to sanctify His name and prevent it from being profaned. In short, the Lord does everything for His name's sake, because He deserves the glory due His name. And we shall ascribe to the LORD the glory due His name; worship the LORD in the splendor of His holiness (Ps. 29:2).

May 29

Seek the Lord

But if from there you seek the Lord your God, you will find Him if you seek Him with all your heart and with all your soul. (Deuteronomy 4:29)

He commanded Judah to seek the Lord, the God of their ancestors, and to obey His laws and commands (2 Chron. 14:4). They entered into a covenant to seek the Lord, the God of their ancestors, with all their heart and soul (2 Chron. 15:12). So the Israelites who had returned from the exile ate it, together with all who had separated themselves from the unclean practices of their Gentile neighbors in order to seek the Lord, God of Israel (Ezra 6:21). All who would not seek the Lord, the God of Israel, were to be put to death, whether small or great, man or woman (2 Chron. 15:13). When they go with their flocks and herds to seek the Lord, they will not find Him; He has withdrawn Himself from them (Hosea 5:6). But if from there you seek the Lord your God, you will find Him if you seek Him with all your heart and with all your soul (Deut. 4:29). Afterward the Israelites will return and seek the Lord their God and David their king (Hos. 55:6). "In those days, at that time," declares the Lord, "the people of Israel and the people of Judah together will go in tears to seek the Lord their God" (Jer. 50:4).

The poor will eat and be satisfied; those who seek the Lord will praise Him – may your hearts live forever! (Ps. 22:26). Glory in His holy name; let the hearts of those who seek the Lord rejoice (1 Chron. 16:10; Ps. 105:3). The lions may grow weak and hungry, but those who seek the Lord lack no good thing (Ps. 34:10). Seek the Lord while He may be found, call on Him while He is near (Isa. 55:6), for it is time to seek the Lord, until He comes and showers His righteousness on you (Hos. 10:12). Evildoers do not understand what is right, but those who seek the Lord understand it fully (Prov. 28:5). Seek the Lord and live (Amos 5:6). Seek the Lord, all you humble of the land, you who do what He commands (Zeph. 2:3). And the inhabitants of one city will go to another and say, "Let us go at once to entreat the Lord and seek the Lord Almighty." (Zech. 8:21). And many peoples and powerful nations will come to Jerusalem to seek the Lord Almighty and to entreat Him (Zech. 8:22). The rest of mankind may seek the Lord, even Gentiles who bear my name, says the Lord (Acts 15:17).

Reflection: When we seek the Lord, we will find Him if we seek Him with all our heart and with all our soul (Deut. 4:29). This echoes to the first and the greatest commandments: "Love the Lord your God with all your heart and with all your soul and with all your mind." (Matt. 22:37-38). Seeking the Lord means seeking his presence. We need to love God's close presence as our refuge, glory, and strength. We need to direct our heart to love God's glory. Seeking the Lord is setting of the mind and heart on Him. It is the conscious fixing or focusing of our mind's attention and our heart's affection on God. In other words, seeking the Lord is seeking Him with an ardent love (Matt. 22:37-38). With daily devotion including prayers and Bible reading, we can approach God's presence step by step. We can come to the Outer Court by asking, the Inner Court by seeking, and the Holy of Holies by knocking (Matt. 7:7-11; Luke 11:5-13). Nevertheless, in order to come to His close presence, we must seek His face (2 Chron. 7:14). Prayer doesn't necessarily lead us to seek His face, because it may merely seek His help. Seeking His face is beyond that. Seeking His face is devotion that reach higher level, and bring us to deeper relationship with God. It is a spiritual exercise that we humble ourselves before man, submit ourselves to the Lord, examine our relationship with the Lord, and deepen it. It is a spiritual exercise that we confess our sins in front of the Lord, and reconcile with our brethren who hurt us. It is a spiritual exercise that we are willing to pay any prices in order to enter the presence of God, by fasting, diligent devotion. It is a spiritual exercise that we wait upon the Lord, until He gives us assurance, and fulfills His promises. Only by doing so, can we enter the glorious and intimate presence of God.

May 30

Serve the Lord (I)

And now, Israel, what does the LORD your God ask of you but to fear the LORD your God, to walk in obedience to him, to love him, to serve the LORD your God with all your heart and with all your soul, and to observe the LORD's commands and decrees that I am giving you today for your own good? (Deuteronomy 10:12-13)

(Moses pronounced curse against Israel:) Because you did not serve the LORD your God joyfully and gladly in the time of prosperity, therefore in hunger and thirst, in nakedness and dire poverty, you will serve the enemies the LORD sends against you. He will put an iron yoke on your neck until he has destroyed you (Deut. 28:47-48).

(However, in the Book of Jeremiah:) "'In that day,' declares the LORD Almighty, I will break the yoke off their necks and will tear off their bonds; no longer will foreigners enslave them. Instead, they will serve the LORD their God and David their king, whom I will raise up for them (Jer. 30:8-9).

Do not turn away from the LORD, but serve the LORD with all your heart (1 Sam. 12:20). Serve the LORD your God, so that his fierce anger will turn away from you (2 Chron. 30:8).

Reflection: Moses exhorts Israel: "And now, Israel, what does the LORD your God ask of you but to fear the LORD your God, to walk in obedience to him, to love him, to serve the LORD your God with all your heart and with all your soul, and to observe the LORD's commands and decrees that I am giving you today for your own good?" (Deut. 10:12-13). To serve the Lord our God with all our heart and with all our soul means that we must be in union with the Lord before we serve Him. We must be in union with Him in legal, as His servants; in life, as His children; and in love, as His bride (Spurgeon). Without being in union with Him in life and in love, we cannot serve Him with all our heart and with all our soul. On the other hand, we will be His slaves, not His children (Rom. 8:14-15). Without being in union with Him in life and in love, a pastor will be a hired hand, not a shepherd (John 10:12).

May 31

Serve the Lord (II)

But as for me and my household, we will serve the LORD. (Joshua 24:15)

(Joshua said to all the people:) "Now fear the LORD and serve him with all faithfulness. Throw away the gods your ancestors worshiped beyond the Euphrates River and in Egypt, and serve the LORD. But if serving the LORD seems undesirable to you, then choose for yourselves this day whom you will serve, whether the gods your ancestors served beyond the Euphrates, or the gods of the Amorites, in whose land you are living. But as for me and my household, we will serve the LORD" (Josh 24:14-15).

Joshua said to the people, "You are not able to serve the LORD. He is a holy God; he is a jealous God. He will not forgive your rebellion and your sins (Josh. 24:19). If you forsake the LORD and serve foreign gods, he will turn and bring disaster on you and make an end of you, after he has been good to you." But the people said to Joshua, "No! We will serve the LORD." Then Joshua said, "You are witnesses against yourselves that you have chosen to serve the LORD." "Yes, we are witnesses," they replied (Josh. 24:19-22). And the people said to Joshua, "We will serve the LORD our God and obey him." (Josh. 24:24).

Now serve the LORD your God and his people Israel (2 Chron. 35:3). Serve the LORD with fear and celebrate his rule with trembling (Ps. 2:11). We too will serve the LORD, because he is our God (Josh. 24:18).

Reflection: Joshua dedicates himself and his household to serving the Lord. This is one of important reasons that he is able to lead Israel. Without being a God-pleased head of his household, he won't be able to become a God-pleased leader of Israel. Moreover, Joshua warns against idolatry. In the whole history of Israel's spiritual journey, idolatry is the most important issue Israel has dealt with. History repeats himself. As Christians in the New Testament era, idolatry is the most important issue in our spiritual journey. "For everything in the world—the lust of the flesh, the lust of the eyes, and the pride of life—comes not from the Father but from the world" (1 John 2:16). In the final analysis, all these sins are idolatry. The lust of the flesh is idolatry of mammon, the lust of eyes is the idolatry of sex, and the pride of life is idolatry of success. Without dealing with idolatry, we won't be able to serve the Lord faithfully, because, we may even put our ministry and success in the ministry above the Lord Himself, thus may be committed to idolatry, ironically.

JUNE 1

THE ARK OF THE COVENANT AND THE MIRACLES

The flow of the Jordan was cut off before the ark of the covenant of the Lord. When it crossed the Jordan, the waters of the Jordan were cut off. (Joshua 4:7)

The ark of the covenant of the Lord led Israelites and found them place to rest (Num. 10:33). The ark of the covenant of the Lord guided the Israelites, who however had to keep a distance with it (Josh. 3:2-4). The ark of the covenant of the Lord went into the Jordan ahead of them (Josh. 3:11, 14). The flow of the Jordan was cut off before the ark of the covenant of the Lord. When the ark of the covenant crossed the Jordan, the waters of the Jordan were cut off (Josh. 4:7; also see Josh. 3:13). The priests who carried the ark of the covenant stood firm on dry ground in the middle of the Jordan, while all Israelites passed by until the whole nation had completed the crossing on dry ground (Josh. 3:17). And under Joshua's command, the priests came up out of the river carrying the ark of the covenant, and the waters of the Jordan came back to their place and ran at flood stage as before as soon as the priests had set their feet on the dry ground (Josh. 4:16, 18). Twelve stones were set up in the middle of the Jordan at the spot where the priests who carried the ark of the covenant had stood, as a memorial to the people of Israel forever (Josh. 4:5, 7, 9).

Under Joshua's command, the Israelites marched around the city of Jericho, with the armed guard going ahead of the ark of the Lord (Josh. 6:7). They carried the ark of the Lord around the city, circling it once every day for six consecutive days (Josh. 6:11-14), and circling it seven times on the seventh day (Josh. 6:15).

Reflection: In the Old Testament, God was manifested in the Ark of the Covenant. The Ark of the Covenant was the manifestation of God's physical presence on earth (the *shekhina*). God performed the miracles of crossing the Jordan and conquering Jericho. How did the ark of the covenant lead the Israelites to enter Canaan? The ark of the covenant went to Jordan ahead of them, and the ark of the covenant came out of the water after the whole nation completed the crossing on the dry ground. The ark of the covenant types Christ. Jordan symbolizes death and hell. Crossing Jordan signifies our baptism, by which we die with Christ, and resurrect with Christ. When we experience the presence of God, experience the resurrection power of Jesus Christ, miracles will happen to us. These miracles don't have to be in the physical sphere, and they are often in the spiritual realm. When we experience the presence of God and the resurrection power of Jesus Christ, our lives will be transformed. And we will win a victory over the power of sin.

Just as in the battle of Jericho, the ark of the Lord guarantees the victory, in our spiritual warfare, Christ will guarantee us victory as long as we experience His presence and resurrection power. With the presence of God and the resurrection power of Jesus Christ, we will prevail over the power of sin.

June 2

The Ark of the Covenant and the Levites

At that time the Lord set apart the tribe of Levites to carry the ark of the covenant of the Lord. (Deuteronomy 10:8)

The tribe of Levi was set apart to carry the ark of the covenant of the Lord (Deut. 10:8; 2 Sam. 15:24; 1 Kings 8:4). They were chosen to do so (1 Chron. 15:2). They carried the ark of God with poles on their shoulders (1 Chron. 15:15). More exactly, the priests, the sons of Levi were assigned this holy duty (Deut. 31:9, 25; Josh. 3:8; 6:6; 8:33; 2 Sam. 15:24). They took up the ark of the covenant and passed on ahead of the people (Josh. 3:6).

Israelites carried the ark of the covenant with joy (1 Chron. 15:25, 28). Priests blew the trumpets regularly before the ark of the covenant (1 Chron. 16:1, 6), and ministered before the ark of the covenant regularly, according to each day's requirements (1 Chron. 16:37).

David assembled all Israel in Jerusalem to bring up the ark of the Lord to the place he had prepared for it (1 Chron. 15:3). He summoned some priests and Levites who were consecrated to bring up the ark of the Lord (1 Chron. 15:14). The ark of God was in the temple of the Lord (1 Sam. 3:3). David appointed some of the Levites to minister before the ark of the Lord, to make petition, to give thanks, and to praise the Lord, the God of Israel (1 Chron. 16:4).

Reflection: The tribe of Levi was chosen and set apart to carry the Ark of the Covenant of the Lord. This Old Testament practice leaves us a principle that only can those who are chosen and set apart carry on the holy duties. We have to be consecrated before we serve the Lord. The history of salvation is virtually the history of election, in which God has chosen and set apart some people for His use. God sets Noah apart from the pervert generation for the ark; He sets Abraham apart from his country, his people and his father's household for the Promised Land; He sets Israel apart from all the peoples of the earth to be His own special treasure (Deut. 14:2); He sets the Levites apart from all the other tribes to carry the ark of the covenant of the Lord, and to perform all the other holy duties. He sets the godly for Himself; He sets the believers apart from the unbelievers;

He sets His church apart from the world; In fact, the church is a group of people whom the Lord has called out of the world. When we are set apart by the Lord, we won't conform to the pattern of this world, but be transformed by the renewing of our mind (Rom. 12:2), then we will be capable of serving the Lord.

JUNE 3

THE ARK OF THE COVENANT AND HIS DWELLING PLACE

Then the king said to Zadok, "Take the ark of God back into the city. If I find favor in the Lord's eyes, he will bring me back and let me see it and his dwelling place again." (2 Samuel 15:25)

Because of the ark of the covenant, the Lord blessed the house of Obed-Edom (1 Chron. 13:14; 15:25; 2 Sam. 6:11, 12). God helped the Levites who carried the ark of the covenant (1 Chron. 15:26). The ark of the covenant entered the City of David (1 Chron. 15:29), and stayed there (2 Sam. 15:29). David thought that if he found favor in the Lord's eyes, He would let him see the ark of God and His dwelling place (2 Sam. 15:25). David felt guilty that the ark of the covenant of the Lord was under a tent while he himself was living in a palace of cedar (1 Chron. 17:1; 2 Sam. 7:2). He had it in his heart to build a house for the Name of the Lord as a place of rest for the ark of the covenant (1 Chron. 28:2), so that the ark of the covenant of the Lord and the sacred articles belonging to God might be brought into the temple (1 Chron. 22:19). He prepared a place for the ark of God and pitched a tent for it (1 Chron. 15:1; 16:1; 2 Chron. 1:4). Solomon prepared the inner sanctuary within the temple to set the ark of the covenant (1 Kings 6:19). And he regarded the places the ark of the Lord had entered were holy (2 Chron. 8:11).

Reflection: In the Scriptures, there is a successive line of places where God both has and will place His presence among people on the earth. The first one was the tabernacle, where He was present with His chosen people, Israel. The second one was the Solomonic Temple, which King David desired to build, and King Solomon built in the Promised Land to replace the tabernacle. The third one was the Second Temple, which was rebuilt by the Israelites under the leadership of Ezra and Zerubbable after return from captivity in Babylon. A Third Temple will occur in the Tribulation before the Antichrist appears on the earth. In the Millennium, the Millennial Temple will function in the millennial kingdom. All of these are God's dwelling places in the physical realm. In the spiritual realm, Jesus Christ was the dwelling place of God; the body of a believer is the dwelling place of God; and the universal church is the dwelling place of God. How eager David was to see the Ark of the Covenant and His dwelling place. He had it in his heart to build a house for the Name of the Lord as a place of rest for the ark of the covenant. David craved to dwell in the house of the Lord all the days of his life, to gaze on the beauty of the Lord and to seek him in His temple (Ps. 27:4). David dearly loved the house where the Lord lived, the place where His glory dwelled (Ps. 26:8). David valued God's dwelling place the most (Ps. 84:10). This is the reason why even he has sinned, the Lord's favor has never left him. As long as we crave for God's dwelling place, as David does, we will find favor in His eyes.

June 4

The Ark of the Covenant and the Tabernacle

Then the Lord said to Moses: "Set up the tabernacle, the Tent of Meeting, on the first day of the first month. Place the ark of the covenant law in it and shield the ark with the curtain." (Exodus 40:1-3)

The Lord gave skill to all the craftsmen to make everything He had commanded Moses, including the ark of the covenant law (Exod. 31:6-7). The Israelites did everything just as the Lord commanded Moses, including the ark of the covenant law with its poles and the atonement cover (Exod. 39:35). The ark of the covenant law was placed in the tabernacle, the Tent of Meeting, and the curtain shielded the ark (Exod. 40:2-3, 21). When the camp was to move, the shielding curtain was taken down and covered the ark of the covenant law (Num. 4:5).

The ark of God was called by the Name (2 Sam. 6:2; 1 Chron. 13:6). The Book of the Law was placed beside the ark of the covenant of the Lord (Deut. 31:26), which was enthroned between the cherubim (1 Sam. 4:4; 6:2; 1 Chron. 13:6). The cherubim of gold spread their wings and sheltered the ark of the covenant of the Lord (1 Chron. 28:18). The ark of the covenant was gold-covered, and contained the gold jar of manna, Aaron's staff that had budded, and the stone tablets of the covenant (Heb. 9:4). The ark of the covenant law was placed behind the curtain that separated the Holy Place from the Most Holy Place (Exod. 26:33). And the atonement cover was put on the ark of the covenant law in the Most Holy Place (Exod. 26:34). Sacred anointing oil was used to anoint the Tent of Meeting, and ark of the covenant law, and sacred articles (Exod. 30:22-28). The gold altar of incense was placed in front of the ark of the covenant law (Exod. 40:5).

Reflection: The ark of the covenant law was placed behind the curtain that separated the Holy Place from the Most Holy Place (Exod. 26:33). And the atonement cover was put on the ark of the Testimony in the Most Holy Place (Exod. 26:34). In other words, on the top of the ark of the covenant, there was the atonement cover, which was also called the mercy seat. It conceals the people of God from the ever-condemning judgment of the Law. And this is God's grace. The phrase "mercy seat" connotes the concept of "expiation" or "propitiation". It carries the idea of the removal of sin. In the spiritual sense, Jesus is the Ark of the Testimony. When He died on the cross, the curtain that separated the Holy Place from the Most Holy Place was torn from top to bottom (Matt. 27:51). Because of his death of atonement, we have confidence to enter the Most Holy Place by the blood of Jesus, by a new and living way opened for us through the curtain, that is, his body (Heb. 9:19-20), approach God's throne of grace with confidence, and receive mercy and find grace to help us in our time of need (Heb. 4:16). God's throne of grace is the atonement cover. It implies that the most amazing grace of God is the atonement Jesus has done for us. By the atonement of Jesus, we are able to enter the inner sanctuary of the tabernacle and come before God's throne of grace.

JUNE 5

THE ARK OF COVENANT AND THE LORD'S PRESENCE

The Israelites inquired of the Lord. (In those days the ark of the covenant of God was there.) (Judges 20:27)

The ark of the covenant represents the Lord's presence (Judg. 20:27). The Lord would meet with Moses and gave him all His commands for the Israelites above the cover between the two cherubim that were over the ark of the Testimony (Exod. 25:22; 30:6). Entering the Tent of the Meeting, Moses heard the voice speaking to him from between the two cherubim above the atonement cover on the ark of the Testimony (Num. 7:89). The ark of God was not inquired of during the reign of Saul (1 Chron. 13:3).

Whenever the ark of God went, God's hand was heavy on the idols and their worshipers (1 Sam. 5:1-12). Dagon fell on his face on the ground before the ark of the Lord when the ark of the Lord entered his temple, with his head and hands being broken off (1 Sam. 5:3-4).

Whenever the ark of God was with Israelites, they won victory (1 Sam. 14:18). David and the whole house of Israel were celebrating all their might before the Lord (2 Sam. 6:5). The ark of the Lord saved Israelites from the hand of their enemies whenever it went with them (1 Sam. 4:3). The Philistines were afraid of the ark of the Lord (1 Sam. 4:7). When the ark of the Lord had been in the Philistine territory seven months, the Philistines tried to send away the ark of the Lord with guilt offerings (1 Sam. 6:1-12).

Reflection: Before the Incarnation of God in Jesus Christ, the Ark of the Covenant was God's presence and His self-revelation. The Lord met with Moses and spoke to him above the cover between the two cherubim that were over the ark of the covenant (Exod. 25:22; 30:6; Num. 7:89). And Israelites inquired of the Lord with the ark of the covenant (Judge 20:27). However, the ark of God was not inquired of during the reign of Saul (1 Chron. 13:3). In contrast, David wished to dwell in the house of the Lord all days of his life to gaze on the beauty of the Lord and to seek him in his temple (Ps. 27:4). The scriptures reveal the answer why the Lord abhors Saul and gives His favor to David. David craves for God's presence, and eager to see the Ark of the Covenant and His dwelling place. Since that by the atonement of Jesus, a new and living way opened for us through the curtain that veils the Holy of the Holies, do we have confidence to approach God's throne of grace? In our prayers, when we ask, we enter the Out Court; when we seek, we enter the Holy Place; when we knock, we enter the Holy of the Holies. Have you ever had any experience in these three realms of prayer? Have you ever met Jesus in your daily devotion? If you, like David, craves for God's presence, and eager to see the Ark of the Covenant and His dwelling place, you will experience the glorious presence of God on an intimate and a profound level.

JUNE 6

THE GOSPEL (I)

The god of this age has blinded the minds of unbelievers, so that they cannot see the light of gospel that displays the glory of Christ, who is the image of God. (2 Corinthians 4:4)

(Paul says,) I am so eager to preach the gospel (Rom. 1:15). I am not ashamed of the gospel, because it is the power of God that brings salvation to everyone who believes (Rom. 1:16). For in the gospel the righteousness of God is revealed – a righteousness that is by faith from first to last, just as it is written: "The righteous will live by faith." (Rom. 1:17). This will take place on the day when God judges people's secrets through Jesus Christ, as my gospel declares (Rom. 2:16). I have fully proclaimed the gospel of Christ (Rom. 15:19). He gave me the priestly duty of proclaiming the gospel of God (Rom. 15:16). Christ did not send me to baptize, but to preach the gospel – not with wisdom and eloquence, lest the cross of Christ be emptied of its power (1 Cor. 1:17). When I preach the gospel, I cannot boast, since I am compelled to preach. Woe to me if I do not preach the gospel (1 Cor. 9:16). What then is my reward? Just this: that in preaching the gospel I may offer it free of charge, and so not make full use of my rights as a preacher of the gospel (1 Cor. 9:18). I do all this for the sake of the gospel, that I may share in its blessings (1 Cor. 9:23). By this gospel you are saved, if you hold firmly to the word I preached to you (1 Cor. 15:2). And even if our gospel is veiled, it is veiled to those who are perishing (2 Cor. 4:3). The god of this age has blinded the minds of unbelievers, so that they cannot see the light of gospel that displays the glory of Christ, who is the image of God (2 Cor. 4:4). The gospel I preached is not of human origin (Gal. 1:11). I became a servant of this gospel by the gift of God's grace given me through the working of His power (Eph. 3:7).

Reflection: In the Scriptures, light and darkness, a pair of antitheses, are metaphors to describe righteousness and sin, or good and evil. And there is paradox pertaining to light and darkness. For instance, the opening of Adam's and Eve's eyes by Satan led to blindness to God. Their eyes became open to the dark world of sin. Since then, sinners cannot see the glory of Christ, and they have been brought into Satan's power. Sin has blocked their access to the light and truth of God (2 Cor. 4:4). However, Christ has destroyed death and has brought life and immortality to light through the gospel (2 Tim. 1:10). And the gospel is the power of God that brings salvation to everyone who believes (Rom. 1:16), because the light of gospel displays the glory of Christ, who is the image of God (2 Cor. 4:4). God is light; in Him there is no darkness at all (1 John 1:5). Jesus Christ is the radiance of God's glory (Heb. 1:3). If we walk in the light, as He is in the light, we have fellowship with one another, and the blood of Jesus, His Son, purifies us from all sin (1 John 1:7). However, the god of this age has blinded the minds of unbelievers, so that they cannot see the light of gospel that displays the glory of Christ, who is the image of God (2 Cor. 4:4). The gospel is veiled to those who are perishing. Praise the Lord, we were once darkness, but now we are light in the world (Eph. 5:8). As children of light (Eph. 5:9), we are a chosen people, a royal priesthood, a holy nation, God's special possession, that we may declare the praises of Him who called us out of darkness into His wonderful light (1 Pet. 2:9).

JUNE 7

THE GOSPEL (II)

He said to them, "Go into all the world and preach the gospel to all creation." (Mark 16:15)

And this gospel of the kingdom will be preached in the whole world as a testimony to all nations, and then the end will come (Matt. 24:14). And the gospel must first be preached to all nations (Mark 13:10). The gospel is bearing fruit and growing throughout the whole world (Col. 1:6).

Scripture foresaw that God would justify the Gentiles by faith, and announced the gospel in advance to Abraham: "All nations will be blessed through you." (Gal. 3:8). This mystery is that through the gospel the Gentiles are heirs together with Israel, members together of one body, and sharers together in the promise in Christ Jesus (Eph. 3:6). It has been revealed through the appearing of our Savior, Christ Jesus, who has destroyed death and has brought life and immortality to light through the gospel (2 Tim. 1:10). Remember Jesus Christ, raised from the dead, descended from David. This is my gospel (2 Tim. 2:8).

We speak as those approved by God to be entrusted with the gospel (1 Thess. 2:4). This is the gospel that you heard and that has been proclaimed to every creature under heaven (Col. 1:23). With the help of our God we dared to tell you His gospel in the face of strong opposition (1 Thess. 2:2). Our gospel came to you not simply with words but also with power, with the Holy Spirit and deep conviction (1 Thess. 1:5). Because we loved you so much, we were delighted to share with you not only the gospel of God but our lives as well (1 Thess. 2:8). He called you to this through our gospel, that you might share in the glory of our Lord Jesus Christ (2 Thess. 2:14).

Reflection: God did not have to entrust us with the Great Commission. He could have called the angels instead of us, or He could have the mission done by Himself. The reason God has called us to preach the gospel is that He loves us so much that He wants us to share in His glory: "He called you to this through our gospel, that you might share in the glory of our Lord Jesus Christ" (2 Thess. 2:14). Among all the creation, we have been chosen to preach the gospel to all creation (Mark 16:15). In Genesis, God entrusts human-beings dominion over all creation. In the Gospel, God entrust human-beings Great Commission to preach the gospel to all creation. When talking about the Great Commission, we always mention Scriptural verses, such as Matthew 28:16-20, or Acts 1:8. We are aware that we are entrusted Great Commission to share the gospel of Jesus Christ in Jerusalem, and in all Judea and Samaria, and to the ends of the earth (Acts 1:8). However, we shall not neglect the Great Commission expressed in the Gospel of Mark that we must preach the gospel to all nations first ((Mark 13:10), then we must go into all the world and preach the good news to all creation (Mark 16:15). We know that the whole creation has been groaning as in the pains of childbirth right up to the present time (Rom. 8:22). For the creation waits in eager expectation for the children of God to be revealed. For the creation was subjected to frustration, not by its own choice, but by the will of the one who subjected it, in hope that the creation itself will be liberated from its bondage to decay and brought into the freedom and glory of the children of God (Rom. 8:19-21).

JUNE 8

THE GOSPEL (III)

Now to him who is able to establish you in accordance with my gospel, the message I proclaim about Jesus Christ, in keeping with the revelation of the mystery hidden for long ages past. (Romans 16:25)

(Paul says) Now brothers and sisters, I want to remind you of the gospel I preached to you, which you received and on which you have taken your stand (1 Cor. 15:1). Whatever happens, conduct yourselves in a manner worthy of the gospel of Christ (Phil. 1:27). Even if you had ten thousand guardians in Christ, you do not have many fathers, for in Christ Jesus I became your father through the gospel (1 Cor. 4:15). God is able to establish you in accordance with my gospel, the message I proclaim about Jesus Christ, in keeping with the revelation of the mystery hidden for long ages past (Rom. 16:25), the gospel He promised beforehand through His prophets in the Holy Scriptures (Rom. 1:2). And you also were included in Christ when you heard the message of truth, the gospel of your salvation. When you believed, you were marked in Him with a seal, the promised Holy Spirit (Eph. 1:13).

It has always been my ambition to preach the gospel where Christ was not known, so that I would not be building on someone else's foundation (Rom. 15:20). Now when I went to Troas to preach the gospel of Christ and found that the Lord has opened a door for me (2 Cor. 2:12). Pray also for me, that whenever I speak, words may be given me so that I will fearlessly make known the mystery of the gospel (Eph. 6:19). Now I want you to know, brothers and sisters, that what has happened to me has actually served to advance the gospel (Phil. 1:12). In all my prayers for all of you, I always pray with joy because of your partnership on the gospel from the first day until now, being confident of this, that he who began a good work in you will carry it on to completion until the day of Christ Jesus (Phil. 1:4-6). And because of my chains, most of the brothers and sisters have become confident in the Lord and dare all the more to proclaim the gospel without fear (Phil. 1:14). I am put here for the defense of the gospel (Phil. 1:16).

Reflection: In the Biblical era, mystery religions and mystery cults were popular in the Middle East and the Asia Minor. Mystery was understood as the esoteric knowledge made known only to select few. Christianity was thought as one of the mystery religions.

However, according to the Scriptures, the mystery of gospel is God's salvation plan that God has kept hidden for ages, and then reveled gradually and progressively in the course of history. In the history of salvation, God has revealed the mystery of Gospel. The revelation of the mystery had been hidden for long ages past (Rom. 16:25). Although the mystery has been kept hidden for ages and generations, it is now disclosed to the Lord's people. To them God has chosen to make known among the Gentiles the glorious riches of this mystery, which is Christ in you, the hope of glory (Col. 1:26-27). What is the mystery? The mystery, as one of the mysteries of the gospel, is the New Creation, in which Christ created in Himself one new humanity out of two, Jews and Gentiles; and in one body, which is the church, the body of Christ, He has reconciled both of them to God through the cross, by which He put to death their hostility (Eph. 2:15-16). Jews and Gentiles have been reconciled through the cross. Reconciliation happened first, then did new creation. The mystery of gospel has been fully revealed by God through His Son, Jesus Christ, who is the ultimate revelation.

June 9

The Gospel (IV)

For if someone comes to you and preaches a Jesus other than the Jesus we preached, or if you receive a different spirit from the Spirit you received, or a different gospel from one you accepted, you put up with it easily enough. (2 Corinthians 11:4)

"Truly I tell you," Jesus replied, "no one who has left home or brothers or sisters or mother or father or children or fields for me and the gospel will fail to receive a hundred times as much in this present age: homes, brothers, sisters, mothers, children and fields—along with persecutions—and in the age to come eternal life (Mark 10:29-30). For whoever wants to save their life will lose it, but whoever loses their life for me and for the gospel will save it (Mark 8:35). Truly I tell you, wherever this gospel is preached throughout the world, what she has done will also be told, in memory of her (Matt. 26:13; Mark 14:9).

For if someone comes to you and preaches a Jesus other than the Jesus we preached, or if you receive a different spirit from the Spirit you received, or a different gospel from one you accepted, you put up with it easily enough (2 Cor. 11:4). I am astonished that you are so quickly deserting the one who called you to live in the grace of Christ and are turning to a different gospel which is really no gospel at all. Evidently some people are throwing you into confusion and are trying to pervert the gospel of Christ. But even if we or an angel from heaven should preach a gospel other than the one we preached to you, let them be under God's curse! As we have already said, so now I say again: If anybody is preaching to you a gospel other than what you accepted, let them be under God's curse! (Gal. 1:6-9). We did not give in to them for a moment, so that the truth of the gospel might be preserved for you (Gal. 2:5).

It is right for me to feel this way about all of you, since I have you in my heart and whether I am in chains or defending and confirming the gospel, all of you share in God's grace with me (Phil. 1:7). Because of the service by which you have proved yourselves, others will praise God for the obedience that accompanies your confession of the gospel of Christ, and for your generosity in sharing with them and with everyone else (2 Cor. 9:13).

Reflection: Evangelism involves message, messenger, and method. God gives us message to preach, which is the gospel. And He chooses messengers to preach this massage. And we, as messengers, have freedom to choose the methods to preach the message. However, we cannot alter the message. Methods may change over the time, but the message will remain the same forever. The message is about Jesus Christ, and Him crucified (1 Cor. 2:2). And any altered message is heresy. In other words, heresy is "a different gospel" the Apostle Paul mentions in today's theme scripture. Unfortunately, heresies have existed since the days of the early church. During its early centuries, the Christian church dealt with many heresies, such as Docetism, Montanism, Adoptionism, Sabellianism, Arianism, Pelagianism, and Gnosticism. During the course of church history, new heresies emerged. Some of them were merely the reincarnation of the old ones in the early centuries of the church history. Heresies are some of Satan's most powerful weapons he uses to try to destroy the church. He mixes lies with the truths, attempts to deceive Christians as he did to Adam and Eve in the Garden of Eden. Satan uses persecutions from outside to try to destroy the church. However, God overpowers him, and turns the curse into blessing, and makes church grow in the midst of persecution. However, heresies are more powerful weapons in Satan's armory. In the church history, we have seen that heresies have done harm to the church. For instance, the liberal theology has caused the decline of the church in Europe. Nowadays, the theology of prosperity which is popular worldwide has been doing severe harm to the church. Remember, in the gospel, there is one message that never changes, that is Jesus Christ and Him crucified (1 Cor. 2:2). This is the core of the gospel message. We must keep the cross at the center of the gospel.

Pearls of Wisdom VOLUME 1

JUNE 10

FEAR OF THE LORD (I)

The fear of the Lord is the beginning of wisdom, and knowledge of the Holy One is understanding. (Proverbs 9:10)

Come, my children, listen to me; I will teach you the fear of the Lord (Ps. 34:11). Now let the fear of the Lord be on you. Judge carefully, for with the Lord our God there is no injustice or partiality or bribery (2 Chron. 19:7). He (Jehoshaphat) gave them these orders: "You must serve faithfully and wholeheartedly in the fear of the Lord" (2 Chron. 19:9). Do not let your heart envy sinners, but always be zealous for the fear of the Lord (Prov. 23:17). The fear of the Lord – that is wisdom, and to shun evil is understanding. (Job 28:28). The fear of the Lord is the beginning of wisdom; all who follow His percepts have good understanding (Ps. 111:10). The fear of the Lord is the beginning of wisdom, and knowledge of the Holy One is understanding (Prov. 9:10). The fear of the Lord is the beginning of knowledge (Prov. 1:7). You will understand the fear of the Lord and find the knowledge of God (Prov. 2:5).

The fear of the Lord fell on all the kingdom of the lands surrounding Judah, so that they did not go to war against Jehoshaphat (2 Chron. 17:10). The church throughout Judea, Galilee and Samaria enjoyed a time of peace and was strengthened. Living in the fear of the Lord and encouraged by the Holy Spirit, it increased in numbers (Acts 9:31).

Reflection: For the unbeliever, the fear of the Lord is the fear of the judgment of God and eternal death, which is eternal separation from God (Luke 12:5; Hebrews 10:31). For the believer, the fear of the Lord is something much different. The believer's fear is reverence and awe of God (Hebrews 12:28-29). The fear of the Lord is the beginning of wisdom, and knowledge of the Holy One is understanding. God is holy, just and righteous. To fear the Lord is to recognize His holiness, justice, glory, majesty and power. When we fear the Lord, we are in awe of His holiness, justice, glory, majesty and power. On the other hand, when we are in awe of His holiness, justice, glory, majesty and power, we are trembled in fear. When we are trembled in fear of the Lord, we don't dare to sin. The fear of the Lord produces true faith that helps us shun evil. The fear of the Lord helps us trust in the Lord, because we come to realize how holy, just and righteous He is. The fear of the Lord helps us to know God, know His attributes and characters. The fear of the Lord brings us to a deeper relationship with Him. The fear of God is respecting Him, obeying Him, submitting to His discipline, and worshipping Him in awe. True wisdom, understanding, and knowledge begin from the fear of the Lord, from respecting Him, obeying Him, submitting to His discipline, and worshipping Him in awe. True wisdom urges us to serve Him faithfully and wholeheartedly in the fear of the Lord.

June 11

Fear of the Lord (II)

Humility is the fear of the Lord; its wages are riches and honor and life. (Proverbs 22:4)

The fear of the Lord is pure, enduring forever. The decrees of the Lord are firm, and all of them are righteous (Ps. 19:9). The fear of the Lord adds length to life, but the years of the wicked are cut short (Prov. 10:27). The fear of the Lord leads to life; then one rests content, untouched by trouble (Prov. 19:23). The fear of the Lord is a fountain of life, turning a person from the snares of death (Prov. 14:27). Through love and faithfulness sin is atoned for; through the fear of the Lord evil is avoided (Prov. 16:6). Better a little with the fear of the Lord than great wealth with turmoil (Prov. 15:16). Humility is the fear of the Lord; its wages are riches and honor and life (Prov. 22:4).

The spirit of the Lord will rest on Him – the Spirit of wisdom and of understanding, the Spirit of counsel and of might, the Spirit of the knowledge and fear of the Lord. And He will delight in the fear of the Lord. He will not judge by what He sees with his eyes, or decide by what He hears with His ears (Isa. 11:2-3). He will be the sure foundation for your times, a rich store of salvation and wisdom and knowledge; the fear of the Lord is the key to this treasure (Isa. 33:6).

Reflection: Humility is the fear of the Lord; its wages are riches and honor and life. The Apostle Paul's experience is a perfect example. He has more reasons than anyone else does to put confidence in the flesh: he was circumcised on the eighth day, of the people of Israel, of the tribe of Benjamin, a Hebrew of Hebrews; in regard to the law, a Pharisee (Phil. 3:5). He is a student of Gamaliel who is recognized as one of the top scholars of Jewish Law. He is high-born, high-bred, and high-browed. He has privilege, prestige, and power. However, although having more reasons to put confidence in flesh, Paul considers everything a loss because of the surpassing worth of knowing Christ Jesus the Lord. He considers everything rubbish that he may gain Christ, which is the pearl of great price. Like a merchant looking for fine pearls, Paul has found one of great value, and abandoned everything he had in order to gain Christ. As a matter of fact, Paul has imitated Christ, who has diminished His divine power, and relinquished His divine prestige and privileges, and taken the humble position of a slave and been made in the likeness of men, and become obedient to death—even death on a cross! (Phil. 2:6-8);

and paradoxically, God has exalted Him to the highest place and given him the name that is above every name (Phil. 2:9), just as the Prophet Isaiah prophesizes, "The Lord is exalted, for he dwells on high; he will fill Zion with his justice and righteousness. He will be the sure foundation for your times, a rich store of salvation and wisdom and knowledge; the fear of the Lord is the key to this treasure (Isa. 33:5-6).

JUNE 12

GLORY AND POWER (I)

Yours, Lord, is the greatness and the power and the glory and the majesty and the splendor, for everything in heaven and earth is yours. Yours, Lord, is the kingdom; you are exalted as head over all. (1 Chronicles 29:11)

I have seen your sanctuary and beheld your power and your glory (Ps. 63:2). You are worthy, our Lord and God, to receive glory and honor and power, for you created all things, and by your will they were created and have their being (Rev. 4:11).

At that time people will see the Son of Man in clouds with great power and glory (Mark 13:26; Luke 21:27). Then will appear the sign of the Son of Man in heaven. And then all the peoples of the earth will mourn when they see the Son of Man coming on the clouds of heaven, with power and great glory (Matt. 24:30). He was given authority, glory and sovereign power; all nations and peoples of every language worshiped Him. His dominion is an everlasting dominion that will not pass away, and His kingdom is one that will never be destroyed (Dan. 7:14). His divine power has given us everything we need for a godly life through our knowledge of Him who called us by His own glory and goodness (2 Pet. 1:3).

Reflection: The Father and the Son are the same in substance and essence, equal in glory and power. In the Old Testament the token of the divine presence is the "cloud of glory" (called "the glory" in the New Testament). It is the divine nature itself that is denoted by the "glory." The Son is the radiance of the glory of the Father and the exact representation of his being (Heb. 1:3). The Son is of the same kind of Person as the Father, out of the intense relationship which they have, being able to reveal and expound Him to the perceptions of mankind. It was because of this intimacy which He had with the Father that He could represent Him to His creation. Thus the "Son" in His relation to "God" is represented here by light beaming forth from light, and by exact impress—the perfect image produced by stamp or seal. However, in order to fulfill the mission to save the world, the Son has diminished His divine power, and relinquished His divine prestige and privileges, and taken the humble position of a slave and been made in the likeness of men, and become obedient to death—even death on a cross! (Phil. 2:6-8). He has initiatively and intentionally concealed the greatness and the power and the glory and the majesty and the splendor of the Son of God; He has initiatively and intentionally veiled glory and honor and power of the Son of God. Nevertheless, paradoxically, through crucifixion and resurrection, He has been exalted as head over all. God has exalted Him to the highest place and given him the name that is above every name (Phil. 2:9). He has been given authority, glory and sovereign power; all nations and peoples of every language worship Him. His dominion is an everlasting dominion that will not pass away, and His kingdom is one that will never be destroyed. At the end time, when He returns, people will see the Son of Man in clouds with great power and glory, as the sign of the Son of Man in heaven. And then all the peoples of the earth will mourn when they see the Son of Man coming on the clouds of heaven, with power and great glory (Matt. 24:30). God's people will praise Him: "Yours, Lord, is the greatness and the power and the glory and the majesty and the splendor, for everything in heaven and earth is yours. Yours, Lord, is the kingdom; you are exalted as head over all" (1 Chron. 29:11).

June 13

Glory and Power (II)

After this I heard what sounded like the roar of a great multitude in heaven shouting: "Hallelujah! Salvation and glory and power belong to our God." (Revelation 19:1)

In a loud voice they were saying: "Worthy is the lamb, who was slain, to receive power and wealth and wisdom and strength and honor and glory and praise (Rev. 5:12). Then I heard every creature in heaven and on earth and under the earth and on the sea, and all that is in them, saying: "To Him who sits on the throne and to the Lamb be praise and honor and glory and power, for ever and ever (Rev. 5:13). To Him be glory and power for ever and ever! Amen (1 Pet. 4:11; Rev. 1:6). To the only God our savior be glory, majesty, power and authority, through Jesus Christ our Lord, before all ages, now and forevermore! Amen (Jude 1:25). Amen! Praise and glory and wisdom and thanks and honor and power and strength be to our God for ever and ever. Amen (Rev. 7:12). And the temple was filled with smoke from the glory of God and from His power, and no one could enter the temple until the seven plagues of the angels were completed (Rev. 15:8). After this I heard what sounded like the roar of a great multitude in heaven shouting: "Hallelujah! Salvation and glory and power belong to our God." (Revelation 19:1)

Reflection: Because of the Son's complete submission to the Father, and His motivation which was fully toward pleasing Him and in harmony with His purposes, the Father has invested Him with all His power, and positioned him with the authority to use that power at his own initiative. "Therefore God exalted him to the highest place and gave him the name that is above every name, that at the name of Jesus every knee should bow, in heaven and on earth and under the earth, and every tongue acknowledge that Jesus Christ is Lord, to the glory of God the Father" (Phil. 2:9-11). And through the Son, the Father receives glory, majesty, power and authority that are due onto His name (Jude 1:25). At the end time, "salvation and glory and power belong to our God." (Rev. 19:1). And this fulfills Jesus' prayer: "Father, the hour has come. Glorify your Son, that your Son may glorify you." (John 17:1). At His first coming, the Son of God has diminished His divine power, and relinquished His divine prestige and privileges, and taken the humble position of a slave and been made in the likeness of men, and become obedient to death—even death on a cross! (Phil. 2:6-8). He was born in a manger, from a lowly woman. He was raised in an ordinary and not well-to-do family. By doing these, He has initiatively and intentionally concealed the greatness and the power and the glory and the majesty and the splendor of the Son of God; and has veiled glory and honor and power of the Son of God. Paradoxically, in the Book of Revelation, we have seen that His glory and power, greatness and majesty, honor and splendor of the Son of God will be fully revealed and completely manifested.

JUNE 14

PROPHECY (I)

For prophecy never had its origin in the human will, but prophets, though human, spoke from God as they were carried along by the Holy Spirit. (2 Peter 1:21)

And if a prophet is enticed to utter a prophecy, I the Lord have enticed that prophet, and I will stretch out my hand against him and destroy him from among my people Israel (Ezek. 14:9). Above all, you must understand that no prophecy of Scripture came about by the prophet's own interpretation of things (2 Pet. 1:20). For prophecy never had its origin in the human will, but prophets, though human, spoke from God as they were carried along by the Holy Spirit (2 Pet. 1:21). It is the Spirit of prophecy who bears testimony to Jesus (Rev. 19:10).

Now brothers and sisters, if I come to you and speak in tongues, what good will I be to you, unless I bring you some revelation or knowledge or prophecy or word of instruction? (1 Cor. 14:6). Tongues, then, are a sign, not for believers but for unbelievers; prophecy, however, is not for unbelievers but for believers (1 Cor. 14:22). Follow the way of love and eagerly desire gifts of the Spirit, especially prophecy (1 Cor. 14:1). Do not neglect your gift, which was given you through prophecy when the body of elders laid their hands on you (1 Tim. 4:14).

Reflection: Prophecy in essence is "a message from God". To prophesy is to proclaim a message from God. And the one who proclaims a message from God is a prophet. In the Old Testament, Samuel, Elijah, and Elisha are well-known prophets who verbally deliver messages from God to Israel. And some other prophets, such as Isaiah, Jeremiah, Ezekiel, and Daniel put the messages from God in a written form. The prophets always start their prophecies with the sentence: "this is what the Lord says". Prophecy never has origin in human will (2 Pet. 1:21). And no prophecy of Scripture came about by the prophet's own interpretation of things (2 Pet. 1:20). Moreover, a true prophet must not lead Israel to idol worship, and his prophecies about the future must be fulfilled. And prophet who fails to meet these two criteria is a false prophet. Furthermore, fulfilled prophecy serves as an irrefutable evidence for the Scriptures' divine origin. Biblical prophecy contains twin aspects which are designed to act in harmony with one another. One is foretelling which predicts the future by announcing the will of God and his plans for his people. The other is forthtelling which applies to the present circumstances by preaching the message from God and the salvific truth to His people. In addition, many prophecies in the Scriptures are dual prophecies, which means that they have both a short-term and long-term fulfillments, or present and future applications. Among all the prophecies in the Scriptures, the Messianic prophecies are the ones of primary importance. Messianic prophecies can be found throughout the Old Testament which points to the first advent of the Messiah. Messianic prophecies play key roles in the revelation of God, because the Incarnation of Christ is the ultimate divine revelation.

JUNE 15

PROPHECY (II)

Blessed is the one who reads aloud the words of this prophecy, and blessed are those who hear it and take to heart what is written in it, because the time is near. (Revelation 1:3)

(Jesus told John,) "Do not seal up the words of the prophecy of this scroll, because the time is near (Rev. 22:10). "Look, I am coming soon! Blessed is the one who keeps the words of prophecy written in this scroll" (Rev. 22:7). Blessed is the one who reads aloud the words of this prophecy, and blessed are those who hear it and take to heart what is written in it, because the time is near (Rev. 1:3).

(Paul says,) Concerning the coming of our Lord Jesus Christ and our being gathered to him, we ask you, brothers and sisters, not to become easily unsettled or alarmed by the teaching allegedly from us—whether by a prophecy or by word of mouth or by letter—asserting that the day of the Lord has already come (2 Thess. 2:1-2). (Jesus says:) I warn everyone who hears the word of the prophecy of this scroll: If anyone adds anything to them, God will add to that person the plagues described in this scroll. And if anyone takes words away from this scroll of prophecy, God will take away from that person any share in the tree of life and in the Holy City, which are described in this scroll (Rev. 22:18-19).

Reflection: Our intellectual curiosity compels us to figure out how the end time prophecies will be fulfilled in the way human reason can understand. Unfortunately, prophecies will not be understood until the time comes for them to be fulfilled. However, we don't have to be discouraged, because the purpose of biblical prophecies is not for head but for heart. "Blessed is the one who reads aloud the words of this prophecy, and blessed are those who hear it and take to heart what is written in it, because the time is near." (Rev. 1:3). What matters to God is not how much we understand His salvation plan with our intellectual faculties, but how we obey His commandments with our heart. As children of God, our responsibility is not to figure out the mysteries of God, such as end time prophecies, that God keeps hidden from us, but to obey His commandments that have been written in black and white in the Scriptures. "The secret things belong to the Lord our God, but the things revealed belong to us and to our children forever, that we may follow all the words of this law." (Deut. 29:29). Obedience is the highest virtue of Christian faith. And it is the secret to receiving blessings from God, as the Scriptures reads, "Blessed is the one who reads aloud the words of this prophecy, and blessed are those who hear it and take to heart what is written in it, because the time is near." (Rev.1:3). Hearing the word of God and taking to heart is the key to receiving blessings.

June 16

Salvation (I)

The Lord is my rock, my fortress and my deliverer; my God is my rock, in whom I take refuge, my shield and the horn of my salvation. (2 Samuel 22:3; Psalm 18:2)

The Lord is my light and my salvation (Ps. 27:1). Surely God is my salvation; I will trust and not be afraid. The Lord, the Lord himself, is my strength and my defense; he has become my salvation." With joy you will draw water from the wells of salvation (Isa. 12:2-3). He is the horn of my salvation (2 Sam. 22:3; Ps. 18:2). The Lord is the strength of His people, a fortress of salvation for His anointed one (Ps. 28:8). He has become my salvation (Exod. 15:2; Ps. 118:14, 21; Isa. 12:2). I will lift the cup of salvation and call on the name of the Lord (Ps. 116:13). Then my soul will rejoice in the Lord and delight in His salvation (Ps. 35:9). Show us your unfailing love, Lord, and grant us your salvation (Ps. 85:7). May your unfailing love come to me, Lord, your salvation, according to your promise (Ps. 119:41). I trust in your unfailing love; my heart rejoices in your salvation (Ps. 14:7).

I wait for your salvation (Ps. 119:166). I long for your salvation (Ps. 119:174). My soul faints with longing for your salvation (Ps. 119:81). My eyes fail, looking for your salvation (ps. 119:123). As for me, afflicted and in pain – may your salvation, God, protect me (Ps. 69:29). I pray to you, Lord, in the time of your favor; in your great love, O God, answer me with your sure salvation (Ps. 69:13). Contend, Lord, with those who contend with me; fight against those who fight against me. Take up shield and armor; arise and come to my aid. Brandish spear and javelin against those who pursue me. Say to me, "I am your salvation." (Ps. 35:1-3). Restore to me the joy of your salvation (Ps. 51:12).

Reflection: The expression "the horn of salvation" appears in the Scriptures several times to connote the saving power. As they, in the biblical era, were used for fighting, protection, and securing dominance, animal horns became symbols of strength, power, and victory. "A horn is a sign of power (Deut. 33: 17)—literally of an ox (Num. 23: 22) or metaphorically of a people (1 Kgs. 22: 11). In Dan. 7: 8 the horns refer metaphorically to kings. So the 'horn of salvation' (Ps. 18: 2) indicates the saving power of the king. The four horns on the corners of altars (Exod. 27: 2) afforded sanctuary to a fugitive who clung to them. The horn of salvation in Luke 1: 69 (NRSV marg., AV) denotes royal saving power, now belonging to the Messiah." (Oxford Biblical Studies Online). Animal horns are used as a shofar trumpet which is used for Jewish religious purposes, especially in the occasion of Rosh Hashanah, the Jewish New Year. In the Old Testament, the word "horn" also refers to the protrusion at each of the four corners of the altar (Exod. 27:2), which connotes the purification and atonement for sin. In other words, it implies the power of salvation from God. In the New Testament, the horn of salvation refers to Jesus Christ: "Praise be to the Lord, the God of Israel, because he has come to his people and redeemed them. He has raised up a horn of salvation for us in the house of his servant David" (Luke 1:68-69). Apparently, the horns on the altar in the Old Testament which signify purification and atonement for sin, serve as type to symbolize Jesus Christ, who offers purification and atonement for sin on the cross. Because His precious blood shed on the cross not only covers our sinful acts, but cleanses our sinful nature, His salvation is strong, powerful, and triumphant.

June 17

Salvation (II)

Truly my soul finds rest in God; my salvation comes from Him. (Psalm 62:1)

Salvation comes from the Lord (Jonah 2:9). The salvation of the righteous comes from the Lord (Ps. 37:39). He brings salvation on the earth (Ps. 74:12). All the ends of the earth will see the salvation of our God (Isa. 52:10). All the ends of the earth have seen the salvation of our God (Ps. 98:3).

Our salvation is nearer now than when we first believed (Rom. 13:11). Surely His salvation is near those who fear Him (Ps. 85:9). Salvation is far from the wicked, for they do not seek out your decree (Ps. 119:155). Do not let them share in your salvation (Ps. 69:27). If my house is not right with God, surely He would not have made with me an everlasting covenant, arranged and secured in every part; surely He would not bring to fruition my salvation and grant me my every desire (2 Sam. 23:5).

In repentance and rest is your salvation, in quietness and trust is your strength (Isa. 30:15). With joy you will draw water from the wells of salvation (Isa. 12:3). It is good to wait quietly for the salvation of the Lord (Lam. 3:26). Christ was sacrificed once to take away the sins of many; and He will appear a second time, not to bear sin, but to bring salvation to those who are waiting for Him (Heb. 9:28), who through faith are shielded by God's power until the coming of the salvation that is to be revealed in the last time (1 Pet. 1:5).

Reflection: Rest is important to our salvation. The psalmist says, "Truly my soul finds rest in God; my salvation comes from Him." (Psalms 62:1). The Sovereign God, the Holy One of Israel, says: "In repentance and rest is your salvation, in quietness and trust is your strength." (Isa. 30:15). The Sovereign Lord, the Holy One of Israel spoke through the prophet Isaiah to Judah when the Assyrian Empire was about to besiege Judah, one of its vassal states. King Hezekiah turned to Egypt instead of the Lord for help. The Lord spoke through Isaiah, "Woe to the obstinate children," declares the Lord, "to those who carry out plans that are not mine, forming an alliance, but not by my Spirit, heaping sin upon sin (Isa. 30:1). King Hezekiah sinned because he didn't look to God for protection, who is Judah's rock and shelter (Ps. 18:2). The failure of King Hezekiah as well as Judah reminds us that God is the only one to whom we must seek help. Our salvation comes only from the Lord. When we look to Him, we must repent and rest in Him. Our salvation is a result not of our own efforts, but of His grace. We ought to build and deepen personal relationship with Him, in repentance and rest, draw water from the wells of salvation. As a matter of fact, only in Jesus Christ can we find true salvation, who offers us rest of salvation. Watchman Nee points out "the Rest of Salvation" in Matthew 11:28-29, "The rest in verse 28 is spoken of this way: 'Come to Me all who toil and are burdened, and I will give you rest.' This rest is the rest of salvation. Verse 29 is the rest of victory. The first rest is the rest of being reconciled with God. The second rest is the rest within us. The first rest is the rest of our salvation. The second rest is our rest on earth." (Collected Works of Watchman Nee, The (Set 1) Vol. 17: Notes on Scriptural Messages (1)).

JUNE 18

SALVATION (III)

He has clothed me with garments of salvation and arrayed me in a robe of His righteousness. (Isaiah 61:10)

Lord, be gracious to us; we long for you. Be our strength every morning, our salvation in time of distress (Isa. 33:2). Godly sorrow brings repentance that leads to salvation and leaves no regret (2 Cor. 7:10). In repentance and rest is your salvation, in quietness and trust is your strength (Isa. 30:15). God makes salvation its wall and rampart (Isa. 26:1). May your priest, Lord God, be clothed with salvation, may your faithful people rejoice in your goodness (2 Chron. 6:41). He has clothed me with garments of salvation and arrayed me in a robe of His righteousness (Isa. 61:10).

Salvation and glory and power belong to our God (Rev. 19:1). Salvation belongs to our God, who sits on the throne, and to the Lamb (Rev. 7:10). Now have come the salvation and the power and the kingdom of our God, and the authority of His Messiah (Rev. 12:10). Salvation is found in no one else, for there is no name under heaven given to mankind by which we must be saved (Acts 4:12), for God did not appoint us to suffer wrath but to receive salvation through our Lord Jesus Christ (1 Thess. 5:9). He became the source of eternal salvation for all who obey Him (Heb. 5:9). How shall we escape if we ignore so great a salvation? This salvation, which was first announced by the Lord, was confirmed to us by those who heard him (Heb. 2:3).

Come, let us sing for joy to the Lord; let us shout aloud to the Rock of our salvation (Ps. 95:1). Sing to the Lord, all the earth; proclaim His salvation day after day (1 Chron. 16:23). Sing to the Lord, praise His name; proclaim His salvation day after day (Ps. 96:2). Sing to the Lord a new song, for He has done marvelous things; His right hand and His arm have worked salvation for him (Ps. 98:1). Let us rejoice and be glad in His salvation (Isa. 25:9). Let the earth open up, let salvation spring up, let righteousness flourish with it (Isa. 45:8). He will be the sure foundation for your times, a rich store of salvation and wisdom and knowledge (Isa. 33:6).

Reflection: The first pieces of garments human beings have ever worn were the fig leaves which Adam and Eve tried to dress themselves when they sinned. Unfortunately, those pieces of garment were unable to cover their sins, because they tried to cover their own sins with self-righteousness. However, God prepared and provided them "coats of skins and clothed them" (Gen. 3:7, 21), that symbolized the righteousness from the Lamb, Jesus Christ. So is it today. If we try to come to God dressed in our works of righteousness, we can never make it, for "all our righteousness acts are like filthy rags" in the presence of a holy God (Isa. 64:6). "For he has clothed me with garments of salvation and arrayed me in a robe of his righteousness" (Isa. 61:10). The garments of salvation and the robe of righteousness are the appropriate attires we must put on when coming to His presence. And true righteousness comes from God through our faith in Christ. Any merit-based religion is unable to provide us salvation, because righteousness cannot be attained by our own efforts. In the parable of the wedding banquet (Matt. 22:1-14), the king had prepared wedding attire for every guest to wear. A guest who didn't put on the weeding attire was thrown into the darkness. In this parable, the king represents the King of the kings, and the Lord of the lords. The wedding banquet symbolizes our union with Christ, as the church is the bride of Christ. The wedding attire signifies the garments of salvation and the robe of righteousness the Lord has prepared for us, and the righteousness comes from Christ. We must put on the garments of salvation and the robe of righteousness God has prepared us in Christ to come into the union with Christ.

JUNE 19

SALVATION (IV)

I tell you, now is the time of God's favor, now is the day of salvation. (2 Corinthians 6:2)

He (the Lord) says, "In the time of my favor I heard you, and in the day of salvation I helped you." I tell you, now is the time of God's favor, now is the day of salvation (2 Cor. 6:2). In the day of salvation I will help you (Isa. 49:8). I will show my salvation (Ps. 50:23). My salvation is close at hand and my righteousness will soon be revealed (Isa. 56:1). My salvation will not be delayed. I will grant salvation to Zion, my splendor to Israel (Isa. 46:13). My righteousness draws near speedily, my salvation is on the way

(Isa. 51:5). My salvation will last forever, my righteousness will never fail (Isa. 51:6). My righteousness will last forever, my salvation through all generations (Isa. 51:8).

(The Lord says,) For Zion's sake I will not keep silent, for Jerusalem's sake I will not remain quiet, till her vindication shines out like the dawn, her salvation like a blazing torch (Isa. 62:1). I will clothe her priests with salvation, and her faithful people will ever sing for joy (Ps. 132:16). With long life I will satisfy him and show him my salvation (Ps. 91:16). My own arm achieved salvation for me (Isa. 63:5).

(The Lord says,) I will also make you a light for Gentiles, that my salvation may reach to the ends of earth (Isa. 49:6). I have made you a light for the Gentiles, that you may bring salvation to the ends of the earth (Acts 13:47).

Reflection: The Scriptures tell us that we live in the day of salvation: "For he says, 'In the time of my favor I heard you, and in the day of salvation I helped you.' I tell you, now is the time of God's favor, now is the day of salvation." (2 Cor. 6:2). Charles Spurgeon explains, "This day is the day of salvation because, 'He has made Him, who knew no sin, to be sin for us that we might be made the righteousness of God in Him.' There could have been no day of salvation if a Savior had not appeared! And if that Savior had not become our Substitute and Surety, salvation would have been denied us by the stern voice of Justice. But now Christ has come into the world and died for sin—and because He has finished all the works which He undertook, the Lord our God proclaims for us the day of salvation. Notice that, according to the context, this is the day of salvation because we may now be reconciled to God." (Charles Spurgeon, sermon, "THE DAY OF SALVATION"). In the day of salvation, everyone has to repent, to change from self-centered life to Christ-centered life. The day of the final judgment is imminent. We have no time to waste. We have no excuse to delay repentance. We have no time to waste and not to accept Christ as our Lord and Savior. We have no excuse not to "'Love the Lord your God with all your heart and with all your soul and with all your strength and with all your mind'; and, 'Love your neighbor as yourself.'" (Luke 10:27). We have no excuse not to serve the Lord with our body, soul, and spirit. We have no excuse not to proclaim the gospel and advance the Kingdom, as both John the Baptist and Jesus call for repentance as the kingdom of God has come near (Matt. 3:2; Mark 1:15).

June 20

John the Baptist

John the Baptist appeared in the wilderness, preaching a baptism of repentance for the forgiveness of sins. (Mark 1:4)

He went to all the country around the Jordan, preaching a baptism of repentance for the forgiveness of sins (Luke 3:3). The whole Judean countryside and all the people of Jerusalem went out to him (Mark 1:5). Confessing their sins, they were baptized by him in the Jordan River (Mark 1:5; Matt. 3:6). Even tax collectors came to be baptized (Luke 3:12, 7:29). But the Pharisees and the experts in the law rejected God's purpose for themselves, because they had not been baptized by John (Luke 7:30). Now the Pharisees who had been sent questioned him, "Why then do you baptize if you are not the Messiah, nor Elijah, nor the Prophet?" "I baptize with water," John replied, "but among you stands one you do not know. He is the one who comes after me, the straps of whose sandals I am not worthy to untie." This all happened at Bethany on the other side of the Jordan, where John was baptizing (John 1:24-28). John said to the crowds coming out to be baptized by him, "You brood of vipers! Who warned you to flee from the coming wrath?" (Luke 3:7).

(John said to people), "I baptize you with water. But one who is more powerful than I will come, the straps of whose sandals I am not worthy to untie. He will baptize you with the Holy Spirit and fire (Luke 3:16; Matt. 3:11; Mark 1:8). And I myself did not know Him, but the one who sent me to baptize with water told me, 'The man on whom you see the Spirit come down and remain is the one who will baptize with the Holy Spirit.'" (John 1:33). John baptized with water, but in a few days you will be baptized with the Holy Spirit (Acts 1:5).

Reflection: For a long time, the Jews had used baptism in ritual cleansing ceremonies of Gentile proselytes. As a trailblazer and the forerunner of Jesus Christ, John the Baptist administered the first baptism in the New Testament to the nation of Israel just prior to the ministry of Jesus Christ. By doing this, he reminded the Jews that it wasn't just the Gentiles who needed cleansing. As God's chosen people, the Jews needed to repent and turn away from sin as well. Unlike the later Christian baptism which represents a rebirth in Christ, John's baptism is the baptism of repentance (Matt. 3:11, Acts 19:4), which demonstrates one's recognition of his sin, his desire for spiritual cleansing, and his commitment to following God's law in anticipation of the Messiah's arrival. John paved the way for Christ by calling people to acknowledge their sin and their need for salvation.

His baptism was a purification ceremony meant to ready the peoples' hearts to receive their Savior, although the baptism of John was insufficient to save (see Acts 18:24–26; 19:1–7). Moreover, his baptism fulfills Old Testament prophecy which predicts an end to Judah's exile, and a road that leads the captives back to their land. God will cleanse His people, end their exile, and bring them the new heaven and the new earth (Isa. 65:17-25). Furthermore, the prophecy that the baptism of John has fulfilled will be further, completely and ultimately fulfilled through the ministry of Jesus Christ.

JUNE 21

JESUS AND BAPTISM

As soon as Jesus was baptized, He went up out of the water. At that moment heaven was opened, and he saw the Spirit of God descending like a dove and alighting on Him. (Matthew 3:16)

Before the coming of Jesus, John preached repentance and baptism to all the people of Israel (Acts 10:37). John's baptism was a baptism of repentance. He told the people to believe in the one coming after him, that is, in Jesus (Acts 19:4).

At that time Jesus of Nazareth came from in Galilee and was baptized by John in the Jordan (Mark 1:9; Matt. 3:13). When all the people were being baptized, Jesus was baptized too (Luke 3:21). But John tried to deter Him, saying, "I need to be baptized by you, and do you come to me?" (Matt. 3:14). As soon as Jesus was baptized, He went up out of the water. At that moment heaven was opened, and he saw the Spirit of God descending like a dove and alighting on Him (Matt. 3:16). After this, Jesus and His disciples went out into the Judean countryside, where He spent some time with them, and baptized. John was also baptizing at Aenon near Salim, because there was plenty of water, and people were coming and being baptized (John 3:22-23).

(Jesus said to James and John,) "You don't know what you are asking," Jesus said, "Can you drink the cup I drink and be baptized with the baptism I am baptized with?" (Mark 10:38). "We can," they answered. Jesus said to them, "You will drink the cup I drink and be baptized with the baptism I am baptized with" (Mark 10:39). (Jesus said to His disciples,) I have a baptism to undergo, and what constraint I am under until it is completed (Luke 12:50).

Reflection: Seen as the new Elijah, John the Baptist prophesizes and ushers in the coming Messiah (Mal. 4:5–6; Matt. 11:1–14). Although different than the baptism Jesus institutes, John's baptism shares points of contact with the baptism Jesus commands in calling repentance and cleansing of sin as prerequisites to enter the Kingdom of God. Although the meaning of Christian baptism is rooted in the baptism of Jesus, the baptism Jesus receives from John the Baptist differs from the practice of Christian baptism. The baptism of Jesus marks inauguration of his public ministry, when the outpouring of the Holy Spirit on Jesus at His baptism signified this ordination to ministry. As soon as he was baptized, the heavens opened for Jesus in order that He saw the Spirit descended. And that veil that had separated us from God was torn down in Jesus' case. He walked under an open heaven. And from then on, Jesus always walked under an open heaven, until His death on the cross, when the heavens were shut for Him, yet opened for us. Right before Jesus ascended to the heaven, the heaven was opened for Him again (Acts 1:9-11). As a matter of fact, Jesus Christ didn't have to receive the baptism from John, as he was the sinless Lamb of God who didn't need the cleansing of sin. However, he received baptism from John not as the Son of God, but as a man, a Jew who was under the Law. He received baptism from John as a true Israelite in order to fulfill all righteousness (Matt. 3:15).

JUNE 22

BAPTISM (I)

We were therefore buried with Him through baptism into death in order that, just as Christ was raised from the dead through the glory of the Father, we too may live a new life. (Romans 6:4)

Your whole self ruled by the flesh was put off when you were circumcised by Christ, having been buried with Him in baptism, in which you were also raised with him through your faith in the working of God, who raised Him from the dead (Col. 2:11-12).

Or don't you know that all of us who were baptized into Christ Jesus were baptized into His death? (Rom. 6:3). Now if there is no resurrection, what will those do who are baptized for the dead? If the dead are not raised at all, why are people baptized for them? (1 Cor. 15:29). They (the Israelites) were all baptized into Moses in the cloud and in the sea (1 Cor. 10:2). We were all baptized by one Spirit as so to form one body – whether Jews or Gentiles, slave or free – and we were all given the one Spirit to drink (1 Cor. 12:13). There is one body and one Spirit, just as you were called to one hope when you were called; one Lord, one faith, one baptism; one God and Father of all, who is over all and through all and in all (Eph. 4:4-5).

(Paul says,) All of you who were baptized into Christ have clothed yourselves with Christ (Gal. 3:27). Is Christ divided? Was Paul crucified for you? Were you baptized in the name of Paul? (1 Cor. 1:13). So no one can say that you were baptized in my name (1 Cor. 1:15). Christ did not send me to baptize, but to preach the gospel – not with wisdom and eloquence, lest the cross of Christ be emptied of its power (1 Cor. 1:17).

Reflection: As one of the two ordinances Jesus Christ has instituted for the church, baptism is a symbol of His death, burial, and resurrection. Baptism identifies us with Jesus Christ in death to sin, burial of old nature, and resurrection to newness of life. We participate in His death, burial, and resurrection. We die with Him, be buried with Him, and resurrect with Him. Pay attention to this order: death, burial, and resurrection, which is contrary to the natural order of a man's life: birth, life, and death. This distinctive order reveals one of the secrets to the Kingdom of heaven. In the spiritual realm, death comes first, then does life. All of us who were baptized into Christ were baptized into His death. We were therefore buried with him through baptism into death in order that, just as Christ was raised from the dead through the glory of the Father, we too may live a new life (Rom. 6:3-4). Now if we died with Christ, we believe that we will also live with him (Rom. 6:8). Yes, it is contrary to the physical realm. In the physical realm, life comes first, then does death. In the spiritual realm, death comes first, then does life.

June 23

Baptism (II)

And this water symbolizes baptism that now saves you also – not the removal of dirt from the body but the pledge of a clear conscience toward God. It saves you by the resurrection of Jesus Christ. (1 Peter 3:21)

Whoever believes and is baptized will be saved. But whoever does not believe will be condemned (Mark 16:16).

Peter replied, "Repent and be baptized, every one of you, in the name of Jesus Christ for the forgiveness of your sins. And you will receive the gift of the Holy Spirit" (Acts 2:38). Those who accepted his message were baptized, and about three thousand were added to their number that day (Acts 2:41). (Peter said,) Then I remembered what the Lord had said: "John baptized with water, but you will be baptized with the Holy Spirit." (Acts 11:16).

When they believed Philip as he proclaimed the good news of the kingdom of God and the name of Jesus Christ, they were baptized, both men and women (Acts 8:12). When they arrived, they prayed for the new believers there that they might receive the Holy

Spirit, because the Holy Spirit had not yet come on any of them; they had simply been baptized in the name of the Lord Jesus (Acts 8:15-16). Then Peter said, "Surely no one can stand in the way of their being baptized with water. They have received the Holy Spirit just as we have." (Acts 10:47). So he ordered that they be baptized in the name of Jesus Christ (Acts 10:48). On hearing this, they were baptized in the name of the Lord Jesus (Acts 19:5). And now what are you waiting for? Get up, be baptized and wash your sins away, calling on His name (Acts. 22:16).

Reflection: Although we were buried with Him through baptism into death in order that we may live a new life (Rom. 6:4), baptism itself does not have saving effect. Peter says, "And this water symbolizes baptism that now saves you also – not the removal of dirt from the body but the pledge of a clear conscience toward God. It saves you by the resurrection of Jesus Christ." (1 Peter 3:21). Peter stresses that insofar as baptism is "an appeal to God for a good conscience," (or is "a pledge of a good conscience toward God"), it saves. In other words, Peter is saying, "Baptism is the God-ordained, symbolic expression of that call to God. It is an appeal to God - either in the form of repentance or in the form of commitment." (See John Piper's Desiring God). As one of the two ordinances Jesus Christ has instituted for the church, baptism serves as a sign of covenant Jesus Christ, the head of the church, has made with His bride, church, just as the Lord has made a covenant with Abraham. It serves as the pledge of a clear conscience toward God. The Mosaic Law of purification emphasizes the outward commandments and rituals, whereas baptism ordained by Christ emphasizes the holiness of Christian's inner life.

June 24

The Blood of Christ (I)

For you know that it was not with perishable things such as silver or gold that you were redeemed from the empty way of life handed down to you from your ancestors, but with the precious blood of Christ, a lamb without blemish or defect. (1 Peter 1:18-19)

Remember that at that time you were separate from Christ, excluded from citizenship in Israel and foreigners to the covenants of the promise, without hope and without God in the world. But now in Christ Jesus you who once were far away have been brought near by the blood of Christ (Eph. 2:12-13). I speak to sensible people; judge for yourselves what I say. Is not the cup of thanksgiving for which we give thanks a participation in the blood of Christ? And is not the bread that we break a participation in the body of Christ? Because there is one loaf, we, who are many, are one body, for we all share the one loaf (1 Cor. 10:15-17). The blood of goats and bulls and the ashes of a heifer sprinkled on those who are ceremonially unclean sanctify them so that they are outwardly clean. How much more, then, will the blood of Christ, who through the eternal Spirit offered himself unblemished to God, cleanse our consciences from acts that lead to death, so that we may serve the living God! (Heb. 9:13-14). For you know that it was not with perishable things such as silver or gold that you were redeemed from the empty way of life handed down to you from your ancestors, but with the precious blood of Christ, a lamb without blemish or defect. He was chosen before the creation of the world, but was revealed in these last times for your sake (1 Pet. 1:18-20).

Reflection: The blood of Christ is the basis of the new covenant. The new covenant is designed for eternal life. The Messiah-Servant (Isa. 42:1-7) was the covenant - He was the basis of the relationship between God and His people. It is only through Jesus Christ that we can have an eternal relationship with God. And this relationship is on the basis of the new covenant. Just as the old covenant was ratified with blood, the new covenant was ratified through the blood of Christ. The blood of Christ sealed, ratified, and made valid the new covenant. Through the new covenant which was sealed by the blood of Christ, God saves us from eternal condemnation and death, offers us forgiveness and remission of sin, dispenses eternal life. With the blood of Christ, our salvation is secured forever. The old covenant was made with the blood of the sacrifices (Heb. 9:18.20); whereas the new covenant was made with the blood of the Son of the eternal God. As the Jews didn't believe the original sin, which is the sinful nature of man, the blood of the sacrifices which made the old covenant between God and Israel only has temporary effect. It could only cover the sinful acts that were committed by Israel in the past year. In contrast, as it not only covers our sinful acts, but cleanse our sinful nature, the precious blood of Jesus Christ with which He has made the new covenant with the church, has eternal effect. Therefore, the new covenant has replaced, fulfilled, and completed the old covenant.

June 25

The Blood of Christ (II)

Remember that formerly you who are Gentiles by birth and called "uncircumcised" by those who call themselves "the circumcision" (which is done in the body by human hands) remember that at that time you were separate from Christ, excluded from citizenship in Israel and foreigners to the covenants of the promise, without hope and without God in the world. But now in Christ Jesus you who once were far away have been brought near by the blood of Christ. (Ephesians 2:11-13)

In him we have redemption through his blood, the forgiveness of sins, in accordance with the riches of God's grace that he lavished on us (Eph. 1:7-8). Brothers and sisters, since we have confidence to enter the Most Holy Place by the blood of Jesus, by a new and living way opened for us through the curtain, that is, his body, and since we have a great priest over the house of God, let us draw near to God with a sincere heart and with the full assurance that faith brings, having our hearts sprinkled to cleanse us from a guilty conscience and having our bodies washed with pure water (Heb. 10:19-22). How much more, then, will the blood of Christ, who through the eternal Spirit offered himself unblemished to God, cleanse our consciences from acts that lead to death, so that we may serve the living God! (Heb. 9:14).

Reflection: Because of the blood of Christ, we, the Gentiles have been brought into a covenant relationship with God. In the Old Testament, God made a marriage covenant with Israel by Torah, the Mosaic Law, which served as the *ketubah* (marriage contract). And circumcision stipulated by the Mosaic Law served as a ring owned by the groom that was given to the bride under the wedding canopy. As the sign of the old covenant, circumcision rendered to the Jews a strong sense of pride. On the other hand, the Gentiles were called "uncircumcised" by the Jews, who were excluded from this covenant relationship with God. However, when Jesus came to the world, He paid *mohar* (the bride price) with His precious blood, and made the new covenant with His precious blood, as He said to His bride, the church, "This cup is the new covenant in my blood." (1 Cor. 11:25; also see Matt. 26:28, Mark 14:24, Luke 22:20). The new covenant serves as the *ketubah* (marriage contract). And circumcision of the heart by the Spirit, not by the written code serves as the ring owned by Christ, the groom that was given to the church, the bride. Therefore, we have confidence to enter the Most Holy Place by the blood of Jesus (Heb. 10:19), and approach God's throne of grace with confidence, so that we may receive mercy and find grace to help us in our time of need (Heb. 4:19). The new covenant does not render us sense of spiritual pride; instead, it renders to us full assurance of forgiveness of sins, and cleansing of guilty conscience.

June 26

The Blood of Christ (III)

For you know that it was not with perishable things such as silver or gold that you were redeemed from the empty way of life handed down to you from your ancestors, but with the precious blood of Christ, a lamb without blemish or defect. (1 Peter 1:18-19)

The high priest carries the blood of animals into the Most Holy Place as a sin offering, but the bodies are burned outside the camp. And so Jesus also suffered outside the city gate to make the people holy through his own blood (Heb. 13:11-12). He said, "For this is my blood of the covenant, which is poured out for many for the forgiveness of sins" (Matt. 26:28). He did not enter by means of the blood of goats and calves; but he entered the Most Holy Place once for all by his own blood, thus obtaining eternal redemption (Heb. 9:12).

Now have come the salvation and the power and the kingdom of our God, and the authority of his Messiah. For the accuser of our brothers and sisters, who accuses them before our God day and night, has been hurled down. They triumphed over him by the blood of the Lamb and by the word of their testimony (Rev. 12:10-11). For you know that it was not with perishable things such as silver or gold that you were redeemed from the empty way of life handed down to you from your ancestors, but with the precious blood of Christ, a lamb without blemish or defect (1 Pet. 1:18-19).

In him we have redemption through his blood, the forgiveness of sins, in accordance with the riches of God's grace that he lavished on us (Eph. 1:7-8). Is not the cup of thanksgiving for which we give thanks a participation in the blood of Christ? And is not the bread that we break a participation in the body of Christ? (1 Cor. 10:16).

Reflections: Redemption was a common practice in the ancient societies, including Roman Empire, where slave trade was a major business. Redemption was a technical term for money paid to buy back and set free prisoners of war or to emancipate slaves from their masters. If a person wanted to free a loved one or friend who was enslaved, he would pay the redemption price, purchasing or redeeming that slave for himself and then granting him freedom, testifying to the deliverance by a written certificate. In the Biblical era, to the Jews, the word "redemption" brought to mind the picture of God's deliverance from Egyptian bondage. Such a deliverance experience gave them hope for the redemption of Israel from bondage to Roman Empire. They anticipated the LORD would send them a Messiah who would accomplish this task. Unfortunately, Jesus Christ, the Son of God came to the world, and paid the price of redemption with His precious blood from bondage to sin, but not bondage to Rome. Hence, many Jews' Messianic hope came into air when they didn't see Jesus fulfilled their expectation. Before redemption from Christ, we were held in bondage of sin, and were hostages in Satan's kingdom of darkness. Christ has ransomed us with His precious blood. "In him we have redemption through his blood, the forgiveness of sins, in accordance with the riches of God's grace that he lavished on us" (Eph. 1:7-8). Redemption has been made not through any perishable things such as silver or gold, but through the precious blood of the Son of

God. Redemption is such a costly payment that nobody is able to pay. God Himself has made this payment with the infinitely priceless blood of Christ, and once for all, thus obtaining eternal redemption. Ever since then, we are no longer held captive by Satan, instead, we have become God's possession. Furthermore, Christ has not only cleansed us from our sin with His blood, but sanctified us with His blood. His Blood has not only poured out for us for the forgiveness of sins, but made us holy.

JUNE 27

BLOOD AND COVENANT (I)

Moses then took the blood, sprinkled it on the people and said, "This is the blood of the covenant that the LORD has made with you in accordance with all these words." (Exodus 24:8)

He (Moses) said, "This is the blood of the covenant, which God has commanded you to keep." (Heb. 9:20). Because of His covenant with His people, the Lord will free prisoners from the waterless pit (Zech. 9:11). However, His people brought foreigners uncircumcised in heart and flesh into His sanctuary, desecrating His temple while they offered Him food, fat and blood, and they broke His covenant (Ezek. 44:7).

When Moses had proclaimed every command of the law to all the people, he took the blood of calves, together with water, scarlet wool and branches of hyssop, and sprinkled with the blood both the tabernacle and everything used in its ceremonies. In fact, the law requires that nearly everything be cleansed with blood, and without the shedding of blood there is no forgiveness (Heb. 9:19-22). The blood of goats and bulls and the ashes of a heifer sprinkled on those who are ceremonially unclean sanctify them so that they are outwardly clean (Heb. 9:13). The high priest enters the Most Holy Place every year with blood that is not his own (Heb. 9:25). The first covenant was not put into effect without blood (Heb. 9:18).

Reflection: "When God deals with men, He does through a covenant. And He will not deal with us except through a covenant, nor can we deal with Him except in the same manner." (see Charles Spurgeon, "The blood of the everlasting covenant"). Blood has profound significance in God's salvation plan, and plays a key role in God's covenants with His people. The first covenant was not put into effect without blood (Heb. 9:18). Without shedding of blood, there would have been no covenants, because without blood, there would have been no atonement for sin; and without atonement for sin, there would have been no covenants. The purification of sins is the prerequisite for covenants. The

Abrahamic Covenant was a blood covenant (Gen. 15:9-21), so was Mosaic Covenant (Exod. 19-24). However, all of these covenants were only "copies," or "shadows," of the better covenant to come (Hebrews 9:23). The better covenant is the "New Covenant" which is in the blood of Christ. Anyway, a blood covenant is a promise made by God that He will choose a people for Himself and bless them. "The blood is one of the strangest, the deepest, the mightiest, and the most heavenly of the thoughts of God. It lies at the very root of both Covenants, but specially of the New Covenant." (Andrew Murray). The blood of Old Covenant, which is the blood of beasts has merely figuratively atoned for our sinful acts, whereas the blood of the New Covenant, which is the blood of the Lamb of God has permanently and effectively not only covered our sinful acts, but cleansed our sinful nature. And it has broken the power of all sin forever. "The blood of the New Covenant is redemption blood, a purchase price and ransom from the power of Sin and the Law." (Andrew Murray); just as the Apostle Peter says, "For you know that it was not with perishable things such as silver or gold that you were redeemed from the empty way of life handed down to you from your ancestors, but with the precious blood of Christ, a lamb without blemish or defect." (1 Pet. 1:18-19).

JUNE 28

BLOOD AND COVENANT (II)

Now may the God of peace, who through the blood of the eternal covenant brought back from the dead our Lord Jesus, that great Shepherd of the sheep, equip you with everything good for doing his will, and may he work in us what is pleasing to him, through Jesus Christ, to whom be glory for ever and ever. Amen. (Hebrews 13:20-21)

This is my blood of the covenant, which is poured out for many for the forgiveness of sins (Matt. 26:28; Mark 14:24). In the same way, after supper He (Jesus) took the cup, saying, "This cup is the new covenant in my blood; do this, whenever you drink it, in remembrance of me." (1 Cor. 11:25; Luke 22:20).

Even the first covenant was not put into effect without blood (Heb. 9:18). And so Jesus also suffered outside the city gate to make the people holy through His own blood (Heb. 13:12), who have been chosen according to the foreknowledge of God the Father, through the sanctifying work of the Spirit, to be obedient to Jesus Christ and sprinkled with His blood (1 Pet. 1:2). You have come to God, to Jesus the mediator of a new covenant, and to the sprinkled blood that speaks a better word than the blood of Abel (Heb. 12:24). How much more severely do you think someone deserves to be punished who has trampled the Son of God underfoot, who has treated as an unholy thing the blood of the covenant that sanctified them, and who has insulted the Spirit of grace? (Heb. 10:29). Now may the God of peace, who through the blood of the eternal covenant brought back from the dead our Lord Jesus, that great Shepherd of the sheep, equip you with everything good for doing his will, and may he work in us what is pleasing to him, through Jesus Christ, to whom be glory for ever and ever. Amen (Heb. 13:20-21).

Reflection: Resurrection of Christ is not only the biggest miracle in history, but also the biggest mystery in the Bible. Have you ever wondered how God the Father has brought His Son back from the dead? This is mysterious. Fortunately, the Scriptures give us some hints: through the blood of the eternal covenant, the Father brought Christ back to life (Heb. 13:20). This eternal covenant is the covenant of grace which was made before the foundation of the world between God the Father, and God the Son. This is the covenant between God and Christ, between God the Father and God the Spirit, and God the Son as the covenant head and representative of all God's elect. It was sovereignty and grace combined that made this eternal covenant. The blood is the symbol, the token, the earnest, the surety, the seal of the covenant of grace. (See Charles Spurgeon, "The blood of everlasting covenant"). According to the Scriptures, the blood of Christ has two functions: one is for atonement for sin, the other is for pledge of eternal salvation. The blood of Christ was shed on the earth to atone for our sin, and is served as witness in the heaven, to witness His atonement done on the earth. Jesus Christ has made the New Covenant with His church with His own precious blood. And the blood of Jesus Christ, the mediator of the New Covenant, speaks a better word than the blood of Abel (Heb. 12:24). The blood of Abel speaks justice and retribution; whereas the blood of Christ speaks love and forgiveness, as well as grace and mercy. The blood of Christ has served not only as atonement for sin, but as pledge for eternal life as well as the promise of the eternal inheritance. And it secures peace between God and man (Col. 1:20). The blood of the eternal covenant is life-giving blood. Through it, God has brought Christ back from the dead.

JUNE 29

THE DAY OF THE LORD (I)

Wail, for the day of the LORD is near; it will come like destruction from the Almighty. (Isaiah 13:6)

Alas for that day! For the day of the LORD is near; it will come like destruction from the Almighty (Joel 1:15). See, the day of the LORD is coming —a cruel day, with wrath and fierce anger— to make the land desolate and destroy the sinners within it (Isa. 13:9).

The day is near, the day of the LORD is near— a day of clouds, a time of doom for the nations (Ezek. 30:3). Blow the trumpet in Zion; sound the alarm on my holy hill. Let all who live in the land tremble, for the day of the LORD is coming. It is close at hand (Joel 2:1). The LORD thunders at the head of his army; his forces are beyond number, and mighty is the army that obeys his command. The day of the LORD is great; it is dreadful. Who can endure it (Joel 2:11)? The great day of the LORD is near— near and coming quickly. The cry on the day of the LORD is bitter; the Mighty Warrior shouts his battle cry (Zeph. 1:14).

Multitudes, multitudes in the valley of decision! For the day of the LORD is near in the valley of decision (Joel 3:14). The day of the LORD is near for all nations. As you have done, it will be done to you; your deeds will return upon your own head (Obad. 1:15).

Reflection: In the Hebrew bible, the meaning of the phrase "the Day of the Lord" refers to temporal events such as the invasion of a foreign army, the capture of a city and the suffering that befalls the inhabitants. It is used first by Isaiah in his book and later used in other prophetic and apocalyptic texts in the Scriptures. In the New Testament, the "Day of the Lord" may also refer to the writer's own times, or it may refer to predicted events in a later age of earth's history including the final judgment and World to Come. The expression may also have an extended meaning in referring to both the first and second comings of Jesus Christ (New Interpreter's Dictionary of the Bible). No matter in the Old or New Testament, the Day of the Lord is associated with judgment. The Day of the Lord is when God's judgment has come. And the Day of the Lord is an eschatological term which connotes the End of the World, or the Doomsday. In general, most Christians believe that the Day of the Lord is a reference to a time of catastrophe and judgement for the wicked or a time of glorious renewal and salvation for believers. The Day of the Lord is a span of time during which God personally intervenes in history, directly or indirectly, to accomplish some specific aspects of His plan, and a period of time or a special day that will occur when God's will and purpose for His world and for mankind will be fulfilled. The ultimate or final fulfillment of the prophecies concerning the Day of the Lord will come at the end of history when God, with wondrous power, will punish evil and fulfill all His promises. In other words, the Day of the Lord is the day of consummation of God's plan.

June 30

The Day of the Lord (II)

For you know very well that the day of the Lord will come like a thief in the night. (1 Thessalonians 5:2)

Woe to you who long for the day of the LORD! Why do you long for the day of the LORD? That day will be darkness, not light (Amos 5:18). Will not the day of the LORD be darkness, not light— pitch-dark, without a ray of brightness (Amos 5:20)? You have not gone up to the breaches in the wall to repair it for the people of Israel so that it will stand firm in the battle on the day of the LORD (Ezek. 13:5). Be silent before the Sovereign LORD, for the day of the LORD is near. The LORD has prepared a sacrifice; he has consecrated those he has invited (Zeph. 1:7).

Concerning the coming of our Lord Jesus Christ and our being gathered to him, we ask you, brothers and sisters, not to become easily unsettled or alarmed by the teaching allegedly from us—whether by a prophecy or by word of mouth or by letter—asserting that the day of the Lord has already come (2 Thess. 2:1-2), for you know very well that the day of the Lord will come like a thief in the night (1 Thess. 5:2). The day of the Lord will come like a thief. The heavens will disappear with a roar; the elements will be destroyed by fire, and the earth and everything done in it will be laid bare (2 Pet. 3:10).

Reflection: The Old Testament passages dealing with the day of the Lord often convey a sense of imminence, nearness, and expectation. The Scriptures indicate that "the day of the Lord" will come quickly, like a thief in the night (Zeph. 1:14-15; 2 Thess. 2:2), and therefore Christians must be watchful and ready for the coming of Christ at any moment. Repeatedly, Jesus told of the increasing deception that will come in the Last Days. He commanded us to watch and stay alert so we would not be deceived and get caught off guard. The essential elements of Jesus' warning are that no one knows when He will return, and we have to be in a state of preparedness, always watching for His imminent return. Jesus warned that we should always be prepared because no one except the Father knows the hour of His return (Matt. 24:36–44). The day and hour when our Master, Jesus Christ will return will remain unknown. As His servant, our responsibility is not to speculate when He is coming back, but to prepare ourselves for the Day of the Lord. We ought to develop our relationship with Him in our daily devotion, put our faith in practice, diligently serve Him and our brethren, live a life of holiness, share the gospel with the lost. Every day we must make ourselves ready as if He is coming back on the same day, so that one day when He comes back, He will commend us, "Well done, good and faithful servant! You have been faithful with a few things; I will put you in charge of many things. Come and share your master's happiness!" (Matt. 25:21).

Pearls of Wisdom VOLUME 1

Made in the USA
Coppell, TX
18 January 2026

68524478R00136